COMMUNICATIVE SPEAKING AND LISTENING

COMMUNICATIVE SPEAKING AND LISTENING

FOURTH EDITION

by
Robert T. Oliver
Harold P. Zelko
Paul D. Holtzman
The Pennsylvania State University

HOLT, RINEHART AND WINSTON, INC.
New York / Chicago / San Francisco / Atlanta
Dallas / Montreal / Toronto / London

Library of Congress Catalog Card Number: 68-16612

2678902

Printed in the United States of America

2 3 4 5 6 7 8 9

For
Margaret—Sarah—Ingrid

Preface

This fourth edition of *Communicative Speech* reflects many changes both in the judgment of its authors and in the focus of the speech profession. Nothing is stable but flux. This ancient observation has much pertinence for our generation. What is taught in our classrooms often loses pertinence by the time students graduate. The problem is campus-wide; our own profession and beginning course in speech are not immune to it.

In an official publication of the Speech Association of America it has recently been observed that the emphasis upon public speaking as the main focus in the basic course is fast diminishing. The change that is taking place is clearly recorded in the philosophy and contents of this edition.

The first edition in 1949 was organized to serve college courses in public speaking. The revision of 1955, consisting of seventy-five percent new writing, presented "speech education as a centralizing focus of a liberal and humane preparation for fruitful living and effective citizenship." The book, also, was planned for public speakers, but with a chapter added on the needs and the problems of listeners. The edition of 1962 involved a partial change in the authorship (because of the death of Dallas Dickey), with considerable new emphasis upon the informal daily speech needs of individuals—as speakers and as listeners—and with further development of the psychological and social psychological consequences of oral communication.

This new edition is so completely rewritten as to constitute virtually a new book. At least ninety percent is completely rewritten—not merely restyled, but rethought, redesigned. The focus is upon the complete communication needs of individuals, in the speaking–listening transaction, wherever and however it occurs. The authors have endeavored to develop the problems of oral discourse in the context of the broad panoply of insight encompassed by the humanities and social sciences, and in terms of the immediate and prospective needs of students. The new title, *Communicative Speaking and Listening*, reflects the broader treatment of the total process of human communication.

The current edition has been shortened and, we believe, deepened. We have tried rigorously to exclude not only needless repetition but also materials reflective merely of common-sense observation. When the results of research (by scholars in speech, psychology, social psychology, sociology, or any other field) appear to be relevant and helpful, we have sought to base our observations upon the established conclusions. When judgments have to be formed through critical and evaluative interpretations, we have sought to relate what is generally concluded by experts in speech with the conceptions of philosophers, anthropologists, and other students of human behavior. Part of our concern has been to help readers who use this book to view their problems in speech as an integral parcel of their composite intellectual and social life. It is our observation that when the nature of oral communication is viewed realistically, the inquiry relates closely and significantly to the studies being conducted in the whole broad spectrum of socially centered or individually centered education.

We trust that the changes made will render the book even more practical. We have dealt with concepts and with understandings. Our concern is far more with how the student thinks than with what specific things he should do. We have tried always to direct attention not only to the needs, and the ways of solving them, of immediate participants in oral discourse, but also to the social and intrapersonal factors and effects. The book has become in this sense a commentary upon the influences exerted through oral discourse. But in our view this change of focus does not at all detract from its usefulness as a guide to specific individuals in specific ways of improving their insight and skill in dealing with particular problems in speaking and listening. Quite to the contrary. It is our conviction that genuine and lasting improvement is impossible without a clear understanding by the student of the underlying sociopsychological and philosophical problems that are involved. And we believe that the desired improvements are unlikely to occur unless the student also understands the urgency of the need and the effects that are likely to follow. Hence, we believe it is not inapt to consider this revision as a handbook or guide to speech improvement.

Moreover, we have come seriously to question the hypothesis that the best way to teach general competence in all kinds of oral communication is through the presentation of public speeches. We ourselves have long employed the general arguments which have been used to justify this approach—that, for conversation and all forms of discussion, problems need to be analyzed, purposes identified, ideas organized sequentially in terms of projected listener responses, and that the ideas also need to be clarified, supported, and made appealing. We have said, as have our colleagues across the country, that these elements can best be taught by having students give speeches in which such factors may be identified—and that students will then transfer these skills to their daily conversation.

No doubt such transfers are accomplished to some unmeasured degree. Also, we believe that it is wise and pragmatic for students to be taught to become effective listeners to sustained discourse and skilled in the presentation of a wide variety of public speeches. We think, however, that the insights and skills associated with normal daily oral discourse can be identified and can be taught directly. This has been our aim in this revision. And for those who are teaching public speaking or speech making as a main emphasis, this revised edition will provide valuable guidelines.

Among the many changes that have been made, even casual readers will notice that the number of chapters is reduced from seventeen to fourteen; that the chapter on listening has been eliminated—not because this communication problem is being deprecated but because it is deemed of such transcendent importance that it is treated in every chapter, concurrently with the problems of speaking; that the chapter on visual aids has been eliminated, with relevant materials on this topic included in the chapter on development and proof; that the treatment of purposes has been developed in accordance with the general agreement by social scientists upon the multiplicity and interpenetrability of human needs, motives, and aims; that the chapter on the speech to entertain has been replaced by one on speaking and listening aimed to enhance sociability; that the chapters on persuasion and exposition have been wholly recast to deal with persuasive and informative problems and functions, rather than with special modes of public speeches subsumed under these titles; and that every chapter, from first to last, has been reconstituted to develop a unified theme: the nature of man as a symbolic communicator and the ways by which communication is transacted through the cooperation of speakers and listeners in a society which takes its form primarily as a forum of communicative interchanges.

In our view this revision has been developed within the agelong tradition of rhetoric, in accordance with the insights and knowledge from studies in communication theory, interpreted in terms of generalized educational concepts and aims. We trust it will help readers to enhance their abilities as social participants through improved speaking and listening; and we hope it may contribute to their success as well-rounded individuals and useful citizens.

R. T. O.
H. P. Z.
P. D. H.

UNIVERSITY PARK, PENNSYLVANIA
FEBRUARY 1968

Contents

PART FOUR: COMMUNICATIVE FUNCTIONS AND FORMS

Part One

Fundamental Considerations

1 · *Oral Communication: Theory and Practice*

The earliest known writings of men deal directly with problems of effective oral communication. These manuscripts were written by advisors for their leaders over four thousand years ago in the early civilizations of Egypt and of China.[1] From those days until the present, part-time and full-time teachers of speech have attempted to improve the personal effectiveness of their students. These mentors include many familiar names. The great teachers of ancient Athens gave special attention to oral communication. Isocrates founded a school for the education of speakers. Aristotle contributed *The Rhetoric* on the principles and practice of persuasive speaking. Plato in "The Gorgias" declared that without education in effective speech good men can not achieve good results for themselves nor render proper service to others. The great Romans, Cicero and Quintilian, wrote speech texts.[2]

[1] See Giles Wilkeson Gray, "The Precepts of Kagemni and Ptah-Hotep," *Quarterly Journal of Speech,* 32 (1946), pp. 446–54. Also Robert T. Oliver, *Culture and Communication,* Springfield, Ill.: Charles C Thomas, 1962, pp. 76–155; and *The Roots of Asian Rhetorics,* in preparation for publication by The Pennsylvania State University Press.

[2] The interested student will be surprised by the modern relevance

In modern times old knowledge and old assumptions are being challenged and sometimes modified in the so-called information explosion. Especially is this true in those disciplines which study how man interacts with man: psychology, sociology, political science, anthropology, linguistics, and the direct descendant of ancient rhetoric, speech. The assumptions underlying the development of this textbook reflect knowledge gained from those disciplines, both old and new. The reader will want to test his own assumptions against the following:

1. Speaking and listening abilities are directly related to human achievement, human satisfaction, and the richness of one's living.
2. Speaking and listening abilities are not gifts but rewards of learning.
3. There is nothing so practical as a valid theory of communication—the content of the speech profession.
4. A proper model (or analogy) of human communication is not one of transmission of messages but one of a transaction between speaker and listener, both in the active process of give and take.
5. Only occasionally do people prepare speeches. More often they prepare themselves for listening and speaking transactions.
6. Advice to speakers and listeners in search of a set of practical theories should be based not on old traditions but on tested traditions, not on custom but on research and guided experience.
7. Self-expression is only one component in speaker–listener transactions. A student who would improve his abilities in oral communication focuses not on his own expression but on finding ways to improve the responses of others.

It is not surprising that people often face a course in oral communication with reluctance and fear. Small wonder if they think they are being called upon merely to perform or to express or to concentrate on their own speaking behavior. For the reader who adopts our assumptions, at least some of the reluctance and fear must fade, giving way

---

of Aristotle's *The Rhetoric,* available in Modern Library Edition (trans. W. Rhys Roberts, 1954) and in paperback (trans. Lane Cooper, Appleton-Century-Crofts, 1960); Quintilian's *Institutes of Oratory* (Loeb Classical Library edition, 4 vols., 1922, Latin text with English translation on facing pages). For a general introduction to Greek and Roman rhetorical theory (and to the history of rhetoric in the West), see Lester Thonssen and A. Craig Baird, *Speech Criticism: The Development of Standards for Rhetorical Appraisal,* New York: The Ronald Press Company, 1948.

to the excitement of new insights and the possibility of new perceptions of how human beings interact. To help in the process, it will pay to examine each of these assumptions and their validation in some detail.

Oral Communication and Human Achievement

What is "human" about human achievement is the creative co-operation that goes into it. How does a person achieve his goals? He does so, as speaker, by eliciting from listeners signs that they understand or feel or believe or enjoy or do what he thinks they should; and he does so, as listener, by eliciting from speakers what will lead him to understand, to feel appreciated, to make a wise decision in controversy, to enjoy human adventure and thought, or to spur him to needed action. Here are some examples:

—An architect finds an elegant, innovative solution to his client's problem. The architect may or may not succeed in having the plan adopted. His achievement will depend in large part upon his listening and speaking abilities.

—A doctor knows that his prescribed treatment can be undermined by his patient's excessive worrying. For both of them, listening and speaking will be the means to achievement—or failure.

—A student knows that his legal rights have been violated by a threatening college patrolman. Each stands to gain or lose in the conversations that follow.

If one examines opportunities for achievement in a modern society, he is most apt to find at least two human beings interacting in oral communication, with both standing to gain or to lose: the placement interview, a first date, a school or college class, the meeting of the boy's or the girl's parents, a counseling or psychiatric session, a report to the PTA or a professional society, conversation at a cocktail party or a church social. Marshall McLuhan, the stimulating commentator on the effects of communication media, insists that in the age of television it is not written but oral communication that is once more becoming the channel of interaction that binds our lives, that determines our destinies.

In these interactions we achieve and we gain satisfaction—if we are prepared for them. Being prepared for communication does not necessarily mean knowing what we will say or hear. It means knowing what we are trying to accomplish and providing ourselves with the necessary perceptions—perceptions of the situation, of the subject matter and, probably most of all, perceptions of the other person, whether speaker or listener.

An achieving individual in our society is not the one who has learned proper rote motions. He is the one who can adapt to changing conditions while achieving a purpose. He is prepared to find a way rather than to be stuck with old platitudes. He is a skillful speaker and listener dealing with ever new realities. The successful person, one who often achieves satisfaction, seldom recites canned phrases, never assumes he knows all that another has to say.

Oral Communication As Learned Ability

The myth of the "born speaker" and "born listener" has been exploded by teachers and researchers from Aristotle's school among the colonnades to continuing education speech courses in colleges and universities across the land. Yet the myth persists. Why? Each myth-bound person must answer for himself: Does he give up too easily? Probably. Is it unimportant? Is any means to personal fulfillment unimportant? Relearning is often more difficult than first learning. But it is accomplished by students at all educational levels and in adult classes.

Changes toward greater personal effectiveness through speech class learning are confirmed by an abundance of research in communication teaching. Carefully controlled experiments have demonstrated such personal gains by students as greater speaking effectiveness, greater critical thinking ability, greater critical listening ability, even changes in personality in the direction of greater self-sufficiency and reduced anxiety.[3] Long range studies have uncovered acknowledged regrets by thousands of college graduates that they did not learn when they had a chance and vivid testimony of advantages gained from those who did.[4]

[3] Many of these studies have been reported in the professional speech journals: *Speech Monographs, Quarterly Journal of Speech, The Speech Teacher*. See indexes.

[4] For instance, on May 4, 1958, *The New York Times* reported on a survey of nearly four thousand engineers who had received their training at Purdue University. Asked what nontechnical subjects are most important in the engineering curriculum, 99 percent included speech.

A Practical Theory

One learns any new skill best when focusing on a goal or a target. The question is not, "What are the right motions for batting a ball, winning at chess, or playing the guitar?" There is a prior question, "What should I concentrate on when I try to hit a ball, to plan a checkmate, to learn to make my kind of music?"

Practical instruction is like old math: a focus on the mechanics. This has been discarded for the more effective focus on the goals of mathematical manipulations. In old math the student learned his multiplication table because he was required to. In the new math the student learns to multiply because he has a use for it, a goal to achieve with it.

Similarly, in old speech courses one learned some behaviors that were prescribed as good speaking habits. When done without understanding they often turned out to be artificial, stilted, insincere, and unrelated to daily living. The student's focus was on his own behavior; his goal was to achieve the required behaviors prescribed (or seemingly prescribed) by his teacher. In new speech a student seeks his own most effective ways of speaking and listening to achieve communicative goals. His focus is on the target—not on someone else's technique. He values not so much his mastery of techniques as his influence on listeners and speakers.

The assumption that theory is really most practical for the student reflects the discovery that prescribed speaking and listening behaviors are false goals. There is nothing so practical as telling a youngster to keep his eye on the ball. Likewise, we can offer no more practical advice than to aim for and focus on listeners' responses and to challenge speakers to make their talk really meaningful, both in the classroom and beyond.

The content of the speech profession is a constantly changing catalogue of the ways and means of achieving communicative purposes. This content is offered to the student who first learns to take aim. It is of little lasting value to the student who asks only what he should *do,* rather than what he should accomplish.

A Proper Model: Transaction

We depend upon analogies for understanding many things about our worlds. We say worlds, in the plural, for each of us constructs within our perceptual systems a different world, and we respond not so much to a theoretical real world as to our own perceived worlds. This is the process of constructing perceptual maps of reality and of responding not to the reality but to the maps. General semanticists remind us that we must frequently check our maps against the real territory.[5] Otherwise we are prone to respond to a reality that is not there. An example of this mistake can be seen when a summons by a college dean or company manager is assumed (mapped) to be for disciplinary reasons and it turns out to be for announcing an award, a new responsibility, a request for help, or a pay raise.

One system of maps is the language we use. Psycholinguists are currently studying the many aspects of the "world view" problem or "Sapir-Whorf hypothesis," which states that perceptions are culturally determined through the language as it is first learned in that culture.[6] The insightful writer, George Orwell, apparently without knowledge of these linguistic speculations, provided a clear application of this principle in his novel *1984* and its appendix on *Newspeak,* a language designed to control the perceptions (and therefore the behaviors) of the masses.

Because of the influences of language and because of tendencies to "analogize," there is a common, culturally imposed misperception of human communication. The map is that of the transportation of goods, which becomes by analogy a map of the transmission of ideas. Thus, following the model of engineers concerned with transmission of

[5] General semantics is a field that developed with the seminal work of Alfred Korzybski (*Science and Sanity,* 4th ed., International Non-Aristotelian Library Publishing Co., 1958). Concern is with human response to reality and freedom from inappropriate responses to high-level abstractions and projected attitudes (both kinds of maps). For study of general semantics, see J. Samuel Bois, *Explorations in Awareness,* Harper & Row, Publishers, 1957; Harry L. Weinberg, *Levels of Knowing and Existence,* New York: Harper & Row, Publishers, 1959; S. I. Hayakawa, *Our Language and Our World,* Harper & Row, Publishers, 1959. See also the journal, *ETC.: A Review of General Semantics.*

[6] See Edward Sapir, "Communication," *Encyclopedia of the Social Sciences,* New York: Crowell-Collier and Macmillan, Inc., 1933, and *Culture, Language, and Personality,* Berkeley: University of California Press, 1956; Benjamin Lee Whorf, *Language, Thought and Reality,* New York: John Wiley & Sons, Inc., 1956. For a discussion of the limitations of the Sapir-Whorf hypothesis, see Harry Hoijer, ed. *Language in Culture,* Chicago: University of Chicago Press, 1954.

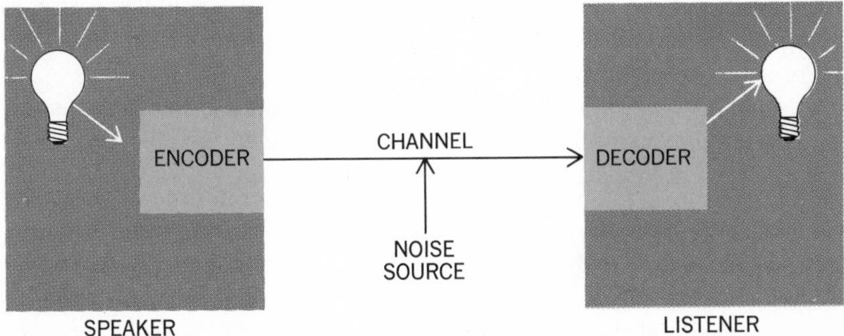

coded messages,[7] speech is assumed to begin when a person has an idea to *convey,* which he then *encodes* for transmission through a *channel* (the air) to someone else's *decoder* and, if there is no *noise* in the channel, the idea arrives—just as it left—in the mind of a *receiver.*

This seems very clear until one examines some realities and some essential differences between communicating human beings and their far simpler transmitting machines.

1. A speaker is not simply initiating a message. He is responding to the occasion, to the listener, to his own motivations, and to a conception of how he wants the listener to respond.

2. A listener is not simply receiving a message. He is responding to the way he perceives the occasion, the speaker's purpose, his own purpose, and his other motivations. A radio receiver, for instance, does not have a purpose; but every person in a communication does—both speaker and listener.

3. A linguistic message—from utterance to recognition—is coded, transmitted, and decoded. But that is not all. Experimental studies indicate that *who* is perceived as the source of the message determines, in part, *what* message is received and, more importantly, how the lis-

[7] See Claude E. Shannon and Warren Weaver, *The Mathematical Theory of Communication,* Urbana, Ill.: University of Illinois Press, 1949. For applications of the theory to oral communication, see Raymond Ross, *Speech Communication: Fundamentals and Practice,* Englewood Cliffs, N.J.: Prentice-Hall, Inc., 1965; also David K. Berlo, *The Process of Communication,* New York: Holt, Rinehart and Winston, Inc., 1960.

tener will respond.[8] Other important determinants of the listener's message and of how the message is formed depend upon what else is going on in the speaker, in the situation, and in the listener, and how all of these are perceived by both.

4. While transmission of messages is analogous to the transmission of goods, the transmission of ideas is not really possible, nor is it the real goal in human communication.

What must emerge clearly from a study of speaking and listening as communication is that (1) transmission is only a part of the human communication process; (2) the message is not the idea; and (3) to understand the idea one must know what is moving listener and speaker and what the communication outcomes are for both.

Another popular model of communication has been offered by Lasswell:[9]

WHO
SAYS WHAT
IN WHICH CHANNEL
TO WHOM
WITH WHAT EFFECT

At first glance this, too, may seem a practical theory. However, it is a model that fails to draw attention to the motives of either speaker or listener and to the social context in which communication takes place. Further, it appears to describe a listener who is passive and who has something happen to him.

Both the transmission model and the Lasswell model represent practical theories for learning about some aspects of communication events. The transmission model is important, for instance, in studying intelligibility or the amount of noise or distortion a message can stand and still get through recognizably. The Lasswell model has had practical application in drawing attention to the responses of speakers and listeners and to the influences of both the sources of messages and the media over which they have traveled.

[8] See Kenneth Andersen and Theodore Clevenger, Jr., "A Summary of Experimental Research in Ethos," *Speech Monographs,* (June, 1963), pp. 59–78.

[9] Harold D. Lasswell, "The Structure and Function of Communication in Society," in Lyman Bryson, ed., *The Communication of Ideas,* New York: Harper & Row, Publishers, 1948, p. 37.

A different model or analogy may be more useful in assisting the speech student to visualize the process, including the complexities of speaker and listener motivation and the essential separation of speakers and listeners. One possibility is a model of *transaction through induction.*

In electronic circuitry the common symbol for a transformer (or induction coil) is:

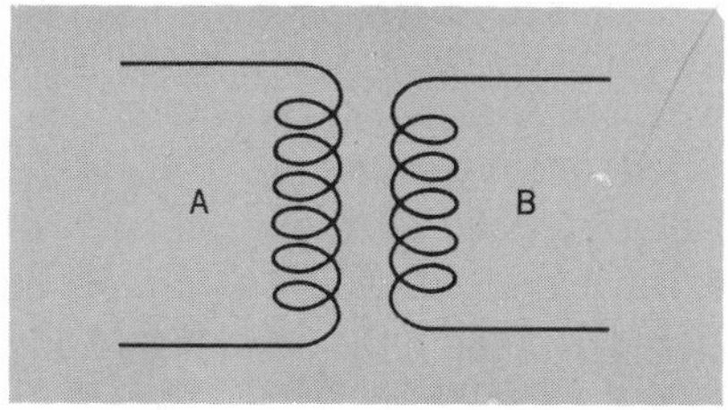

Such transformers are used to change characteristics of electrical current in television sets, fluorescent lighting fixtures, and doorbell circuits. As current flows through A it *induces* current to flow through B or affects the current already flowing through B, although there is no direct contact between them. In fact, they are carefully *insulated* from one another. This common electrical device provides an induction model of communication: whatever flows through one side, for whatever reasons, *influences* what happens on the other side, and vice versa. Electricity is not transmitted, it is induced. There is no direct contact.

So it is with individuals operating together in a communication transaction. There is no transmission of ideas, but—through a complex variety of means—there are efforts by each side to induce thought processes or behaviors as the outcomes of interactions. The idea of transmission from speaker to listener presupposes identical responses to a coded message—whether spoken or heard. The fact is that people simply do not respond identically, for they operate on perceptions based on different experiences, and they apply diverse meanings based on these perceptions and motivations. The idea of induction presupposes a need to adjust speaking and listening behaviors to induce a desired result from the interaction: a speaker chooses what he will say on the basis of a prediction of how it will be perceived by a particular listener or listeners, and a listener chooses his mode of behavior on the basis of a prediction of how it will affect the result of interaction.

A classic example of such adjustment is the asking price in real estate transactions, when the expected listener response is a lower offer, and the predicted communication outcome is settlement on a price between the two figures.

How is this idea practical for the student of oral communication? It helps him place his focus where it belongs: on communicative goals and communicative outcomes. The idea of induction helps the speaker see that there is no best way to encode or interpret an idea. He can see that transmission of a message does not, in itself, constitute communication between human beings; that thought must be given to *who* is being invited to respond, to *what* adaptation can induce interaction leading to the desired outcome, and to *how* listeners' perceptions of the speaker and his purpose and of the social context influence different outcomes. Further, it helps the student—as listener and as critic—interpret with increased understanding the speaking of others.

Preparing Oneself for Communication Transactions

Successes and failures in all communication transactions are determined in part by how well one is prepared for each encounter. This must not be read as, "how well one has prepared what he should say." When one prepares what he will say—when he prepares a speech—he prepares to transmit a coded message. When one focuses on transmitting a message, he is not at that moment apt to be engaging in transaction, though he may have had transaction in mind while preparing the speech. Everyone can remember rote recitations, sometimes ill-conceived as useful speech exercises. At best, these memories are—for the speaker—memories of admiration or of blame for how he spoke, not what thoughts or feelings were induced. At worst, the speaker remembers his anxiety, his insulation from his listeners (a shapeless mass "out there"), and his relief when it was over. What did listeners contribute and gain? Perhaps a polite ear and perhaps some entertainment. But did this remembered speaker ever really interact with the listeners? And they with him? Probably not, unless the speaker was very skilled in handling the manuscript speech (see Chapter 14, Speaking from Manuscript) or the listeners were highly motivated to overcome certain communication barriers.

Even in that speech area called "oral interpretation," the goal of the speaker is not to show off but to invite the listener to become involved in the subject or mood of the poetry or prose, to enhance the communication transaction between writer and listeners.[10] Here, too, effective professional oral interpreters like Hal Holbrook (as Mark Twain), the late Charles Laughton, and even Senator Everett Dirksen, do not prepare the actual written message but prepare for its utterance and for its adaptation to particular groups of listeners.

Any course in effective speaking and listening provides students with the necessary attitudes, understanding, and tools for preparing themselves for oral communication situations. This is so that, as speakers, they can be free to interact with listeners, instead of struggling to remember what they planned to say; and so that, as listeners, they can interact effectively with speakers without being distracted by irrelevant matters.

Sacred Cows and Research

James Winans two generations ago challenged students to recognize that "a speech is not an essay trying to stand on its hind legs." Yet some students persist in the ancient and impractical tradition of going through planned, written motions when speaking in the speech class, without a thought for the consequences in both themselves and their listeners. Modern research substantiates clearly what Professor Winans recognized over fifty years ago: people do respond differently to written and spoken language and differently when spoken language is read and when written language is spoken.[11] A modern student would not

[10] See, for instance, Wilma H. Grimes and Alethea Smith Mattingly, *Interpretation: Writer-Reader-Audience,* Belmont, Calif.: Wadsworth, 1961; Charlotte I. Lee, *Oral Interpretation,* 3rd ed., Boston: Houghton Mifflin Company, 1965.

[11] New research methods have produced new knowledge of these differences. See Milton W. Horowitz and John B. Newman, "Spoken and Written Expression: an Experimental Analysis," *Journal of Abnormal and Social Psychology,* 68 (1964), pp. 640–7; and for a discussion of the implications of the experimental results see Newman and Horowitz, "Writing and Speaking," *College Composition and Communication,* XVI (1965), pp. 160–4. See also Joseph A. DeVito, "Psychogrammatical Factors in Oral and Written Discourse by Skilled Communicators," *Speech Monographs,* XXXIII (1966), pp. 173–6; James W. Gibson, Charles R. Gruner, Robert J. Kibler and Francis J. Kelly, "A Quantitative Examination of Differences and Similarities in Written and Spoken Messages," *Speech Monographs,* XXXIII (1966), pp. 444–51.

dream of treating warts or skin blemishes, as Huckleberry Finn proposed, by tossing a dead cat with proper incantations at a devil in a graveyard at midnight. He would not ignore the more effective treatments available to his doctor through medical research. Yet to some it does not seem inconsistent to study oral communication in the once traditional ways of recitation of written language, even though more effective means are available to speech students through communication research.

Communication research has been conducted rigorously in the field of speech for many years and in other fields as well. It has been recognized that any study of man and his society necessitates careful assessment of the complex communication processes. This book attempts to make available to its readers—those students intent upon learning their own ways to personal effectiveness—the fruits of such research: not just traditional advice, but tested advice whether traditional or new.

Whether or not he acknowledges the choice, each student of speech will decide either to adhere stubbornly to outmoded concepts of rote learning and transmission to passive listeners or to try the realistic and tested modes of communication transactions.

Expression and Communication as Vectors

It was noted earlier that a primary misconception of the communication transaction is the analogy-derived idea of the transmission of ideas. A second common misconception comes from the confusion of self-expression and communication. This confusion produces the concept of a speaker expressing himself without regard for the consequences, either to himself or to others.

All human behavior is, of course, expressive. That is, everyone is always motivated in part by inner personal needs: needs for gratification, for release of hostilities, for freedom from anxiety, for a sense of internal consistency. Expression of these needs determines a part, but only a part, of communicative speaking and listening thought processes and behaviors. The merely expressive listener, for instance, may not contribute constructively in interaction with a speaker who is the object of his hostility, nor would he be apt to entertain a belief that is widely divergent from the truth as he knows it. Similarly, the merely expressive speaker speaks only for his own pleasure or release of tension.

Communicative motivations, on the other hand, urge the speaker to find ways to induce specific thought processes and behaviors in others, or to guide the listener to weigh actively the perceptions aroused by the speaker and then to match these new perceptions with those he already has, in order to help create a communication outcome—a resultant speaker–listener cooperation.

No man is capable of only communicatively motivated behavior. There are, of necessity, always expressive components. At the same time, no man is only expressive in his language behavior, except, occasionally, in the privacy of his dreams, of his solitude, of his withdrawal into insanity, or occasionally in certain phases of psychiatric experiences.

It is important for the student of oral communication to learn to discriminate between expressive and communicative behavior, both in himself and in others. Further, he must recognize that communicative effectiveness may at times require expressive behavior and at other times require its rechanneling, if not its momentary inhibition.

The difference between expression and communication may be illustrated by what one might say and how he might say it if he were to cut himself accidently. If he is alone, he may speak aloud to give vent to feelings of pain, frustration, fear, or anger. If there are others present he will very likely speak quite differently, say different things. In the latter case one feels no less pain, frustration, fear, or anger, but, in addition to the expressive need, there is a communicative need: to evoke help, sympathy, or even admiration for control over profane expression. At the same time, in this example, if the victim's mother is present, her listening might be primarily expressive, compared with that, say, of a visiting doctor. The mother may make little communicative contribution to the transaction, while the doctor may do so by perceiving the situation clearly and providing gratification for perhaps all three communicative desires: help, sympathy, and admiration.

The interplay of expression and communication may be seen more clearly, perhaps, by analogy with the mathematician's vector analysis—without the mathematics. Without knowing it, most people have engaged in vector analysis. The rifleman calls it "Kentucky windage" when he aims slightly upwind of the target. He is estimating what combination of two forces—exploding gunpowder and the wind—is required to land on target. When golfer Arnold Palmer tosses grassblades into the air and watches their fall, he determines both the direction and the force of the wind. For him this will be one vector: a force of a certain magnitude in a certain direction. This will interact with a second vector of greater magnitude in another direction: his drive from the tee. The golfer now predicts a resultant: a third vector representing the flight of the ball as a result of the tee shot in one direction and the wind in another.

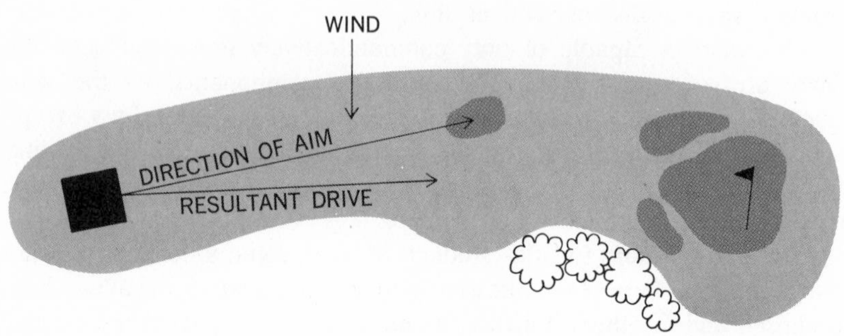

Later, on the green, the golfer does another vector analysis. He computes the force and direction of the the pull of gravity on the sloping green and determines what initial force and direction the putt must have to move the ball into the cup.

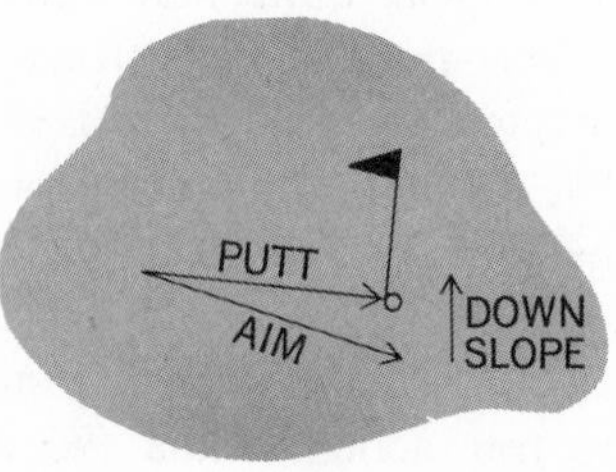

Similarly, people know how much to lean while walking in a strong crosswind; how much to loft a ball so that it will defy gravity until it reaches its destination. In all these cases two primary factors determine the resultant.

By analogy, then, the two interacting primary factors of communicative intent and expressive need determine resultant speaker and listener thought processes and behaviors. Further, two interacting primary vectors of speaker and listener determine resultant communication outcomes: the changes that are wrought in each.

To improve their oral communication abilities, readers are invited to give primary attention to their communicative aims. They do not develop self-expression so much as they adapt to their own expressive needs as speakers or listeners and further adapt to the expressive needs of others in taking communicative aim. This, too, is not an unfamiliar vector analysis. People sometimes put off a communicative attempt when others are in a bad mood, much as the golfer might wait for a gust of wind to die down. At other times we gauge how the expressive needs of others might help the communication along—as the golfer might plan to take advantage of a strong tail wind.

Expressive needs, then, can provide both bonds and barriers to people engaged in communication. They may enhance transaction, or they may insulate speakers and listeners against communicative interaction.

Speaker–Listener Bonds and Barriers

In certain situations people talk and listen easily, their minds stimulated by enthusiasm for an idea or by the company they are in. In other situations they feel reticent, withdrawn, and hesitant to enter into communicative give-and-take. Situations, purposes, topics, and people are all part of the explanation for these differences. A basic problem in personal effectiveness is learning how to recognize and adapt to the bonds and barriers that facilitate and inhibit communication. Bonds between people invite transaction. Barriers insulate people from one another. Both as speakers and as listeners people need to learn how to capitalize on bonds and how to convert barriers into bonds.

"Interested-in-me-ness"

One universal bond between people might be called an "interested-in-me" perception. This is the basis for all rapport between people. Speaking is reinforced when a speaker perceives that his listener is interested. Studies show that speakers have more to say to interested listeners.[12] At the same time, when listeners perceive a speaker as dis-

[12] See Philip P. Amato and Terry H. Ostermeier, "The Effect of Audience Feedback on the Beginning Public Speaker," *Speech Teacher,* XVI (January, 1967): pp. 56–63. This phenomenon is reported also in George C. Homans, *Social Behavior, Its Elementary Forms,* New York: Harcourt, Brace & World, Inc., 1961; see also Bernard Berelson and Gary A. Steiner, *Human Behavior,* Harcourt, Brace & World, Inc., 1964, pp. 143–50 on "Social Reinforcement."

interestedly going through the motions, they tend not to enter the transaction. As columnist Russell Baker put it, "They close their earlids," creating not a bond but a barrier to communication. For both speaker and listener, interest begets interest. Lack of interest insulates.

The important assumption here is that any speaker—by virtue of the fact that he has a genuine communicative intent—is inherently interested in his listener and that there is, therefore, an inherent source of listener interest in the speaker. This mutual interest is not always apparent to one or the other or both. An example may be seen in the once compelling message of the U.S. Navy intercom systems, "Now hear this. Now hear this." Navy men report it has lost some of its force for gaining attention because of repetition and dull-voiced delivery, both signs of disinterest.

On those occasions when apparent disinterest is a barrier, the effective speaker can learn to arouse listener interest—necessarily before attempting to induce other perceptions. Similarly, listeners can, through their behaviors, capture a speaker's interest in them. On those occasions when such mutual interest does not in fact exist, the barrier is more basic, requiring both speaker and listener to re-examine their purposes.

"One-of-us-ness"

A related bond is the "one-of-us" feeling. Speaker and listener perceptions that they are in the same boat invite interaction. But if they feel that they live in worlds apart, they usually are insulated from communication; there is a barrier to mutual induction. Thus, when people first meet one another they usually seek out shared associations and experiences. This is the communicative process of establishing common ground. People learn this communicative bond-building early in life. This is exemplified by one four-year-old—a new girl in her first day in a Pennsylvania nursery school—who was observed to walk up to one of the little boys and say, "I've been to the San Diego Zoo. Where have you been?" The surprised youngster responded, "Well, I've been to the San Diego Zoo, too." The two became inseparable.

Speakers and listeners in communication, no matter what their differences, have endless sources of common ground to bring to bear. They are apt to have had similar experiences, to have read some of the same things, to know some of the same people, to enjoy some of the same television.

A special case of common ground, important in moving listeners to new perceptions and beliefs, is the common premise. This is the particular desire, value, or urgency of both speaker and listener concern and commitment from which acceptance of the speaker's proposal is apt to follow. This more specific aspect of common ground is discussed in Chapter 11.

As in the case of mutual interest, even though speaker and listener have common ground it is not always readily apparent. In a given instance speaker and listener may build a barrier or they may build a bond. They may respond to the knowledge that they identify with different political parties or respond to memories of their experiences together in a community activity. Often their differences may be more obvious to them. Here, again, interaction will depend upon reduction of the insulating barrier. If one or both seek their shared associations and experiences, "one-of-us-ness" can be found and the barrier converted into a bond. Some of the apparent differences between speakers and listeners, which may act as barriers to communication, may occur in status, role, and purpose.

Status

Almost all American institutions are characterized by lines of authority and responsibility, whether in the home, business, government, or volunteer community services. In every activity, someone is in charge, and that someone has someone to whom he reports. While he was president of the United States, Harry Truman displayed on his desk a sign which read, "The Buck Stops Here."

These hierarchies of authority and responsibility are the channels of communication within each social structure. When there are communication barriers blocking these channels, the functioning of the particular social structure suffers. In such instances relative status of speaker and listener is a potential barrier. A barrier between parent and child sometimes shows itself when the child learns from his peers what he seemingly refused to learn from his parent. Similarly in business, industry, and government, status is often a barrier to communicative effectiveness. Not only do status differences block the channels; the fact that two men of equal status are competing for a promotion may constitute a barrier blocking effective interaction.

It would be a mistake to assume that status is necessarily and in all circumstances a communication barrier. On the contrary, it can enhance interaction. People with the enlarged duties and responsibilities of authority need all the help they can get. When this is acknowledged, status often becomes a bond, not a barrier. When a speaker with a problem reaches someone along the hierarchy who has enough authority to do something about the situation, interaction is facilitated.

However, when status is a barrier, it can often be converted into a bond. This will happen when both speaker and listener have genuine communicative intent ("interested-in-me-ness"). Their relationship of subordinate and superior necessarily means that they serve some important function together; there is potential "one-of-us-ness." Boss and employee serve the same company; congressman and constituent both care about conditions in their own district; committee chairman and member are both assigned to finding solutions for the same problems. Behind every status barrier there is apt to exist the bond of a larger unity.

Role

Status is not a constant in our lives. Each person functions in many social groups and institutions, serving in a variety of changing roles of authority and responsibility.

Speakers and listeners have varying expectations for each others' behaviors and even for each others' personalities. These depend upon the situation, the subject under discussion, and the relationships between communicators—including varying status relationships. These factors, in turn, determine the roles that speakers and listeners play and the roles that they expect of each other.[13]

Thus, in every communication transaction, how one behaves is determined in part by how he conceives of his role and how he wants others to perceive that role or, as Erving Goffman explains, how he chooses to present himself.[14]

Playing a role is an inevitable part of every communication transaction. Occasionally there is conscious awareness of role. It is not uncommon for a person to talk about "changing hats," as when a sales manager might say, "As your boss I approve of your long hours on the road, but as your brother-in-law I deplore your neglect of your family." More often, however, role is an unconscious function and, as such, can be a barrier to communication. Why is it that people will accept criticism from one person and reject it from another? Because the role of hostile critic can be a barrier-builder, while that of helping critic can cement a bond. It should be noted that it is not a speaker

[13] Sociolinguists describe communicative behavior and "language as the revealer of the individual's locale, his social roles and position and his cultural level." (Joyce O. Hertzler, *A Sociology of Language*, New York: Random House, Inc., 1965. See especially pp. 372–410.)

[14] See Erving Goffman, *The Presentation of Self in Everyday Life*, New York: Doubleday & Company, 1959.

role or listener role which alone binds or separates; it is each role in relation to the role expected by the other.

Certain social roles are indeed changed as easily as one changes hats. Others are more permanent, such as those relating to where one grows up, one's position in the socioeconomic scheme of things, one's vocation, even one's sex. Some roles are superficial, easily analyzed, and convertible into bonds. For example, when Robert Kennedy spoke on civil rights to law school students and faculty in Georgia—his first major speech as Attorney General of the United States—he presented himself not in the role of advocate of civil rights laws but in the role of enforcer. Further, he reminded listeners of their own roles as people committed to respect for existing laws.[15]

Other roles represent deeper psychological forces. Maladjustment is seen by some psychiatrists as disturbances of communication. And they see psychotherapy as aiming at "improving the communication system of the patient."[16] One system of psychotherapy deals with such disturbances or barriers by enabling people to recognize how their handling of communication situations is dictated by their playing of relatively rigid roles, as described in *The Games People Play*.[17]

In speech classes students sometimes find themselves playing games rather than dealing with each other realistically in their speaking and listening roles. It may be worthwhile to consider a few examples of such classroom games for their value in providing insights and perhaps motivating new perspectives on speech class realities.

Speaker and Listener Games That Build Barriers

ELOCUTION is a game in which students see their roles as being proper or correct. These are the pseudo-communication behaviors that one puts on only for speech (or other) teachers because it is what they seem to expect. This game is usually played awkwardly and uncomfortably. There is no effort to interact with one's classmates, no interest in classmates' responses, no communication and, worst of all, there develops a barrier to growth in personal effectiveness.

[15] For a report on this speech and its effects, see Thomas A. Hopkins, *Rights for Americans: The Speeches of Robert F. Kennedy,* Indianapolis, Ind.: Bobbs-Merrill Company, Inc., 1964, pp. 13–26.

[16] From Jurgen Ruesch and Gregory Bateson, *Communication: The Social Matrix of Psychiatry,* New York: W. W. Norton & Company, Inc., 1951, p. 19.

[17] Eric Berne, *Games People Play: The Psychology of Human Relationships,* New York: Grove Press Inc., 1964.

DON'T BUG ME (with reality) is a game in which students reject the notion of real communication affecting real changes in the feelings and cognitions of student speaker and listeners in the classroom. The student who plays this game might be asked what his listeners knew or believed before he started speaking and respond with a startled, "Huh?!?"

WAKE ME UP WHEN IT'S MY TURN is a listener version of the speaker game, DON'T BUG ME (with reality). In this game the listener is merely waiting for his turn to play one of the barrier-building speaker games. He assumes that what the speaker has to say has no reality and is of little consequence. Further, the WAKE ME UP part of the game is usually a false front for the kinds of tension and anxiety which accrue to students who are getting ready to play ELOCUTION. This listening game is apparent in group discussions when a participant is constantly contributing without regard for or response to what others have been saying.

LOOKIT ME—LOOKIT HOW I DO is a game that is related to ELOCUTION. But it is played without awkwardness and discomfort. LOOKIT ME—LOOKIT HOW I DO is a role the student is ready to play with special pride and flourish at every opportunity. He is insensitive to the groans of his peers. If he is criticized for failing to invite listeners to focus on a significant idea, he might counter by asking, "But wasn't I fluent?"

BUT I SAID is a game in which the student speaker blames the (stupid) listeners for misunderstanding or disagreement. He believes the message is the communication. When it is pointed out that his listeners are confused about or are rejecting his idea, he quickly defends himself, beginning, "But I said . . ."

By way of summary, barriers block potential communication when speaker or listener misconstrues his role and those of others—whether consciously or unconsciously. The student of effective oral communication needs to develop increased sensitivity to role—both in himself and in others—and increased flexibility of role to meet changing circumstances. Those who play barrier-building games—in or out of speech classes—are usually confused regarding the purposes both of oral communication and of exercises for improving one's personal effectiveness.

Purpose

As status tends to determine role, so role in turn tends to determine speaking and listening purposes. In a transmission model of communication, the speaker's purpose is to transmit a message. In an induction model both speaker and listener have purposes. Speakers' purposes are to induce certain responses in their listeners and to profit in some way from the transactions. Listeners' purposes are to gain from the transactions also and perhaps to influence speakers.[18]

While barriers arise when there is no communicative purpose, they arise more often when speaker's and listener's purposes are at odds with one another. In arguments regarding students' rights, for instance, college officials and student activitists are apt to be focused on different problems and to have different communicative purposes. Unless they first discover each others' purposes, speakers and listeners are separated by a barrier. Thus, often the first goal of a speaker is to convert this barrier into a bond by showing how his purpose relates to his listeners' purposes, or by effectively inviting them to share his purpose.

Speaker–listener bonds provide the essential opportunities for interaction. Consequently—at the outset of any communication—existing barriers must be broken down or converted into bonds. When the channels of interaction are thus opened, speaker and listener can interact to the extent that they are sensitive to each other's communicative behaviors.

Communicative Feedback

All the theory and practice, all the speaker–listener bonds, all of the speaker–listener behaviors in effective oral communication in a modern society rely on *feedback:* the reading of responses. Earlier we discussed communication as mutual induction; as always a give-and-take operation. Without sensitivity to response, there is no "take"; hence, no real transaction.

The process by which a speaker guides himself by noting the reactions of his listeners is sometimes known as "circular response." The speaker and his message serve as stimuli to listeners, and their

[18] Explaining communication as a transaction, Raymond A. Bauer states this idea of two-way speaker–listener relationship when he says, ". . . the model which *ought* to be inferred from the data of research is of communication as a transactional process in which two parties each expect to give and take from the deal approximately equitable values." "The Obstinate Audience: the Influence Process from the Point of View of Social Communication," *American Psychologist,* 19 (1964), pp. 319–28.

reactions, in turn, serve as further stimuli to him. Talk, thus, is a very lively process, with constant reaction being perceived back and forth. This is a principal reason why genuine talk ought to be—or to seem to be—extemporaneous: speech resulting from careful preparation to transact, but taking its final form and being modified in its development while the speaker is actually talking with his listeners. In this context the distinctions between public speaking (and listening) and conversation are far less significant than their similarities. Good talk takes place when speaker and listener jointly participate. It is, in fact, a creation of the listeners, just as it is of the speaker.

Mention was made earlier of the games that students sometimes play in the speech class situation and of the barrier-building which results. Much more rewarding than these games are the ways that students find to provide feedback and to capitalize on feedback in order to accomplish genuine communicative purposes:

—The speaker's attitude seems to announce that he is watching for the interest and understanding or belief of his listeners.

—The speaker recognizes the signs when his classmates are puzzled or unbelieving. He acknowledges this feedback and, if he is prepared, tries to find new ways to understanding or acceptance—saying something like, "Let me put it this way, . . ."

—The listener offers clear signs that, much as he wants to understand or go along, the speaker has lost him or is threatening to turn him off.

—The listener encourages the speaker with facial expressions or verbal responses indicating strength of response, from "Uh-huh," to "It's news to me," to "How about that!"

To increase one's abilities in oral communication, then, one must increase his awareness of feedback functions in order to give more feedback and in order to adapt more to feedback. Each student of communicative speaking and listening has a responsibility to increase his *response ability.*

Conclusion

The purpose of this chapter has been to present the premises for serious study of the theory and practice of oral communication. The reader stands warned that it is not an easy study but that it can be a rewarding one. It is difficult because old perceptions of speaking and listening—and of the study thereof—must be replaced by new knowledge, new conceptions, and even new attitudes. The study is rewarding, for it promises the joy and achievement that accrues from personal effectiveness in all the human transactions that comprise one's life story.

Stress has been placed on the idea that communication is far more than message transmission; that though human minds cannot be in direct contact, they can operate effectively in mutual induction. This is done not by merely preparing messages but by first preparing oneself for interaction with others in varying communication situations, and then—on the basis of that preparation—to speak; or, in special circumstances, to compose a speech. Part of this preparation calls for sensitivity to the communication bonds and barriers; development of a sense of communicative purpose, both as speaker and as listener; and an increased awareness of human communication feedback systems.

Finally, the student is urged to treat the classroom as a real situation and to engage in real transactions with his classmates, to avoid games or going through motions, and to provide and respond to genuine feedback.

Exercises

• *Questions for Discussion*

1. What is your own attitude concerning your work in speech? What are your assumptions? Have they been modified by what is written in this chapter? How will your attitude and assumptions affect what you may do to improve your abilities in speaking and listening?

2. What do you think the study of oral communication should do for you? Why would engineers recommend speech in the engineering curriculum?

3. What are the basic differences between expression and communication? Do you need to increase your abilities in both? Why?

4. What is meant by *communicative barriers* and *communicative bonds?* Give some examples of each that are not mentioned in this chapter. Using your own examples, illustrate how a barrier may be converted into a bond, and vice versa.

5. Discuss the meanings, in relation to communicative speaking

and listening, of *rapport, common ground, status, role,* and *purpose.* Explain how each of these factors should enter into your preparation as well as into your classroom speaking and listening. To what extent are they important also in conversation and group discussion?

6. How is language used in communication—and why and how must it be supplemented? Explain, "The message is not the communication."

7. Explain *feedback* and *circular response.* How are they related to oral communication? How are they related to the extemporaneous method of speaking? How does *extemporaneous* differ from *memorized* and *impromptu* speaking? What are the similarities and differences between public speaking and conversation?

• *Projects for Speaking and Listening*

1. Analyze your own personality in a brief essay which you will show to your instructor and keep for your own guidance during the remainder of your speech course. How does your image of yourself correlate with your role, or roles, and status in your group of chosen associates? What convictions are you especially eager to communicate and fortify in speaking with your classmates? What do you hope to learn from them?

2. Learn something important about one classmate: important because he will be a listener throughout the course. Prepare to speak for two minutes, making this one idea about your classmate understandable and memorable to the class.

3. Prepare to speak for three minutes in order to illustrate some way in which oral communication is a necessity in a democratic society, in business, in the professions, or in your present activities as a student. In speaking, try to draw upon your own direct experiences and observations. Make the speaking–listening experience real by building it around a concrete problem or situation and by citing people who are well known to your listeners. Phrase as a single, specific purpose what you want to accomplish, such as, "I want my listeners to realize how ability in oral communication helps a teacher (or lawyer, or businessman, or citizen) to carry out his responsibilities effectively." Select one or several specific examples or illustrations which might help you achieve this response from your listeners. Conclude by summarizing your examples and restating your theme. Find out if there are questions or comments on your idea.

4. Analyze and compare your own point of view on any of the

assumptions regarding speaking and listening set forth in this chapter. Prepare to speak for three minutes in an attempt to get your classmates to accept your point of view.

5. Observe speaking and listening behaviors in the classroom as the course proceeds. Keep a record of what games are played. Discover barrier-building games not described in this chapter. Name the games.

6. Keep a supply of lined 3 by 5 cards to be used as listener feedback cards. For each speaker note (1) what you think the idea was which he wanted you to accept, (2) whether you understand or believe it, and (3) how important the idea is to you. Present the feedback cards to the speakers immediately after each class.

2 · Standards of Effective Communication

After roundly applauding a speaker they had just heard, two college students leaving the hall where he had spoken were overheard in the following conversation. "Mighty fine speaker," said the first. "Yes, indeed," said the other. "But what did he say?" Their responses indicate several things. The first listener may have been commenting on the over-all effect produced by the speaker, which included the impact of his personality and his manner of presentation. This listener may have responded favorably to the speaker as a person; or he may have felt that a speech should be judged primarily by its skill in presentation. He may have felt the style of the speech was artistically pleasing. The second listener indicated by his comment a basic concern with the content of the speech. His "Yes, indeed" showed an appreciation for the delivery, but he may have felt that the ultimate test of a speech is the worth of the message it conveys.

Diversity of Standards

These comments by two listeners suggest that there are varied standards by which any speech should be (and is) evaluated. They also suggest that listeners vary in what they seek to find, and in what they do find, in a speech. Both speakers and listeners play vital roles in the communicative process. Each has a duty to the other. Each also has duties to himself. And, more broadly, each has some responsibility for creating and maintaining the quality of the society of which they both are a part.

A student engaged in learning to improve his ability in oral communication might well wonder what should be the focus of his attention. Is the primary question the accuracy and pertinence of what is said? Is the problem one of analysis to determine the orderly arrangement of ideas? Is the question an ethical one, relating to the moral quality or social effects of the presentation? Should the attention of speaker and listener be directed primarily toward the actual act of communication—or should it be broadened to consider the various factors influencing the preparation and also the varied effects that might result from the occasion?

The many ways of evaluating speech communication have often been considered by members of the speech profession.[1] Always a basic test is whether the speaker accomplished a clearly defined and reasonably formulated purpose—whether he knew what he was trying to accomplish, and the degree to which the speech succeeded in attaining that goal. Concurrently, another test is whether the listeners gained from the speech any new understanding, or renewed enthusiasm, or an aroused curiosity. When oral communication occurs, the natural question is: what difference did it make? How did it affect the speaker? How did it affect the listeners? Did it change their understanding or their behavior? Did it result in any action that might not otherwise have taken place? If so, was the effect socially and ethically desirable or undesirable? This basic test consists of looking at oral discourse in terms of the purpose of speaker and listeners, and, as our brief list of questions indicates, even this test becomes complicated when its implications are explored.

Another way of viewing speech communication is to inquire into the skills of the speaker and of the listeners. Was the subject matter

[1] For a variety of viewpoints and methods of evaluating speeches, *cf.* Paul D. Holtzman, "Speech Criticism and Evaluation as Communication"; Robert T. Oliver, "The Eternal (and Infernal) Problem of Grades"; Thomas M. Sawyer, Jr., "A Grading System for Speech Classes"; Wesley Wiksell, "New Methods for Evaluating Instruction and Student Achievement in a Speech Class," *The Speech Teacher*, 9 (January 1960), pp. 1–19.

well analyzed? Were the main ideas clearly organized in support of a definite theme? Were supporting materials interesting and factual? Were all assertions logically supported? Did the speaker adapt his style and manner to the audience? Did the listeners discern the main ideas and did they evaluate them in relation to the purpose the speaker sought to achieve? Did they signal their reactions to him helpfully or were their responses distracting and indicative of indifference or hostility?

The difficulty of establishing standards by which to evaluate oral discourse is illustrated by the diversity of disciplines interested in it. Originally, the study of oral discourse was in the province of rhetoric. Then philosophers began to point out that the way in which a matter is discussed affects vitally the way in which it is evaluated, and many philosophers agreed that the standard by which discourse should be evaluated is the "symbolic transformation," which occurs when any fact is translated into words or other meaningful symbols.[2] Sociologists became concerned with oral discourse as a stream of influence flowing through society.[3] Linguists,[4] anthropologists,[5] social psychologists,[6] and many others, some using a new name, "Communicologists,"[7] have looked at oral communication through the lenses of their own specialties and therefore evaluate it by their own standards. To resolve the question of how standards should be set, and of what they are, is indeed difficult.

[2] Two such philosophers whose writings on this problem are of special interest to students of speech are Grace Andrus de Laguna, *Speech: Its Functions and Development,* New Haven, Conn.: Yale University Press, 1928; and Susanne Langer, *Philosophy in a New Key,* Cambridge, Mass.: Harvard University Press, 1938.

[3] A helpful introduction to the sociological approach to the study of speech is Hugh Dalziel Duncan, *Communication and Social Order,* New York: Bedminster Press, 1962.

[4] Benjamin Lee Whorf, "Science and Linguistics," in J. B. Carroll, ed., *Language, Thought and Reality,* New York: Wiley & Sons, 1956, pp. 207–19.

[5] Margaret Mead, "Some Cultural Approaches to Communication Problems," in Lyman Bryson, *The Communication of Ideas,* New York: Harper & Row, Publishers, Inc., 1948, pp. 9–26.

[6] Carolyn W. Sherif, Muzafer Sherif, and Roger Nebergall, *Attitude and Attitude-change,* Philadelphia, Pa.; W. B. Saunders Company, 1963.

[7] For an interesting discussion of this concept, see Keith Brooks, ed. *The Communicative Arts and Sciences of Speech,* Columbus, Ohio: Charles E. Merrill, 1967, pp. 98–106.

Starting with the Present

For an average student who is undertaking the study of speech, however, the task is relatively simple. What is of principal concern to him is his present status as speaker and listener, and what changes he would like to achieve. This is a process of self-evaluation and of establishing goals for himself. Each individual approaches this task with the realization that he already has developed a broad complex of speaking and listening habits, some of which are helpful to his generalized life aims, some harmful. These communication habits are closely akin to his personality attributes. They help to make him what he is: whether good or bad, at least distinct from all others. Some of the habits are largely external mechanics and can readily be changed. For example, one speaker does not look at his listeners when he talks, sometimes he cannot be heard, or he talks too fast. If we quickly say that good standards call for looking at the listener, talking loud enough to be heard, and talking at a suitable rate, these can be reached relatively soon. On the other hand, if a speaker tends to be self-centered, this characteristic may interfere with good communication, and it may take him longer than usual to reach the standard of becoming more listener-centered.

Our modern standards come both from those who were chiefly speakers and those who were primarily rhetoricians or scholars in current communication theory. Aristotle's *Rhetoric* is still one of the major reference points for all speakers. His standards are high, as are those of Quintilian, whom we quoted in the first chapter as an exponent of the traditional ideal of ethics and goodness as basic prerequisites for the good speaker. These writers were true rhetoricians, but they were not great speakers. In the classical era from which they came, Cicero is perhaps the outstanding combination of writer of sound rhetoric as well as an outstanding orator of his day, having practiced well the principles as enunciated in his book, *De Oratore*.

As we move through history and cite examples of men who set and practiced high standards and who exercised great influence through their speaking ability, many names come to mind. The forceful, impassioned speaking of Patrick Henry, who inspired the colonists toward revolution; the clear, reasoned logic of Daniel Webster; the energetic, crusading style of William Jennings Bryan; the dynamic sincerity of Theodore Roosevelt; and the strong personal appeal of John F. Kennedy all have contributed to our knowledge of the principles of effective speech.[8]

Standards of Oral Communication

The speaker must relate his own self-assessment to standards recognized to be fundamental to good speech communication. Our problem is to determine the kinds of standards which we should apply to ourselves here and now, within the present environment and today's society. There are several governing factors which can serve as bases for establishing standards that will be helpful as we attempt to improve communicative speaking and listening.[9]

1. *The goal is improvement in all oral communication, not merely formal public speaking.* The need we all have is for a wide variety of abilities suited to a wide variety of uses: social conversation, interviews, group discussion, impromptu talks, and the informal, short speeches in community clubs and other gatherings. We will also be called upon for oral reports in business or professions, and a variety of responsibilities within the complex business climate make greater demands on oral communication. Managers in industry have been found to spend a majority of their time talking and listening with subordinates and superiors. The professions such as law, the ministry, and teaching require constant good speech communication. Leadership in community life requires the ability to make formal speeches as well as informal discussion ability. So it is that one must consider the variety of speech communication needs he will be called upon to meet. The fact that most of these are informal and often require immediate and ready speech rather than a prepared talk becomes a vital factor in establishing standards.

[8] An example of what famous men say of their own speaking is Eugene E. White and C. R. Henderleider, "What Harry S. Truman Told Us about His Speaking," *The Quarterly Journal of Speech,* 40 (February, 1954), pp. 37–42; see also H. L. Ewbank, Sr., *et al.,* "What Is Speech? A Symposium," *The Quarterly Journal of Speech,* 41 (April, 1955), pp. 145–53.

[9] For other discussions of standards; *cf.* James H. McBurney and Ernest J. Wrage, "Standards of Good Speech," *The Art of Good Speech*, Chapter II, Englewood Cliffs, N.J.: Prentice-Hall, Inc., 1953; Robert T. Oliver, "Standards of Good Speech," *Effective Speech for Democratic Living,* Chapter II, Englewood Cliffs, N.J.: Prentice-Hall, Inc., 1959; and Eugene E. White, "A Positive Approach to Speaking," *Practical Speech Fundamentals,* Chapter II, New York: Crowell-Collier and Macmillan, Inc., 1960.

2. *The democratic character of our time has led to emphasis upon conversational talk with our listeners, rather than exhortations directed at them.* Our society values the exchange of ideas, the sharing of information, the cooperative solution of problems. We are developing a growing awareness of our social and ethical responsibilities toward one another and a greater respect for the thinking, judgment, and feelings of others. This feeling of mutual respect has led to a desire to talk things over with cooperative listeners rather than to talk down to them in the manner of an authoritarian orator. This does not mean that we underrate the value of enthusiasm, force, energy, and sincerity that have universally characterized great oratory; it does mean that we adapt these qualities to cultivate a more intimate and conversational manner that will bring us closer to our listeners and to their reaction. This change in social circumstances has led to a change in speaking effectiveness—and this also affects our standards.

3. *The immediate problem in a beginning speech course is self-improvement in oral communication.* Our prospect for doing this will be enhanced if we relate standards closely to the learning process. How can we best achieve systematic progress? This focus demands that our standards involve ourselves as learners. Placing the emphasis on learning rather than on doing makes an essential difference in the attitude we must bring to speaking assignments in the speech class.[10] Whether one fully understands and accepts this difference will largely determine how much improvement he may hope to accomplish. It is an essential condition prerequisite to becoming a successful student of speech communication.

Some of this objective involves unlearning bad habits. This must be done in any endeavor. In athletics, the would-be tennis player may need to change the way he grips the racket in order to gain an ability to stroke the ball rather than to "pat" it. The would-be typist must unlearn the "hunt and peck" method in mastering the touch system.

So it is with good speaking which demands using a tighter organization, a more purposive ordering of materials, an audience-centered view of methods, a variety of types of speaking, all of which may be unfamiliar. Gradually more and more skills will have to be remembered and the process of speaking will come to seem more and more complex as one gives up some of his old habits picked up through hit-or-miss methods or random experience. Some requirements for good speaking

[10] For an analysis of communication and learning, see David K. Berlo, *The Process of Communication,* Chapter IV, New York: Holt, Rinehart and Winston, Inc., 1960.

may even be resisted. Many students, for example, declare that outlining does not help them—on the contrary, that it interferes with their freedom of thought.

In other words, there is a natural tendency to resist giving up the old, partially successful methods for the sake of new ones that in the long run will be much better. But the unlearning and the use of tried and proven methods are both essential if the course in speech is to have lasting results.

4. *All standards must be considered in relation to listeners.* This is to realize that every principle, concept, method, and technique making up the essentials of good speech communication is for the purpose of achieving some kind of listener response. None of these is simply for the self-satisfaction or self-expression of the speaker alone. He will, therefore, constantly strive to consider the usefulness of any standard in relation to its effect on specific listeners.

As we think, then, of the standards which should govern good speaking, we should view them according to these four factors: (1) what is needed is improvement in a wide variety of forms of oral discourse; (2) in order to be effective, speech today must be addressed to listeners as co-participants in the communicative process; (3) the goal is not only to speak well but to learn to speak better; and (4) all standards must be adapted to particular listeners. With these factors in mind, we shall now consider the standards that apply to all of us under these circumstances.

We have established five major qualities or norms under which all standards can be considered: the ethical standard, the logical standard, the artistic standard, the educational standard, and the results standard.

The Ethical Standard—for Speaking

Ethics is concerned with moral values.[11] As we apply the ethical standard to the work one does in a speech course, the following questions will need to be considered:

[11] The problem of ethics in speaking has been discussed by many writers. *Cf.* Lionel Crocker, "Truth through Personality," *The Quarterly Journal of Speech,* 39 (April, 1953), pp. 1–5; Robert T. Oliver, "The Ethics of Persuasion," *The Psychology of Persuasive Speech,* Chapter II, New York: MacKay, 1957, and Karl Wallace, "An Ethical Basis of Communication," *The Speech Teacher,* 4 (January, 1955), pp. 1–9.

1. *Is the speaker being truthful in what he says about the subject?* This question suggests that speakers should not deliberately lie to their listeners; facts should not be misinterpreted or misrepresented, authorities should not be misquoted, and, if illustrations or examples are invented, the listeners should be told they are hypothetical, not real. Failure to represent a subject truthfully also may result from the speaker's lack of understanding of it. In dealing with a subject of great complexity and on which he has only limited knowledge, a speaker cannot say or imply to his audience that he knows all there is to know. If a speech is based on just one magazine article (which may be prejudiced), listeners may be misled. Before one tells others what to think about a subject, he must be willing to take enough trouble to be sure he understands it himself.

Philosophers declare that there is an ethical responsibility to be *morally thoughtful,* by which they mean that misrepresentation resulting from careless thinking or lack of information is in itself a form of deception. And when the full facts of a subject can be ascertained by thoughtful examination of research sources, there is a genuine moral obligation to study them more fully.

2. *Are reasonable requirements for both the facts and opinions presented being satisfied?* What is true about racial relations, for example, may be extremely difficult to determine; but when something regarding this (or any other subject) is stated as a fact, it should first be ascertained that the fact is true. Many people seem not to realize that there is a similar requirement for reasonable validation of their publicly stated opinions. One indeed may have a right to his own opinion, however foolish it may seem to others; but listeners have an equal right to know on what the opinion is based. An opinion is frequently no better than the facts or inferences that support it.

If an opinion is based on false information, superficial observation, or false reasoning, it is unethical to present it to listeners as something they should take seriously. Meanwhile, as listeners we have need to be aware that intensity of conviction is not necessarily the equivalent of being right. A speaker may display the utmost emotional intensity in support of an idea that is factually unsound. It is common to make a clear-cut distinction between facts and opinions, but it does not mean that speakers have free license to advocate opinions wrongly drawn from unreliable facts. There is no escape from the ethical obligation to be morally thoughtful.

3. *Are the feelings of the listeners being reasonably considered?* If language or stories are vulgar (or thought by listeners to be vulgar),

this would be a clear violation of good taste, which many might find offensive. If derogatory remarks about particular religious views are made, some listeners may be hurt. If the qualities of women, or of Negroes, or of Jews, or of immigrants, or of Orientals are disparaged, they as well as other listeners may be offended. When the feelings of even one person in an audience are hurt, others will be offended, even if they themselves were not hurt. This is not to say that such subjects are always to be avoided. What is important is that in talking on any sensitive or controversial subject, a respectful and responsible consideration for opposing points of view and feelings must be demonstrated by the speaker.

It is unfair, and therefore unethical, to use the opportunity as a speaker to attack a viewpoint which the listeners do not have adequate opportunity to defend. And it debases the value of oral communication to present a point of view with such vituperation and bitterness that it invites or perhaps compels replies in a similarly quarrelsome vein. The important consideration is to respect both one's own views and those of the people to whom one talks.

The Logical Standard—for Speaking

Man's mind is basically orderly. He likes to think that it is systematic, analytical, and logical. He, therefore, can attend better to speeches that are well thought out in terms of purpose and scope; that are clearly and logically organized; and that show sound thinking, depth of thinking, and good support and evidence for the points being made.

1. *The structure of the speech should be clear and easy to follow.* Rhetoricians from Aristotle to the present day have described a design for good speaking; and listeners like speakers who observe a "pattern of expectation." A speech should have an introduction, body, and conclusion. A speaker is expected to make clear and definite transitions from one point to the next. If he fails to do so, the result may be a response of confusion from the listener, and an inability to understand clearly or fully. A listener's response in the desired direction may well depend on the ease with which he can follow what is being said.

2. *Materials, proof, and evidence should be sound.* This requirement relates to the developmental materials the speaker uses in enlarging upon and proving his ideas. There is a fundamental rule that people attend to the concrete and specific. It is much more difficult to hold interest when talking in generalities and abstractions. Listeners can detect the difference between "hot air" and worthwhile information.

Credibility of source and accuracy in the use of materials are factors that weigh heavily toward listener understanding and acceptance. When controversial opinions are proposed, they must be supported and proved with more meaningful materials. In this usage, the question in the mind of the listener that must be answered is, "Does the evidence support this speaker's opinions or assertions?"

3. *Clear and logical reasoning must stand out over fuzzy thinking.* While it is true that all listeners do not draw the same inferences or conclusions from the same facts or evidence, the average person can detect illogical and unsupported claims. The requirement for sound and accurate materials is of course closely related to this one, for reasoning is the process of drawing inferences or conclusions from facts or information, or from other conclusions already accepted or proved. The ability to think analytically is also a closely related standard, as well as that of showing a clear and logical structure in one's talk. When the subject is laid out clearly and all of its parts stand out and then are put together by the speaker in an understandable sequence, this all adds to his credibility as a logical person and tends to make his points more acceptable, partly because the speaker's image is enhanced favorably.

The Artistic or Esthetic Standard—for Speaking

Speech, like music, painting, or any other art, has one legitimate function in simply giving pleasure to both speaker and listeners.[12] There should be true pleasure in any good communication artistically accomplished, deriving from our appreciation of the artistry of the speaker. Although we think of the artistic in terms of other qualities primarily, even the principle of the logical standard in the preceding section contributes toward artistry. For surely art includes such qualities as good structure, interesting materials, and the inducement of logical thought processes.

1. *Language should be suitable.* One speaking situation might call for very formal diction, another for a colloquial style. Artistry primarily demands an appropriate style to fit the circumstances and that this style be consistent throughout, or, if inconsistent, that there be a clearly obvious reason. For example, in a technical discussion of a new medical discovery, the language might most suitably be technical; nevertheless,

[12] A speech rated for giving pleasure while also conveying a serious message is Russell H. Conwell, *Acres of Diamonds,* New York: Harper & Row, Publishers, 1943.

for interest effect, a colloquial expression might be used. Both speaker and listener should understand instantly why this change is being made and how it relates to the over-all nature of the speech. Language adapted to the listeners will also be more appealing to them.

2. *The manner of the speaker can affect his artistry.* It is not always necessary or even desirable that the speaker be formal in his dress and general bearing. For some situations and for some subjects, a very large measure of informality might be better. What is important, from the standpoint of artistry, is that the speaker should "suit his manner to the words, his words to the manner"; that he should adopt a method that is understood by his listeners, so they may judge what he is doing on criteria of appropriateness.

It is of course impossible to separate manner from appearance. The initial impression of the listener probably comes from sheer physical appearance. It should be obvious that appropriate dress and even the way one walks to the platform and is seated as he is being introduced would contribute to his total image. Then his facial expression, his degree of sincerity and enthusiasm, and his directness would all be important to the shaping and retaining of a favorable image by his listeners.

3. *Naturalness contributes to artistry.* Frequently throughout this book we will be warning that speaking is not a performance, that one tries to communicate rather than to impress his listeners with his own skill. They react favorably to his skill when it is not obvious, when it is a part of his natural self. Much speaking is not effective because the speaker is obviously more concerned with whether he is doing it well than with what he is trying to communicate to listeners. Suffice it to say here that whenever the listeners think of a talk as a performance (good or bad), it is probably violating the esthetic standard. A speech conforms to the demands of this standard when the manner of composition and presentation are both so well managed that they are not thought about separately. Style should not get in the way of either content or delivery. But it is also true that the very act of doing anything well (including speaking) is a source of pleasure both to the doer and the receiver.

The Results Standard—for Speaking

In terms of our emphasis upon the achievement of the desired response as the ultimate aim of all good speech communication, one basis for judging any talk is to consider its effects. If a speaker is trying to sell a vacuum cleaner or to win votes, to borrow money or to reconcile an aggrieved friend, an obvious standard by which to judge the quality of his talk is to ask whether—or to what extent—it succeeded. "I tried to explain the meaning of *metempsychosis,* and now they do understand it," a speaker may say in justification of his speaking. Or, "My aim was to entertain them, and they laughed all the way through mv talk." The results standard is a natural and proper test that, along with the others, is always applicable.

It must be kept in mind that results are generally neither obvious nor uncomplicated. It is possible to accomplish a great deal through a communicative transaction without any results being immediately apparent. Often a genuine change of attitude or of convictions is a slow process. Listeners may be deeply influenced by what a speaker says to them even though the influence may not be apparent either to them or to him at the time. Listeners who scoff at an idea when they first hear it may, as time passes, come to think much better of it. An apology which is angrily rejected may, on later consideration, become the basis for recognizing an endangered friendship. A salesman who warns a potential customer not to buy a particular item often creates confidence which leads to future sales. Sometimes the evidence of failure is misleading. And equally misleading may be the evidence of success. Listeners who laugh heartily at a speaker's jokes may, nevertheless, lose respect for him because of his vulgarisms or crudity. An audience may understand an explanation of a process, while revising downward their regard for the speaker's intelligence because he belabors the obvious. Sometimes, too, a speech may suggest to the listeners ideas of value which were not even intended by the speaker; and it also happens that speakers may discover more meaning in their own words than they realized were in them. Results, in many ways, are less measurable than might be assumed.

Assessment of results must also be qualified by the following considerations:

1. *The end may not justify the means.* Entertainment achieved through vulgarisms or by ridicule of others or by such self-debasement that it may weaken the respect of the listeners for the serious views of the speaker is success purchased at too high a cost. Persuasion achieved by misrepresentation of facts or by attacks against the integrity of honest people is in direct violation of the ethical standard. Clarity of understanding that is gained by oversimplification actually results in a misconception of the real truth of the matter discussed. If a sound conclusion is supported by shoddy rationalization, the effect in part is to undermine respect for and ability in logical reasoning. We are

never justified in pleading that audience reactions are the final test of the merit of the speaking unless the means used to secure a favorable reaction are thoroughly laudable.

2. *The listener's reaction is secondary to the conviction of the speaker concerning the actual truth of the matter.* If one is interested solely in gaining a favorable response from listeners, he might be tempted to accept their way of thinking instead of leading them to his own more correct views. For example, a confirmed Democrat would be in violation of his own fundamental political purposes if he sought approval of a Republican audience by advocating election of Republican candidates. The "effect achieved," then, only means good speaking when the response secured conforms to the facts as the speaker understands them, and to the principles in which he believes.

3. *The effect must be adjudged in terms of the nature of the problem.* Success in gaining understanding from listeners on how to fill out the stub of a checkbook or how to thread a needle is not a very significant achievement for a classroom speech. Whether one can really explain effectively remains to be tested when he deals with a more complicated problem—such as how to estimate the relation of profits to costs in the operation of a business, or how a complicated instrument works. Demosthenes, often acclaimed the world's greatest orator, failed when he tried to persuade the Athenians to unite against the threat of Philip of Macedonia. Woodrow Wilson failed when he tried to persuade the United States Senate to approve membership in the League of Nations. They failed in achieving their desired response, yet they achieved perhaps other important purposes in speaking out on their deep convictions.[13] Duty may impel a speaker to undertake tasks of such magnitude, or that meet so much opposition, that he cannot achieve a favorable audience response. If we should judge speech only by the standards of immediate success, we might well be tempted always to speak on popular sides of issues or to try to explain only very elementary ideas or processes.

Political analyst William V. Shannon, in the New York *Post,* August 6, 1961, discussed the relationships of this standard to Adlai Stevenson's unsuccessful campaign for the presidency. "Stevenson's campaign ended in defeat, but the mere fact of victory or defeat is not always and at all times the most important fact, in politics or

[13] For a discussion of speakers who risked position and reputation to speak up for almost impossible causes, *cf.* John F. Kennedy, *Profiles in Courage,* New York: Harper & Row, Publishers, Inc., 1956.

in anything else. . . . What matters is not whether a candidate wins or loses but whether he contributes anything to the dialogue by which our people gradually amass their common wisdom and, hopefully, go forward. Adlai Stevenson in defeat did more to contribute to our understanding of ourselves and the world in which we live than have many victors. That is justification enough."

4. *The effect aimed for should be reasonably adjusted to the reaction possibilities of the listeners.* If one speaks on equality of races on two different occasions, once to a group in Augusta, Maine, and then to an audience in Augusta, Georgia, his basic point of view would be the same for both situations; but he might wisely try to accomplish something different in speaking to the Georgia audience from what he would try in Maine. This simply takes into account the fact that some things may easily be accomplished with a single speech (such as getting a young lady to go to the movies); whereas other objectives (such as improving the study habits of your younger brother) may require many talks, perhaps by several people. In judging a speech by its effects, then, we need to inquire whether the effect sought was within the realm of reasonable attainment.

5. *Factors wholly outside the speech situation must not be overlooked.* The mood, background, and prior knowledge of the subject by listeners are some of the factors affecting the results. An attempt to entertain a listener might fail because he had just received bad news from his family or news that he had failed to be selected by a fraternity. Similar disturbances, such as not feeling well, might interfere with a listener's interest or even ability at the time to understand or to be persuaded. Again, relatively unskilled speaking (for instance, an explanation of the physical complexities of water) might seem to succeed if the particular listeners (perhaps unknown to the speaker) had recently heard a lecture on the same subject by their chemistry professor.

The importance of the results standard should not be undervalued. All good speech is presumably aimed to accomplish the speaker's specific purpose in terms of the desired listener response. It is entirely proper to estimate its success or failure in terms of its effect, but not without careful consideration of these five reservations.

The Educational Standard—for Speaking

Up to now, our standards have dealt primarily with the qualities a speech should have to achieve what the speaker desires concerning the listener reaction and response. This standard is concerned with what good speaking objectives and standards will do to further your education. The course in speech is a part of the entire educational program in which you are engaged.[14] We are thus discussing the following educational values that may accrue for speakers and listeners.

1. *Is your speaking helping you to learn and become accustomed to disciplined methods of thinking and behaving that will help you to be a more dependable member of any group?* In a speech class, it is important that every speaker be fully prepared at specific times, and in specific ways. You cannot fail to speak when your turn comes (unless you are ill). Moreover, you are given a stated period of time for your talk. If you use very much more time than this, you steal that time away from other students, or from the opportunity of the instructor to teach the whole class through the medium of oral evaluations. This same type of discipline, of course, is also taught in classes in English composition, mathematics, and laboratory sciences—in any class in which work is to be done on a regular schedule. The difference is that you cannot fail to meet your responsibilities in speech without direct damage to other people. Reliability is a highly regarded asset.

2. *Does the speech serve a worthwhile function in broadening your intellectual perspective, or in deepening understanding, both of you and your listeners?* If the subject or its development is superficial, neither you during its preparation nor the listeners during its presentation will learn much of value. One attribute of positive value a speech may have is that it be intellectually challenging or stimulating. In preparing a talk, or in listening to it, you can make a contribution to your education. Some of the advice on subject selection for speeches is that you draw from your own experiences and interests. This advice is sound; but in following it you should also seek to expand what you already know. If you have a vague notion that you should know something about Milton's use of symbolism in *Paradise Lost,* the fact that you actually do *not* know about it may be a good reason for choosing to speak on it, not for avoiding it. What you learn as you study the subject will help you; and the very fact that it is not common-

[14] Many writers have discussed the educational values of speech. *Cf* Irving Lee, *How to Talk with People,* New York: Harper & Row, Publishers, Inc., 1952; Earl J. McGrath, *Communication in General Education,* Dubuque, Iowa: Wm. C. Brown Company, 1949; and Robert T. Oliver, "Who Says You Should Be a Better Speaker?", *Today's Speech,* XI (April, 1963), pp. 16–17.

place knowledge means that when you speak your listeners will also gain additional information. "Is what I am doing intellectually valuable?" is a sound guide to follow in preparation for speaking.

3. *Does your talk function to increase your own skill in speaking?* If you are not very good at telling jokes, perhaps there is value for you in attaining this skill. Instead of accepting the limitation upon your communicative abilities, work at this particular weakness until you do improve. Similarly, you may have trouble in organizing your ideas clearly, or in making effective internal summaries as your talks progress from one point to another, or in using questions that genuinely arouse listeners to a sense of active participation. Your first two or three talks presented to the class should serve a diagnostic purpose, as you and your instructor discover what kinds of problems you in particular need to solve. When this is determined, you should try successively in every speech thereafter to make substantial progress in mastering those problems. What you can do well you naturally most enjoy doing; but what you do poorly is what you most need to concentrate upon.

4. *Does your speaking contribute to the meaningful integration of your total learning, thinking, and feeling?* Your speech is a significant way of expressing your whole personality. If your work in college is helping you to attain a richer and truer understanding of social conditions, of economic problems, of political issues, of natural science, and of human relations, this increased competence should be reflected in your talks. You may not always wish to talk seriously about vital problems, but surely you should progress in the direction of becoming an educated person.

Your college experience includes a wide variety of subjects studied with many different professors, as well as a wide range of new social experiences, including bull sessions on varied topics. Somehow, all these new experiences need to be brought together into a master integration. Your political ideas are affected by what you learn in economics, sociology, and other courses. How you think about personal and national problems should be influenced by your course in logic and perhaps by work in natural science, as well as in the humanities and social sciences. Achieving a genuine integration of all you learn and of all you feel and believe should be one of your major concerns. There will be no better opportunity to do this than in your speech class. Your speeches should draw together your wide range of new and old information, as laboratory exercises to demonstrate your growing understanding and sensitivity; and, similarly, your opportunity to listen to your classmates will afford stimulating experiences in integrating your total education and growth process.

Standards of Effective Listening

Listening may not be as easily evaluated as speaking, for much of it is covert. Still there are criteria that can be applied—some by observers and speakers and others by the listeners themselves. The basic consideration is: to what extent does the listener contribute appropriately to the communication transaction? This is different from simply asking if the listener contributed the response desired by the speaker. In some situations it may be appropriate for a listener to reject the idea of the speaker. A listener may very appropriately reject a proposal that he change his mind about, say, legalized gambling, if he discovers that the speaker is violating the ethical or logical standard.

Effective listening is far more than playing a game of sit-up-and-pay attention. Everyone knows how to look as if he were listening while thinking of other matters. But there are contributions to be made—to oneself, to the speaker, and to the other listeners.

The Ethical Standard—for Listening

In a society built on the principle that major issues are decided by the people, those people have an ethical responsibility to expose themselves to available persuasion on the issues. Not only must they listen, but they must listen ethically; not quite like the popular cartoon strip character who insisted, "Naturally, I'll listen to the opposition political candidate. I pride myself on being unprejudiced, open-minded, and objective, so I will listen fairly to what I know will be a lot of hog-wash!"

Freedom of speech is a constitutional guarantee to listeners as well as speakers. A democracy cannot offer its people freedom of expression only. But the democratic form of government does offer freedom of communicative speech on the assumption that listeners will make responsible use of the advocacy of others. The primary ethical principle of persuasion in our society is this listener ethic.

This principle includes the notion that listeners can be judged and can judge themselves on a criterion of appropriateness of contribution: to at least match the standards of the speaker, or, even more, to encourage the speaker more fully to meet his responsibilities. Further, listeners have ethical responsibilities to other listeners. How listeners behave influences the contributions of others.

The Logical Standard—for Listening

Every listener has the additional responsibility to check the logic of the speaker's ideas, to determine if what the speaker proposes follows from accepted premises. When a cigarette commercial suggests, "Try something different for a change, turn to Salem," is it saying that Salem is the only cigarette that is different from other brands? In a recent study a large proportion of students thought the ad said just that.[15]

A listener who meets the logical standard is not easily led into accepting untested speaker's conclusions. He has time to think through logical relationships because listening is much faster than speaking. He is alert to fallacies,[16] the uses and misuses of statistics, and equally alert to detecting valid logic and conclusions that do necessarily follow from properly derived and reported facts.

In short, the effective listener is a critical listener. Improvement in critical listening is a legitimate goal of all students in a course in communicative speech.

The Artistic or Esthetic Standard—for Listening

Listening, like speaking, is an art and can be judged as an art. Some of the unesthetic listener behaviors include what one writer calls "compulsive nodding,"[17] which is a listener game of LOOKIT ME—LOOKIT HOW I DO (at listening). This may at first encourage speakers but soon will bring pleasure neither to the speaker nor to other listeners present. Also, just as a speaker may distract with random movements and fiddling, so listeners may distract—themselves, other listeners, and speakers—with inappropriate, restless movements, reading, and doodling.

Not all listening behaviors show, however. Often the listener himself must judge. Later, however, the speaker and perhaps other listeners may judge the art in part by the results.

[15] Ivan L. Preston, "Logic and Illogic in Advertising," *Journalism Quarterly,* 44 (Summer 1967), pp. 231–39.

[16] See W. Ward Fearnside and William B. Holther, *Fallacy: The Counterfeit of Argument,* Englewood Cliffs, N.J.: Prentice-Hall, Inc., 1959.

[17] Dominick A. Barbara, *The Art of Listening,* Springfield, Ill.: Charles C Thomas, 1958, pp. 113–14.

The Results Standard—for Listening

A communication outcome is a change in speaker and listener. Communicative listening may be judged on the basis of outcomes. The effective listener puts together what he hears with what he knows and determines whether they add up to a new perception of his world. Further, the effective listener communicates his interest in the speaker in order to get maximum speaker contribution. These are the major gains of the communicative listener: solving the problems of needed new perceptions and communicating interest.

Other results are apt to be less desirable. Listeners sometimes merely record, or store the message without interacting with the speaker. This is a frequent listening result in lecture courses, in which the listener sheds the message at examination time. Another result may come from "reverie," the mode of listening in which the result is a kind of daydreaming not unlike the reading experience in which one suddenly realizes that he has been thinking of something else. Finally, just as listening may communicate interest, so may it communicate hostility. The hostile listener is often pleased to note minor errors by the speaker and to dwell on them in his thoughts while missing the rest of what he has to say, and making no other contribution.

Through different listening modes[18] different results accrue. Therefore, listener contributions to a communication transaction will vary in a given instance. A related source of variation in the way listeners meet the results standard lies in the purpose which they bring to the transaction.

The Educational Standard—for Listening

Listening can be judged by its educational contribution—to the listener, of course, but also to the speaker and to other listeners. A "recording" listener, for instance, violates this standard when new perceptions fail to emerge. One's listening should contribute no less than one's speaking to a meaningful integration of total learning, thinking, and feeling. In many ways the primary mode of education is shifting to an increased reliance on listening: a major effect of changing media of communication.

[18] For further discussion of the modes of listening, see Paul D. Holtzman, *The Psychology of Speakers' Audiences,* Chapter 2, Glenview, Ill.: Scott, Foresman and Company, (in press).

The educational standard for judging listening suggests two important tasks for the student. One is the development of improved listening ability. The other is constant application of the developed skill, for in changing times one must always be a learner.

Your Potential for Meeting These Standards

You may have much greater potential than you think. Why not assess your capabilities by appraising yourself as a communicator today? Make an inventory in which you list your assets and liabilities. Your inventory will guide you in ascertaining what standards you can most readily meet, as well as those that might require more work. Keep revising this inventory from week to week.

We have already pointed out that speakers are made. There are no born orators, great actors, champion boxers, or four-minute milers. They all reached success through hard work; having set high goals, they are willing to exert the effort required to reach such goals. Few of us want to be great public speakers. We want to be good speakers, able to communicate with others when the occasion demands it, and we want to be able to meet the challenge of any communicative situation. So the goals we set should be modest and within reach.

Your potential to meet the standards, then, is what you make of it. The chief determining question in accomplishing your objective is the attitude you take toward speech training and its potential importance to you. As long as your attitude is positive, enthusiastic, and sincere, you will do the things necessary to reach the standards you set for yourself. And, as you progress and find yourself reaching and then surpassing these, you will revise them upward, for no one has yet reached the ultimate goal of perfect speaker or listener.

Steps in Guiding Your Development

Once you set your standards, work on them systematically by following the plan and assignments of your speech course diligently and with these suggestions as guidelines:

1. Remember the scope of the total process of communication.
2. Recognize your social and ethical responsibilities as a speaker and listener.

3. Measure your present ability in relation to your standards.
4. In setting goals, consider your potential to meet them.
5. Set aside ample time for work and practice.
6. Prepare for every speech thoroughly; apply the principles in conversation, too.
7. Practice according to your needs.
8. Seize opportunities to speak when you have something to say.
9. Use speaking opportunities to exert your best influence as a person.
10. Apply standards to all communicative situations.

Conclusion

This chapter has aimed to bring into focus those standards for speaking and listening that will serve as a foundation for study and practice, both in the present speech course and throughout life. After examining the problem and the bases of selection, we have arrived at and analyzed five major standards. These should be adopted as guides to follow in working toward improvement in communicative speech. Those standards that seem of greatest significance are the ones that will best motivate toward progress.

Others will always judge us as speakers and communicators: our instructor and fellow students in speech class, our business and social associates in the world at large. How we talk will always be a matter of interest and a source of judgment by our peers. In other words, it is wise to have in mind the standards that other people will measure us by, and it is sensible to attempt to meet them at all times. In the long run, we achieve not much more than we ask ourselves to do. As one takes up the study of communicative speech, the objectives to be gained are much beyond the academic study of a subject and classroom procedures. The standards to set and work for will play a continuing part throughout life.

Exercises

• *Questions for Discussion*

1. How may a speaker who excels according to certain standards offset obvious weaknesses in others?

2. Among the five major standards discussed in this chapter, and the many subdivisions, pick out the ones which you feel mean most to you at this stage of your development, both in yourself and as you like to apply them to speakers you hear. In discussing these, consider why it is that there are similarities and differences in the selection made by different students.

3. Which standards apply with particular force to public speaking? To group discussion? To informal conversation?

4. In general striving for excellence, plan to discuss the principle or question of how high above one's present level should he set his standards initially? After the speech course is half finished?

• *Projects for Speaking and Listening*

1. Pick some nationally or internationally famous speaker whom you admire for his speaking ability and evaluate his speaking in terms of the five major standards. Plan a brief talk in class on this.

2. As you listen to the early speeches of your classmates, write a brief paper indicating which standards seem to be met most effectively and which are most violated. Do they fall into categories related more to speech content, delivery, or the speaker as an individual?

3. By consensus among your classmates, agree on listening to a particular speaker (on television or preferably in person) and each pick out the standard he seems to meet best. Hold panel discussions in class in which you compare your choices.

4. Analyze your present level of ability in relation to the speaking and listening standards, indicating those you meet best and those in which you need maximum effort for improvement. Make a list of all of these and rate yourself on each one presently, using a percentage rating. Then plan to rate these again half way through the course and again at the end of the course.

5. After completing a speaking assignment, comment on the kinds of listening behavior you observed among your audience while speaking.

3 · *Preparing for Communicative Situations*

Whenever two or more people confront one another, however casually, they communicate. Even if no words are exchanged—and even when, as strangers, they scarcely glance at one another—each reveals considerable information about himself (clothes, posture, appearance, mannerisms) and each makes judgments, however fleetingly, about the other. Social contact always involves communication, at least to the extent that attitudes and feelings are revealed and are rightly or wrongly interpreted. Furthermore, even when individuals are alone, much of our thinking involves the impressions we do, or might, or should make upon other people, and we also speculate upon the means of making impressions. In a loose and often ill-considered fashion, much of the waking time of all individuals is devoted either to communicating or to preparing to do so. The theme of this chapter is that preparation can be much improved when it is deliberate and guided.

The Nature of Preparation

Sometimes the preparation is for a specific speaking event. On June 16, 1858, at Springfield, Illinois, Abraham Lincoln accepted the senatorial nomination, which set him upon the road that led two years later to the presidency. His opening words are useful guides to anyone who is preparing for a significant speech—either to give it or to listen to it: "If we could first know where we are, and whither we are tending, we could then better judge what to do, and how to do it." The occasion was important, and Lincoln spent off and on about one month preparing the speech. He wanted to make sure that he said what he himself most wanted to say; and he wanted to be sure he phrased his ideas in ways that would have the maximum probable appeal to his listeners. His preparation reflected the earnestness of his concern.[1]

Another of the greatest speeches in American history was Daniel Webster's second speech in his debate with Robert Hayne, in the United States Senate, on January 26, 1830. Webster was busy at the time with an important case which he was presenting before the Supreme Court, and it was not apparent that he had any time at all to prepare his speech. When a friend expressed amazement at the flow of facts, logic, and eloquence which gushed forth seemingly without preparation, Webster explained: "I was already posted, and had only to take down my notes and refresh my memory. In other words, if he had tried to make a speech to fit my notes, he could not have hit it better. No man is inspired with the occasion; I never was."[2] Webster might have added that his preparation consisted also of wide reading and of an excellent memory for what he had read; for when Hayne made a reference to *Macbeth,* Webster instantly recalled the scene and noted how it might be interpreted in a way not to support but to undermine Hayne's position.

For both listening and speaking, the individual should prepare himself as well as the subject matter; and the preparation should be both immediate and long-term. Furthermore, since communication involves a tight relationship between speaker and listener, each should prepare both himself and the subject in relation to the other. Understanding a subject is only a part of preparing to speak effectively on it or to listen intelligently to a discussion of it. It is necessary also to understand oneself in relation to the subject and in relation to the

[1] A detailed account of Lincoln's preparation for this speech is found in Carl Sandburg, *Lincoln: The Prairie Years,* Toronto: Blue Ribbon Books, 1926, p. 376; and David Donald, *Lincoln's Herndon,* New York: Alfred A. Knopf, 1948, pp. 118–19.

[2] Peter Harvey, *Reminiscences and Anecdotes of Daniel Webster,* Boston, Mass.: Little, Brown & Company, 1878, pp. 149–52.

other participants in the discussion; and also to understand how the attitudes one holds toward himself and toward his listeners affect his interpretation of the subject matter. Feelings and beliefs are closely interwoven. We truly prepare to communicate only when this interrelationship is understood and ideas are re-adjusted accordingly. To plunge ahead without realizing the effects of prejudice, ignorance, or bias and without undertaking to compensate for these influences is to invite communicative blocks and failures. Effective communication begins with clear thinking.

Self-Preparation for Oral Communication

What we know is greatly conditioned and limited by how we know it. The seven blind men of Turkestan who went to see the elephant thought that it was a rope, a trunk, a wall, a spear, a snake, a fan, or a tree, depending on where each of them touched it. In another familiar story several men observing an expanse of landscape thought it was a source of timber, a potential farmstead, a scene to be painted, a good plot for real estate development, a tourist attraction, or a manifestation of the glory of God—depending on their varied experiences and interests. Mark Twain, in his essay, "Letter to a Person Sitting in Darkness," observed that never in all history had there been an aggressive war, since every nation believes it is protecting its vital interests. Understanding depends only in part upon mastering the nature of the subject; it depends even more truly upon controlling the bias or special viewpoint of the individual who is considering the subject.

Communication always involves at least two people; hence, there are always at least two different viewpoints from which the subject of discussion is viewed. Both speaker and listeners suffer from three sources of misunderstanding: (1) their attitudes differ; (2) their experiences have been different; and (3) their viewpoints are different. When preparing for communicative speaking or listening, it is wise to consider your own relationship to each of these three problems and also the probable relation to them of the others who will participate in the discourse. In other words, if you are to hear a speech you will do well to consider in advance what you know concerning the attitudes, experiences, and convictions of the speaker that may color his interpretation of the subject. If you expect to give a speech, you will need to develop your ideas and to phrase them in ways that will take account of these factors among your listeners. And if you are to participate in conversation or a discussion, these factors should influence both how you speak and how you interpret what others say.

1. *Differing attitudes influence individual views of specific subjects.* There are such things as conservative or liberal attitudes, racial and religious prejudices, and partisan loyalties; and there are strong preferences for rural or city life, for or against personal participation in social crusades, and for or against boisterous and extroverted assertiveness. Some individuals are exceedingly practical-minded, some are esthetic, some religious. For some anything new is regarded favorably, for others it has to be old to be considered safe and sound. As one expert in human reactions has said: "Our knowledge of simple facts depends to some extent on the attitudes or views we hold about more general issues, in the sense that if these attitudes were different then the facts we know would be different also."[3] One whose attitude toward women drivers is derogatory will view a specific instance of bad driving by saying, "Just like a woman!"; whereas, if it is a man who makes a stupid blunder he may say, "I wonder what's wrong with that fellow?"

We tend to reinforce our general attitudes by noticing, or at least by emphasizing, only such specific instances as do support them. Instances that run counter to our attitudes we dismiss as being exceptional or unimportant. Political partisans who favor the President are confirmed in their attitude by what he does; but so are those who oppose him. As Walter Lippmann has pointed out: "For the most part we do not first see, then define; we define and then see."[4] Our attitudes are glasses that color reality.

2. *Different experiences influence views of specific subjects.* Students of civil engineering tend to notice the details of the construction of a bridge as they pass along the highway; students of animal husbandry note the number, breed, and condition of cows pasturing in a field. We look for what we are used to looking at. What is easily forgotten is that everyone's experience is exceedingly limited. There is a great deal to be known about any subject which no one person can ever know. And of what is known or knowable, individuals select only those portions that make sense to them in terms of their own experience. Thus, out of the totality of possible meanings, each individual "selects for attention a little of it and groups that little in various

[3] Angus Sinclair, *The Conditions of Knowing,* New York: Harcourt, Brace & World, Inc., 1951, p. 14.

[4] Walter Lippmann, *Public Opinion,* Baltimore, Md.: Penguin Books, Inc., 1946, p. 61.

ways in his attention. This tiny residue is what we call his experience or what he experiences. It is a small selection of a small selection. It is the scraps or fragments of the independent reality."[5] Since other people are forming their judgments upon different "small selections" of data, misunderstandings are frequent. Psychologists have discovered that even identical twins raised in the same family have to a significant extent different experiences and therefore different environmental influences on their attitudes. It is no wonder that ordinary people often disagree sharply about matters that, on casual examination, would seem to be based on experiences shared by them all.

3. *Differing personal viewpoints influence individual interpretations of specific subjects.* Each individual exists in an "egocentric predicament," in that he can only see surrounding reality from his own position. What he sees and how he interprets it depends not only on what is "out there" but also on his own nature. "Nor should this surprise us," as one social scientist observes. "For, as human beings, we must inevitably see the universe from a centre lying within ourselves. . . . Any attempt rigorously to eliminate our human perspective from our picture of the world must lead to absurdity."[6] It is well known that participants in an argument find it difficult even to understand one another's views and seldom report on the details of what was said or what was implied without disagreement. Again, speakers say one thing, but listeners hear something else. It is not so much a matter of one being wrong and the other right as it is that each perceives what is said from his own ego-center.

It is far from new to assert that attitude, experience, and egocentricity do affect and distort the interpretation of facts and situations. Everyone knows this to be true. But everyone knows it with special cogency as it applies to other people. A very natural feeling is that: "Since I know about the dangers of subjective interpretation, I avoid them. It is the other person whose views are distorted." The suspicion should be turned about and directed toward oneself as well. The tendency to select and interpret only tiny fragments of reality as though they were the entire fabric is especially strong when one's most earnest convictions are involved. It is then that one refuses to let facts interfere with his beliefs. What is believed most strongly is precisely what most colors observation and distorts interpretation.

[5] Sinclair, *The Conditions of Knowing,* p. 158.

[6] Michael Polanyi, *Personal Knowledge,* Chicago: University of Chicago Press, 1958, p. 3.

Guides to Objectivity

Genuine communication is often handicapped by this human tendency toward subjective interpretation of data. Mutual understanding is difficult to achieve when every participant has a natural inclination to perceive and interpret from his own viewpoint whatever is communicated. Since this is a universal human characteristic, it obviously cannot be eliminated. A safeguard is to understand that it exists and to act in accordance with that understanding. It should be an established principle that whatever seems to support what one already believes should be regarded with skepticism, for it probably is only partly right. Specifically, in preparing as a speaker or listener for a communicative situation, the following tests may be applied:

1. *Try to disprove the opposite of what you believe, to see how it withstands the strongest attack that can be made against it.* For example, if you are convinced the vote should be extended to everyone at the age of eighteen, do your best to challenge this view and undermine it. See how well the merits of the proposal resist the most cogent criticisms of it.

2. *Examine the proposal you favor from all sides to see whether its various aspects are consistent.* This is a method the great lawyer Robert Green Ingersoll used in appealing to a jury to consider the inconsistencies in the case presented against his client. "A lie never fits a fact, never," he told the jurors. "You can only fit a lie with another lie, made for the express purpose, because you can change a lie but you can't change a fact." Then he applied this general principle to the evidence before them:[7]

> Do you believe that Job Davis spelled sheet—a sheet of paper—'sheat'? That is the way it is spelled in this document. Now let us be honor bright with each other, and do not let the lawyers on the other side treat you as if you were twelve imbeciles. . . . Do you believe that Job Davis, the educated young man, the school teacher, the one who attended Normal School, would put periods in the middle of sentences and none at the end?

If you believe women are worse drivers than men but find the fact is they have proportionately fewer accidents, your conclusion must be re-examined in the light of this evidence.

[7] Frederick C. Hicks, *Famous American Jury Speeches,* St. Paul: West Publishing Co., 1925, pp. 217–20.

3. *Talk over with someone else the ideas you plan to present in your speech—preferably with someone who you know opposes them.* A. Conan Doyle, in his story "Silver Blaze," represents Sherlock Holmes as saying to his friend Dr. Watson: "Nothing clears up a case as much as stating it to someone else." Even when the listener does not respond, the mere experience of phrasing one's ideas to fit the inquiring scrutiny of another mind forces consideration of aspects that otherwise might remain obscure. It is like picking an object up and examining it from another side.

4. *Continue reading and doing research concerning your subject even after you think you have attained an understanding of it.* It is notorious that travelers in a foreign country understand it clearly and confidently during their first few days of visiting in it; but if they remain longer, they begin to discover complexities that were not at first apparent. Journeys of the mind into new topic areas exemplify this same phenomenon. A little reading about the causes of crime may point unerringly to environmental conditions as the real cause; but students of criminology find many contributing factors that are not so easily catalogued.

5. *Cultivate the determination to discover what is true about a subject, even if this may mean reaching conclusions you find personally unpalatable.* As Polanyi phrased it: "The effort of knowing is thus guided by a sense of obligation towards the truth: by an effort to submit to reality."[8] Sigmund Freud constantly stressed the tendency to believe—in obedience to either the "pleasure principle" or the "anxiety signal." But he concluded that normal personalities do have the power to submit their desires to the test of realism.[9] Objective understanding is greatly aided by cultivation of a willingness to accept facts even when they run counter to one's dearest desires or strongest convictions.

Anticipating Speaker–Listener Relationships

The most significant characteristic of communication is that it must be adaptive. Communication means to reach outside of oneself to share ideas, feelings, impressions, or doubts. It always involves not only one's

[8] Polanyi, *Personal Knowledge,* p. 63.

[9] Ernest Jones, *The Life and Work of Sigmund Freud,* New York: Basic Books, Inc., 1961, One vol. ed., p. 404.

own beliefs and desires but also two other vital elements: the nature of the subject matter under consideration and the beliefs and desires of the projected listeners. To be a communicator means to avoid insistence upon one's own intentions sufficiently to view them in relation to both the truth of the matter being discussed and the nature of those with whom the discussion will take place.

Sometimes a speaker may expound a subject or even advance arguments concerning it without consideration of the needs or interests of his listeners. Sometimes members of an audience may turn off their minds and think about something else while a speaker is droning out his message toward (but not to) them. Sometimes a speaker may lash out at his listeners in anger, hurling his feelings in the form of words much as he might throw stones. Such anger is expected to hurt the recipient, but little response is desired except the acknowledgement that he has been hurt. These various kinds of noncommunicative discourse have been described in Chapter 1 as self-expression. More commonly, when one speaks or listens his intention is to establish relationships with others, to enlarge his understanding, to arrive at truer interpretations, to exert his influence, or to enrich his social experience.

Both speaking and listening are more effective when there is specific preparation for the interchange that is to take place. The adaptive preparation that should be undertaken is of five types:

1. *An urge to communicate should be developed—a desire to influence hearers, or to consider critically what a speaker may say.* The communicative attitude cannot be taken for granted. Some things a person may not wish to discuss. Some individuals have a strong tendency to preserve the privacy of their thoughts and feelings. On some occasions everyone feels relatively indifferent to the question of how others may respond. Keenly evaluative listening and effective talk both demand special effort. Just as an athlete needs to prepare his mind and body for maximum effort before a contest, so do communicators before entering into discourse. Being ready for a football game means being trained to the peak of fitness, skilled in the plays to be used, coached on what to expect from the opposition, and eager to make the maximum effort. Much the same process is demanded for effective speaking and listening. As listeners we should intensify our zest to learn what the other participants think and feel about the problem being discussed. As speakers we should have an honest desire to influence the listeners.

2. *Planning for communication should be realistic in terms of*

what the speaker knows and what the listeners may properly expect from him. A college student talking about international relations should keep in mind both his own and his hearers' limitations of knowledge, as well as the intensity of their convictions. A college student could talk realistically to the Rotary Club about what he and his fellow students think about war, or international trade, or race relations—but his experience scarcely warrants his telling them what national policies should be in these areas. On many complicated problems it is more realistic to raise questions than to try to provide answers.

3. *The circumstances under which the discourse will take place should influence the preparation for it.* For example, it makes considerable difference whether one is to be allowed five minutes in which to develop his ideas or may speak at whatever length he desires. It matters whether the occasion will be a dinner, with most of the program consisting of movies, or an afternoon discussion meeting. Whether the participants will be tired from a day's work, or impatient to leave the meeting to attend a football game, or are gathered with a common determination to solve the problem under discussion will be factors influencing both the speaking and listening.

4. *There should be prior thought concerning the common level of understanding of the subject matter to be discussed.* If a speaker should foolishly undertake to tell his listeners what they already know, they will soon cease to listen. Indifference or even resentment will replace interest. If a speaker assumes that his listeners have an understanding of the topic which in fact they lack, his talk will be more complicated or technical than they can understand and they will naturally become confused and dissatisfied. Both speaker and listeners should have a mutual understanding of what their common level of understanding is, so that they can proceed from a sound basis in teaching and in learning from one another.

5. *The speaker, in preparing what he will say, should give careful consideration to what will probably best motivate his listeners in relation to the subject and circumstances of the discourse.* It may be that self-interest is a basic motive for every individual, but on the occasion of a rally to raise funds for people whose homes have been destroyed in a flood, the stronger motive may be a philanthropic desire to help. "What others will think" may motivate listeners concerning their highly visible behavior, such as whether they paint their house and keep their lawns trimmed; but they may not be influenced by what others think when the action they are asked to take is confidential, such as the amount of their annual pledge to their church. However sophisticated

a speaker may be about the nature of human motivation in general, every speech or speaking situation demands special analysis of the motives which will probably be operative under the particular circumstances that are anticipated.

Preparing for a Public Speech

Speaking in public differs from normal conversation and casual discussion in important respects. When a speech is to be presented to an audience, the responsibility is heavy on the speaker to deliver a suitable message. Problems of organization and of sequential development must be solved. There is likely to be some degree of stage fright as the speaker contemplates the nature of his responsibilities. Close adaptation to the listeners is harder when they cannot talk back than it is in the give-and-take of conversation. These are factors which complicate the preparation for a speech.

Preparation for a speech involves getting one's ideas developed, supported, and organized; and it also involves the preparation of one's own communicative feelings. There is probably nothing that will contribute more to a feeling of confidence and the urge to communicate than the assurance of being well prepared. This does not mean simply having enough to say; it depends on the quality of the preparation—upon what has been done and how. The following five factors are all important:

1. *Preparation should be started early*. The maximum time should be utilized, from the moment it becomes known that a speech is to be given on such-and-such a date, for the cluster of ideas and feelings a speaker has about a subject to grow into the fabric of his mental and emotional processes. Only in this way does the speech become part and parcel of himself—truly his own, rather than a collection of data upon which he is merely reporting. When the class in speech first meets it is well to determine how many speeches will be presented during the term, and at least approximately upon what dates, so that preparation for all of them may commence at once. The longer the speech germinates, the sturdier its growth will be.

2. *Preparation should be spread over all the available time*. Part of the preparation for a speech must be accomplished in the library, checking facts, and at the desk, with papers spread out before one. Part of the time may be spent in discussing ideas with friends. Still

other forms of preparation consist of thinking, while listening to a lecture, or while reading for another course, how the facts and ideas encountered might affect the topic for the speech. Ideas may be reconsidered while walking across campus, having lunch, or reading the daily newspaper. If the topic to be discussed is held always in the forefront of one's mind, phrases to illuminate it, illustrations, and new approaches to aspects of it will occur in the midst of other activities. When the student understands that (whatever the topic may be for his speech) he is actually representing through that topic his whole set of values and understandings, he gradually will learn to prepare for speaking during all his waking hours, regardless of what else he may be doing. Studying for an examination in another course does not interfere with this generalized kind of preparation but actually assists it. Whatever keeps the mind alert and intent on analysis of facts and ideas provides grist that may be ground into supporting or illustrative material for the ideas that are to be communicated.

3. *Preparation should be realistically adjusted to the circumstances.* On a particular topic (such as: "What the People I know Think of the War in Vietnam") the principal preparation needed is to search one's mind and memory to cull from experience what is already there. For another topic (such as: "How the United States Became Involved in Vietnam") it is necessary to make a careful search through large bodies of relevant data. For a topic that derives directly from your work-experience or from study in your major field, adequate preparation might consist largely of selecting and organizing materials well known to you. Another time you may deliberately choose to speak on such a topic as, "A Comparison of the Views of Plato and Aristotle on the Nature of Happiness," precisely because you do not know the subject matter and will use your speaking event as a reason for gathering and interpreting information about it. There is no set formula governing preparation that could possibly apply to such diverse circumstances. Preparation should be adequate to enable you to speak sensibly and dependably on the topic you have selected. How much is enough depends on what you undertake to talk about in relation to what you already know and what you wish to accomplish with your listeners.

4. *Preparation should be geared to the needs of the audience.* A specialist in electronics might prepare to speak to electrical engineers on miniaturization in "pocket-TV" sets with confidence that the listeners would readily understand the special information he had to impart; however, for a general audience, he would require much preparation

to develop his facts and ideas in nontechnical terms. Thus, when the speaker knows a great deal more than his audience does about a subject this may require of him more (not less) preparation. On the other hand, if a student were to talk on his hobby of breeding hybrid Iris bulbs to a class in horticulture, he would expect them to demand of him a much deeper and broader knowledge of plant culture than a general audience normally would expect. Thus, when a speaker knows a great deal less than his audience in the general area related to his topic, he will generally need fuller preparation. Also, if a speaker plans to talk to a group on a subject in which he believes the members are uninterested, his preparation will have to encompass ways in which he can relate his topic to various interests they already have—and this, too, will make special demands upon him. The listeners are always a cardinal factor in preparation and their relation to the subject will affect considerably the kind demanded of the speaker.

5. *The preparation should be satisfying to the speaker*. Stage fright breeds upon feelings of inadequacy. If, while an individual awaits his opportunity to speak, he is aware that he is not quite clear as to the point he wishes to make, or that his materials are not well organized, or that he lacks illustrative material that would arouse interest, or that his factual support is weak, fear is a very natural (and proper) reaction. On the other hand, even if one knows he is not an expert speaker but is assured that at least he knows what he is talking about, this assurance of being well prepared creates confidence.

As these foregoing considerations indicate, there is no set formula that prescribes the manner of preparation for speaking. The method will vary with the occasion. Thorough preparation, in any event, is the key to confidence. Preparation should be started early, should be spread over the available time, and should be adjusted to special requirements of the subject, the circumstances, the listeners and the speaker himself.

Preparing for Listening

In some ways listening is the most complex of the communicative skills. It receives less of an individual's attention because its processes are not observable. We see what we read and what we write; we hear what we say; but when we listen, it may appear that our ears are merely recording the sounds available to them. Actually, hearing is a highly selective process. This is indicated in the fact that sleeping parents may not be disturbed by the sound of passing automobiles but will be awakened by a slight cry from their baby in the next room. Another instance is the fact that amidst the buzz of general conversation, one will instantly hear his own name. Less well known is the fact that we unconsciously tune out materials uninteresting to us and tune in items of special interest. There are various kinds of preparation that will significantly improve one's listening ability.

1. Striving to maintain an open mind on the subject to be discussed—so that adverse points of view, or facts that do not accord with one's own preconceptions, are not automatically rejected without consideration.

2. When the subject to be discussed is known in advance, listeners may summarize for themselves what they already know about the subject and perhaps raise questions in their minds they hope the speaker may answer. This provides a readiness and receptivity for his development of the topic.

3. When the speaker is already well known to the listener, he may be prepared for peculiarities in the speaking (such as a guttural tone or a foreign accent) or for special qualities of personality (such as a tendency to exaggerate, to generalize without sound evidence, to be minutely particular in the development of ideas, to present ideas in formless disorganization), or to use some unusual mode of organization (such as stating the reverse of what the speaker believes, then refuting his own statement).

4. The listener should also prepare himself physically for effective listening by being well rested and not impatient to be gone. If he has physical handicaps, such as a hearing loss, he should place himself advantageously to increase his opportunity to hear.

5. The listener should remind himself of his responsibility as a member of the communicating group—remembering that by making his own interest manifest he encourages attentiveness by others; or by openly showing boredom he makes more difficult the tasks of the speaker and also of the other listeners.

The Phases of Preparation for Speaking and Listening

Preparation is a general term which includes preliminary planning, organization, development of ideas, and readying both one's ideas and oneself for speaking and for listening. Some of this preparatory work is discussed in this chapter, but not all of it. Organization of one's ideas is sufficiently important to have a chapter devoted to it; so is the gathering of materials, the development or support of one's ideas, the formulation of the purpose, the devising of factors of interest. Special chapters are also devoted to preparation of speeches to inform, to persuade, and to enhance sociability.

The whole process of preparation may be considered in four major phases, subdivided into twelve stages. The following table may help in the visualization of the whole process; but it should not be assumed that these steps necessarily occur in any special sequence. The important thing is not the order in which they occur but the fact that each step must be accounted for before the preparation is complete.

Steps in Preparing a Speech

Major Steps	Specific Steps
PLAN	1. Choose the topic
	2. Analyze the audience
	3. Arrive at the purpose
	4. Research to gather materials
ORGANIZE	5. Determine central idea and main ideas
	6. Devise an organizational pattern
	7. Construct the outline
	8. Plan the introduction and conclusion
DEVELOP	9. Develop the ideas
	10. Incorporate factors of interest
PRESENT	11. Consider wording and style
	12. Practice sound principles of development and delivery in all communicative situations

While consideration is being given to each of these stages, an equally important concern, as has been stressed throughout this chapter, is that the speaker must also prepare himself. Self-preparation involves also a number of phases—which, as in the preceding table, are not sequential but concurrent. These factors are offered as a checklist of what needs to be accomplished.

Steps in Preparing Oneself to Speak

Major Steps	Specific Steps
ANALYZE	1. Be sure you understand the subject matter 2. Analyze and confront your own biases about it 3. Consider what attitudes your listeners hold toward you and toward the subject
CONTROL	4. Examine the weaknesses of your proposal 5. Consider the consistency of your point of view 6. Pursue your inquiry beyond minimal demands
ADJUST	7. Develop a genuine urge to communicate 8. Relate yourself to the topic realistically 9. Relate realistically to the listeners and to the circumstances
INTEGRATE	10. Give yourself ample time for thought 11. Develop your ideas in terms of all you know, feel, or believe 12. Do not stop short of satisfying yourself

Since communication is always an inclusive process that involves listening and reaction (or feedback) as well as speaking, an effective communicative encounter depends also upon sound evaluative listening. The following guidelines to effective listening should be followed:

Guidelines to Effective Listening

1. Consider how your purposes relate to those of the speaker.
2. Develop an attitude of interest and inquiry concerning the speaker's views of the subject.
3. Be physically prepared: rested, alert, ready to be responsive.
4. Guard against your biases concerning the subject or the speaker.
5. Listen for the speaker's purpose and central idea.
6. Follow the main ideas, noting transitions and summaries.
7. Compare the speaker's reasoning on the subject with your own.

8. **Evaluate his use of facts and his opinions, in relation to your own.**
9. **Note in what ways his presentation is effective or ineffective.**
10. **Relate what you accept from his speech to your general pattern of thinking and acting.**

What to Talk About

Organized talks will be given in the speech class in order that the students may practice the principles of sound reasoning, adaptation to listeners, critical listening, and the other attributes of effective oral communication. If this practice is to result in reshaping the insights and the behavior governing everyday oral communication, the talks presented before the class must be realistic. This demands that they concern matters of common interest and understanding and that they aim toward some kind of practical effect. As in normal conversation, the topics are determined in part by each individual speaker and in part by the predominant interests of the group. Topics for speeches are aspects of the broad concerns which occupy the mind of the speaker's community. For example, in 1967–68, such concerns included the war in Vietnam, student unrest on campuses, integration, crime, teenage behavior in relation to sex and drugs, the draft, the ethics of politicians, safety factors in automobile construction, shifting patterns of international relations, the population explosion, world food shortages, African nationalism, the global responsibilities of the United States, and new developments in electronics, oceanography, and space travel. Of course, there always are multiple subjects of broad public interest. Some are recreational, including sports and travel; some are artistic, including new movements in painting, music, and literature. Some involve controversial or exciting individuals and events.

What is to be talked about in a community is always dictated in part by the community itself. At Fort Lauderdale, Florida, during the Easter holiday, the conversation among the hordes of vacationing students is different from what it is among brokers on the Wall Street stock exchange when the market is active. What is talked about in time of war differs from the normal topics and tone of talk in times of peace. Fashions rise and fall in discourse much as they do for clothing, dancing, slang, and music. When a speaker wishes to know what he should talk about, the first advice is for him to use his eyes and his ears to help him determine what his fellows are predominantly interested in.

However, a speaker's function is not to echo back to his associates what they already know and feel and believe. His function is to exercise his own proper share of influence—and to attain his own satisfactions—by the effective presentation of his own points of view. When everyone is saying something about a significant subject (the military draft, for example), he may wish to try to exercise his own influence in changing their opinions. Similarly, a speaker may wish to speak about a subject precisely because it is not fashionable, is not accepted, or is not appealing to people generally.

There are five guidelines to the selection of a topic for a particular speaking assignment:

1. *Topics should be drawn from the speaker's own interests, convictions, information, and experience.* The principal value anyone has to offer to an audience is what he himself thinks and feels, not what someone else suggests. Merely to summarize for listeners what is found in a magazine or book is an elementary exercise in reporting. A personal contribution emerges if the speaker summarizes the material then explains why he recommends or rejects it. What a speaker has to offer is his own individualized interpretation.

2. *The kind of influence a speaker wishes to exert will help determine what he talks about.* One who aims to be considered a good companion, jolly, relaxed, pleasant, and never demanding may want to limit his topics for talk to sports and other recreations, and may always present what he has to say with a light, gay, and amusing interpretation. One who pictures himself as a serious individual with real concern for problems of ethics, politics, and social conditions will naturally speak about serious problems with the aim of shaping his listeners' reactions toward them.

3. *The choice of topic is limited in part by the nature of the audience.* A speaker should always consider his projected subject in light of how he wishes to relate it to his listeners. It may be that he is deeply concerned by what he considers lax ethical behavior among his contemporaries and feels this would be corrected if there were a general development of interest in religion, or in classical literature, or in the history of ethical thought. Such a speaker would choose his topic in accordance with his interpretation of what his listeners need to hear. Another speaker may tend to go along with the crowd rather than to oppose it and may, accordingly, select for his speeches topics that reflect what his listeners feel is most significant. Always, as has been indicated earlier in this chapter, the speaker needs to find a com-

mon level of understanding and a common bond of interest with his listeners concerning whatever topic he may select. It is useless to talk calculus to students who have not even studied algebra.

4. *The length of time allotted for the speech determines in part the nature of the topic.* Speeches presented in a class must necessarily be restricted in length to a few minutes. This time limitation seriously abridges the range of speech topics. It would be foolish to try to discuss Russian-American relations in five minutes. However, students may always select a broad subject area—such as Russian-American relations, or public health, or race relations, or urban renewal, or any other of their choice—and give a series of speeches about it during the term. In this fashion, various aspects of the general subject may be considered, one at a time, with perhaps a final speech that draws generalized conclusions based on the prior discussions. Evaluative listening is improved if students work on topics in teams of two or more, each team devoting itself to study and discussion of the same general subject area throughout the course. Thus, as the expertness of the speaker increases through his continuing study, so does the penetrating criticism that one or more of his classmates may direct at his presentations. If students do decide to speak on different topics for each assignment, they should exercise care in limiting the focus of their inquiry to a single aspect that can be dealt with adequately in the time available.

5. *Speakers and listeners should not expect to communicate effectively without mutual understanding of the subject under discussion.* It is unrealistic to try to speak on or to listen evaluatively to a subject which is only dimly understood. The ideal speech topic is one that is drawn from the interests and experience of the speaker and his listeners, and concerning which the speaker takes the trouble to assemble fresh information and to do cogent thinking. It is educationally detrimental to try to think about any subject having only incomplete or undependable information. And it is immoral for anyone to try to influence the thinking of listeners concerning a subject which he himself does not understand.

Conclusion

Oral communication, as described in Chapter 1, requires the kinds of preparation, for both speaking and listening, which have been discussed in this chapter. Speakers and listeners need to prepare themselves for effective communication, by realizing that all thinking (including their own) is influenced by egocentricity, by subjective attitudes, and by one's own experiences. Objectivity should be sought as a means of seeing how the subject will be viewed by listeners, and also in an effort to view it without the distortion of one's own prejudices.

Since communication is always a process of mutual interaction, it requires that speakers and listeners must adapt themselves to one another, to the reality of their relationship with the topic, and to the circumstances under which they confront the topic. Preparation for speaking and for listening is a complicated process that involves both general attitudes and specific decisions. What to talk about is a problem in which the nature of communicative responsibilities and the relations between speaker and listeners are involved. How we speak and how we listen depends upon what manner of individuals we are. In this sense the Elizabethan dramatist Ben Jonson was right when he said: "Speak that I may know you, for speech most shows the man."

Exercises

• *Questions for Discussion*

1. What is meant by the assertion in this chapter that effective communication requires not only understanding the subject to be discussed but also understanding oneself in relation to the subject? Why is it also necessary to understand the relation of prospective listeners to the subject and to the speaker? How should this affect preparation for speaking? For listening?

2. How do general attitudes affect the understanding of specific topics? How may this influence be dealt with? How may speakers and listeners deal with this problem in ways that will improve their communication with one another?

3. If a speaker's experiences have been quite different from those of his listeners, how may this difference be a barrier to his communication with them? What may he do to render this difference helpful rather than detrimental?

4. Do individuals you know differ markedly in their urge to communicate? Can this quality be enhanced? Should it be? Can you think of instances in which the urge to communicate should be diminished?

5. What is meant by realistic communication? How may this guideline be employed helpfully in your speech class? How should it be utilized in the discourse held generally in your community? Does

our national or world community suffer significantly from a lack of realism in public discussion?

6. In what ways may preparation for an assigned speech in the speech class be helpful in study for other courses? If work in preparing a speech demands time that should be given to study for other courses, how may this problem be resolved in a way that would be helpful to the work both in speech and in the other courses?

• *Projects for Speaking and Listening*

1. Through class discussion a general subject area may be selected in which virtually all the class members are intensely interested. Subtopics within this general subject may then be developed by each student for a five-minute speech which he will present to the class.

2. All members of the class, having developed speeches on subdivisions of the same general subject, will be prepared to listen evaluatively in terms of their own specialized knowledge and convictions concerning a phase of the subject. Using the guidelines to objectivity, each student should write a brief evaluation (1) of the speech of a specified classmate; and (2) of his own basis for judgment of what the other student presents.

3. Either orally or in writing (depending on class time) describe a speaking situation in which the speaker showed an inadequate understanding of the attitudes, knowledge, experience, or abilities of his listeners. What, specifically, would you advise him to do that he did not do?

4. Discuss the pros and cons of using a different topic for every speech in class versus the method of making all (or most) speeches upon different aspects of a single general subject.

Part Two

Developmental Processes

4 · *Focusing on Communicative Purposes*

All communication, like all other volitional behavior, is purposive. Experts in human behavior agree that everything man does voluntarily is governed by purposes which he may or may not understand. Without purpose there is no meaning. We can understand human behavior and even human nature only in terms of purpose; or, as one psychologist says, "we can hardly consider the structure of experience without its function."[1] It is commonplace to react to utterances by other people with such thoughts as: "Why did he say that?" Or "What did he mean?" Or "What did he really mean?" The assumption always is that we speak with some purpose in mind—though it is also recognized that often the real purpose is realized only fuzzily or perhaps not at all by the speaker. Just as truly, the purpose may be misunderstood partly or wholly by the listener. Purposes always exist; but they are not always apparent.

[1] Dennis E. Broadbent, *Perception and Communication,* London: The Scientific Book Guild, 1958, p. 7.

Paradox of Communicative Purposes

There is a basic paradox concerning purposive communication that must be understood before we can either make our own purposes more operative or infer correctly the purposes of others. The paradox is that all utterance is governed by a dominant purpose but that often the purpose is not what it seems. Berelson and Steiner point out this paradox as follows: "People often act in consistent ways that produce consistent results—and under conditions where they seem to have a choice in the matter. Thus their behavior bears all the external signs of being purposive and goal-directed. Yet they themselves often vehemently deny the motive that would be inferred, or even report the opposite motivation."[2] Their illustration of this principle is a description of a young woman who generally dates ineligible men and who has broken several engagements, thus indicating a fear of or avoidance of marriage, yet who insists she really wants to be married. Maslow reminds us that human motivations are so complex that it is not easy to determine the precise purpose for any act or set of actions. "If we examine carefully the average desires that we have in daily life," he points out, "we find that they have at least one important characteristic, i.e., that they are usually means to an end rather than ends in themselves. We want money so that we may have an automobile. In turn we want an automobile because the neighbors have one and we do not wish to feel inferior to them, so that we can retain our own self-respect and so that we can be loved and respected by others. Usually when a conscious desire is analyzed we find we can go behind it, so to speak, to other more fundamental aims of the individual."[3]

So inscrutable are the real reasons why people do or say things that behavioral experts tend to look for how purposes operate and for what effects they may produce, rather than to try to determine their essential nature.[4] As John Dewey phrased it: "We are held accountable by others for the consequences of our acts. They visit their

[2] Bernard Berelson and Gary A. Steiner, *Human Behavior: An Inventory of Scientific Findings,* New York: Harcourt, Brace & World, Inc., 1964, p. 279.

[3] A. H. Maslow, *Motivation and Personality,* New York: Harper & Row, Publishers, Inc., 1954, pp. 65–6.

[4] Cf. Jurgen Ruesch, *Therapeutic Communication,* New York: W. W. Norton and Company, 1961, p. 41 and *passim.*

like and dislike of these consequences upon us. In vain do we claim that these are not ours; that they are products of ignorance not design, or are incidents in the execution of a most laudable scheme."[5] Both as speakers and as listeners we often fail to understand our own communicative purposes. "Consciousness is not all that we would like it to be; many psychological processes take place in our minds which we may not happen to observe or which we are not capable of observing directly."[6] Despite the vagueness with which we understand either ourselves or others, there is presumed to be a general motivational cohesiveness[7] governing all the behavior of an individual. Each of us is thought to be ambitious or lazy, sympathetic or indifferent, kind or cruel, self-centered or considerate. What we say and how we say it cannot fail to have social consequences for which we are held accountable; and these consequences must reflect our own purposes, although not always clearly enough to render them evident.

The aim of this chapter is to consider the kinds of purposes which may usefully be employed in communicative speaking and listening; how these purposes do, should, and may influence the quality and the effects of the communicative behavior of speakers and listeners; and what speakers and listeners should do to render their purposes more influential.

Complexity of Communicative Purposes

Experts in the study of oral communication have generally agreed that "*Purpose* is a prerequisite for profitable talk of any kind."[8] Many textbooks in speech identify the basic purposes of communication as: to inform, to convince, to persuade, to inspire, and to entertain. Often this list is reduced to three by considering conviction, persuasion, and inspiration as parts of one process, to activate, or to persuade. Experts in cognition often tend to list types of purposive communication as

[5] John Dewey, *Human Nature and Conduct,* New York: Modern Library, Inc., 1930, p. 315.

[6] Heinz Kohut and Philip F. D. Seitz, "Concepts and Theories of Psychoanalysis," in Joseph M. Wepman and Ralph W. Heine, eds., *Concepts of Personality,* London: Aldine Publishing Co., 1963, p. 118.

[7] Kohut, p. 117.

[8] Jon Eisenson, J. Jeffrey Auer, and John V. Irwin, *The Psychology of Communication,* New York: Appleton-Century-Crofts, 1963, p. 259.

comprising sixteen[9] or twenty-eight[10] or even more. The results are diverse primarily because no one has been able to devise a system of precise and mutually exclusive categories. Our purposes as speakers and listeners are always interrelated, overlapping, and either complementary or contradictory. What we wish to accomplish when we communicate with one another is never simple and never single. Our aims as speakers and as listeners are multiform and various.

We may wish to explain, but in order to do so we must persuade our listeners to be interested and often must also persuade them to accept our selection and interpretation of facts necessary for the explanatory process. Meanwhile we must also entertain them, at least to the extent of arousing and maintaining their interest. Similarly, as listeners we may seek entertainment at the expense of misinterpreting parts of what the speaker is saying; or we might argue back with him, even though his main purpose was not to persuade but to inform. The contrary ways in which listeners may interpret (or misinterpret) speakers are indicated by two letters from readers which were printed in the Los Angeles *Herald-Express,* on September 29, 1960, following the celebrated television debate between Presidential candidates Richard Nixon and John Kennedy.

A

While watching the Nixon-Kennedy debate on TV, I could not help admiring Mr. Nixon for his poise, awareness and understanding of the problems facing the United States today and in the future.

One only has to watch the two aspirants together to see the tremendous difference in the two men. Mr. Kennedy seemed unsure, immature and somewhat scared.

B

Of all the knuckle-headed, addle-pated, asinine things to do, the advisors of Richard Nixon did them all when they did not find some excuse for refusing that debate. They threw their own candidate to the wolves when they allowed so close a comparison of the two men.

Even I, a Democrat, cannot gloat over that victory. There was no contest. Poor Richard was slaughtered.

Both listeners heard the same debate; but their interpretations of what they heard were precisely opposite. Much of the meaning came not from the speakers but from within the listeners themselves. The pur-

[9] Charles Morris, *Signs, Language and Behavior,* Englewood Cliffs, N.J.: Prentice-Hall, Inc., 1946, pp. 123–52.

[10] Berelson and Steiner, pp. 257–8.

poses of the listeners dominated what they heard and how they heard it.

Several rather obvious conclusions may be drawn concerning communicative purposes. (1) There is always a purpose or a set of purposes governing any act of speaking or of listening. (2) The purpose is not always fully known even to the one speaking or the one listening. (3) The purpose is usually a complex combination of complementary and contradictory aims. (4) Improved communication results when the purposes of the speaker and the listener either are similar or may readily be reconciled with one another. (5) The speaker may more readily and surely accomplish his communicative mission when he understands well in advance what major purpose or purposes he will wish to accomplish. And (6) a listener may comprehend and evaluate what he hears more readily and accurately when his purpose in listening is appropriate and when he understands what it is. Some of the implications of these conclusions, however, are far from obvious and need careful consideration to help make communication effective. The implications which govern communicative purposes are as follows:

Any communication has a purpose related to oneself (as speaker or listener); to the subject matter under discussion; and to the other participant(s) (as speaker or listeners). This means that at a minimum every member in a communicative situation has at least three intertwined (but not necessarily interrelated) purposes. He will have one purpose or set of purposes related to his own conception of his own well-being: to attract attention to himself; to defend himself against actual or fancied attack; or to enhance feelings of love and respect by the listeners for himself. He will have another purpose or set of purposes relevant to the subject matter under discussion: to clarify its meanings; to represent it favorably or unfavorably; to display his knowledge or to mask his ignorance concerning it. And he will have still other purposes toward the other participants in the communicative situation: to help them to understand clearly and to draw correct conclusions concerning the subject matter; to induce them to think as he would like to have them do concerning himself; and to indicate his feelings toward them. The kinds of purposive intent an individual may have in any given communicative situation cannot be fully catalogued, for they are exceedingly complex. But it should not be overlooked that the purposes always involve feelings about oneself, about the subject matter, and about the other participants.

Some of the purposes may be contradictory. A purpose to spare oneself labor in gathering, interpreting, and organizing data will be contrary to the purpose to impress listeners with the clarity and depth of one's understanding of the subject. A purpose to represent a particular subject matter favorably might run counter to a purpose to represent it accurately. A purpose to enhance the favorable attitude of listeners toward oneself might at least appear to be endangered by a purpose to represent the subject matter quite differently than they perceive it. Such contrariety of purposes is far from rare; it is, rather, entirely normal. Unless dealt with effectively, such a combination of contradictory purposes will only confuse the speaker while he is preparing and presenting his message and the listeners while they seek to comprehend it.

The dominant purposes should be determined in advance and adhered to. For a particular communicative situation, a speaker may decide that his primary purpose is to explain (clarify, inform) how to attain *Satori* through the processes of Zen Buddhism. One listener may decide to listen receptively, seeking to enhance his understanding of the processes. Another may decide to listen with selective emphasis upon evaluation of the speaker's capacity to understand what he is talking about. Or the speaker might select as his purpose the aim to persuade his listeners to become disciples of Zen. Some listeners might weigh his persuasive appeals in order to determine whether or not to accept his counsel; others, who may feel committed to either a favorable or unfavorable reaction to his persuasion, might listen primarily to see what he might say that would clarify their understanding of Zen or of the nature of *Satori*. It is always possible that speaker and listeners may have diverse purposes, and even that several purposes may be wholly or partially accomplished through one communicative interchange. But efficiency in speaking and in listening is considerably heightened when the motivational pattern governing each is clearly understood—and especially when each one understands the immediate and dominant purpose of the other as well as of himself.

The purpose may or may not be signaled to the other participants. If the purpose of the speaker is to teach and of the listeners to learn, it is helpful to both to know what the other intends. If a speaker wishes to demonstrate how a slide rule works, he helps his listeners if he makes it clear to them that this is his aim and his only aim; and they can help him if they make manifest when they understand a step in his explanation and when they remain confused and need further clarification. On the other hand, if a speaker is aiming to persuade his listeners to accept the justice of the existing draft law, he may avoid a too-hasty rejection of his views if he presents them, without argument, in the form of an explanation of this means of securing military manpower, as contrasted with other available means. If a listener feels hostility toward a speaker or toward his views, he yet may gain a fairer understanding of the speaker and of his opinions if he conceals his dislike and listens courteously and intently. The degree to which the purposes of speaker and of listener should be made clearly manifest during a communicative situation, and at what point, are factors in the strategy of communication. But whether or not the purpose should be clearly signaled to the other participants, it should always (as was indicated in the prior paragraph) be clear and be dominant in the thinking of the individual himself. Not telling what you are doing is far different from not knowing what you are doing. And normally, in most communicative circumstances, the real aim of speaker and of listener is aided substantially by making certain the other participants know precisely what that aim is. A shared understanding of the purpose of any group activity usually enhances its success.

Classification of Communicative Purposes

As has been indicated, communicative purposes are multiple; they overlap; they may contradict one another; and speakers and listeners may not always share mutual purposes. Without understanding this complex network of personal and social communicative motives, it is difficult to comprehend the communicative tasks of either speaking or listening. To revert to the opening paragraph of this chapter, the commonplace questions, "Why did he say that?" and "What did he mean?" and "What did he really mean?" are far from easily answered. Yet complex and diverse as human purposes may be, they manifest certain common tendencies that make it feasible to group them into helpful even if not precise categories. The generally accepted division into the categories of *informing, persuading,* and *pleasing* (or enhancing sociability) is probably the most useful.

Inform and Be Informed

Among the many needs which human beings experience is the need to know. Nature hates a mental as well as a physical vacuum. Once curiosity about a subject has been aroused—that is, once attention has been purposively drawn to it—the mind normally is uneasy and dissatisfied until that curiosity is allayed by supplying satisfying answers to its questions. This is a characteristic of listeners that makes them willing and cooperative participants in the communicative process. Speakers should realize that listeners want to know—if and when the proper condition has been created. And the condition is that their curiosity or interest concerning the subject must first be aroused. Naturally, no one is interested in something of which he never has heard. We have to know something about a subject in order to want to know more. The arousal of interest is so important a factor in the communicative situation that a full chapter is devoted to it. For now it is enough to realize that when interest genuinely exists, a mental vacuum is created. The mind reaches out to grasp a subject, for it has become curious about it; but there is nothing (or not enough for full comprehension) there for it to grasp. Consequently there is an emptiness, or a partial vacuum. This vacuum constitutes a psychological urgency to learn, so that the uncertainty may be replaced with the satisfaction of understanding.

Similarly, speakers may be induced by listeners to want to share what they know about a subject, when a mutuality of interest has been established. It is satisfying to teach individuals who manifest an eagerness to learn. An audience readily brings out the best a speaker can offer them by displaying close attention.

The problem of a speaker commences, however, long before he confronts his listeners. He must select his subject, gather information about it, interpret its varied meanings, and organize its sequential development in the preparatory phase. Now he needs to call to his aid imaginative insight and generalized knowledge both of human nature and of his prospective listeners. He must ask himself what they already know about the subject, whether or to what extent they are interested in it, and how more information could be useful to them. His preparation for the speech should be in the form of an imagined dialogue with his projected listeners. The great nineteenth century preacher, Henry Ward Beecher, described to a group of Yale divinity students how he discovered this method as a guide to the development of his own ability in preaching. "There was a reason," he told himself, "why when the apostles preached they succeeded." With great care he studied the "Book of Acts" and the various "Letters" in the *New Testament,* searching for the answer:[11]

I took every single instance in the Record, where I could find one of their sermons, and analyzed it, and asked myself: 'What were the circum-

[11] Henry Ward Beecher, *Yale Lectures on Preaching,* New York: J. B. Ford, 1872, p. 11.

stances? Who were the people? What did he do?' And I studied the sermons until I got this idea: That the apostles were accustomed first to feel for a ground on which the people and they stood together; a common ground where they could meet. Then they heaped up a large number of the particulars of knowledge that belonged to everybody; and when they had got that knowledge, which everybody would admit, placed in a proper form before their minds, then they brought it to bear upon them with all their excited heart and feeling.

What Beecher found out about the apostles and what we find out from his sermons when we read them is that their effectiveness arose in large part from the quality of sharing interest and information. The speaker first made earnest efforts to determine what his potential listeners knew, believed, and felt about the subject. Then, basing his own approach firmly upon that foundation, he was able to lead the listeners on to a new and broader understanding. We learn—and are glad to learn—in terms of what we already know.

Persuade and Evaluate

Among the many human needs is also a need to influence others and to be influenced by them. Man is incurably homogeneous. The amount of conformity in human behavior is remarkable. When social psychologists analyze human personalities, they find at the root of every type a strong tendency to adhere to the values of the group.[12] The sense of belonging is an anchor point of mental health, just as a feeling of being rejected by one's associates is psychologically unsettling. The tides of influence in human relationships flow back and forth, while students of leadership argue whether a leader should advance boldly well in advance of his followers or should try, rather, to phrase for them what they already substantially believe. In either case, it is generally agreed that normal individuals desire both to lead and to be led—to persuade and to be persuaded.[13]

There are many similarities between communication that aims to share information and that which seeks to exert influence. The first is called informative, the second persuasive. Theoretically the difference between them is decisive: the first being simply to clarify meanings, with no indication of what conclusion should be derived from them; whereas the second lays stress upon the desired conclusion. A teacher,

[12] David Riesman, Nathan Glazer, and Reuel Denney, *The Lonely Crowd,* New Haven, Conn.: Yale University Press, 1950.

[13] Bernard M. Bass, *Leadership, Psychology, and Organizational Behavior,* New York: Harper & Row Publishers, Inc., 1959.

for example, might explain to his class the differences, so far as he can identify them, between the two major American political parties; but he would be considered as exerting an improper influence if he tried to persuade his students to adhere to either the Republican or the Democratic Party. Actually, the difference between exposition and persuasion is largely a matter of differential emphasis. In either kind of discourse a pattern of meaning is devised and communicated; in either case the speaker intends to influence his listeners to accept the pattern as he depicts it. The crucial difference—and it is significant—is that the pattern of informative discourse emphasizes that the choice of how to react evaluatively to the subject is left to the listeners; whereas, persuasive discourse undertakes to win acceptance for the conclusion advocated by the speaker.

Experience demonstrates that mere explanation may be motivated by a persuasive intent. For example, a speaker may explain how tax policies differ by showing that an income tax is based on ability to pay; whereas, the sales tax may take five percent of a poor man's total income and only one-tenth of one percent of a rich man's income. Despite the expository nature of the discourse, it probably tends for most listeners to be persuasive. Their tendency will be not simply to say, "I understand," but either to conclude that the income tax is fairer, or to argue back that both groups pay the same amount and that it would be unjust to confiscate wealth through the higher charges which the income tax imposes on larger incomes.

In a free society, persuasion is valued as a kind of communication which aims toward the constructive and peaceable solution of problems. It provides a method for competition among ideas. Decisions in the home, in business, or in the political forum may be reached through free and approved controversy. Persuasion is a highly valued and frequently used kind of communication. When we are persuaded, we receive valued guidance as to what to believe or to do; when we persuade, we provide leadership to guide the behavior of others. Both the exertion and the reception of persuasion are essential ingredients of social living.

Enhance Sociability

A large proportion of social communication aims primarily toward maintaining mutually pleasing social relationships. In a limited sense it is speech designed to entertain. In a broader sense, it encompasses all the multiple instances in which people talk together primarily to cement their bonds of sociability, to signal to one another their mutual enjoyment in being together, and to strengthen their social ties against the inevitable strains and stress of competitive aims and actions.

When a speaker tells a joke, engages in generally whimsical talk, relates an exciting experience, describes unusual facts, or invites a comrade to tell him about a recent trip or an interesting book he has read, the response that is sought is generally simple enjoyment in one another's company. There are many occasions when relaxation, fun, and diversion from the tension of work or worry are the principal social aims. At home and on the job, when tempers are frayed or nerves are tense, when problems accumulate and personal frustrations mount, there is a positive therapeutic need for socializing talk.

Entertainment is one of the basic purposes of oral communication. Viewed broadly as comprising all the verbal interchanges that are designed primarily to preserve and promote sociability, this kind of discourse is both extensive and important. Much of our talk is aimed principally to signal the message: "We are friends" or "We are foes." Much more has little intent beyond pointing out: "This is interesting or "This will please you." Not only do we often speak simply for the purpose of trying to keep people happy; we may listen for the same reason—sometimes to jokes we have often heard before, or to anecdotes that are not as good as our appreciative response seeks to indicate. One way of enriching human relations is by generous giving. And often the best gift is the high and sincere compliment of speaking or of listening with an appreciative acknowledgement of the pleasure we feel in the company of those with whom we are assembled.

Communicative exchanges (speaking and listening) that give pleasure to the participants are valuable in and for themselves. But entertaining speech also serves highly useful supplementary purposes. Whatever else the discourse seeks to accomplish will usually be facilitated if the talk is pleasing. If a speaker wishes to enlighten or to persuade a group, his purpose is deeply serious. But he can reduce tensions, create bonds of good fellowship, and achieve a willingness to listen by interposing relevant anecdotal materials or whimsical comments amidst the serious facts and arguments. No discourse is effective except as it holds the attention of the participants. It often is useful to lighten the mood of listeners while attempting to enlighten their minds.

Focus of the Communicative Purpose

As the foregoing discussion indicates, the varied and interrelated purposes which speakers and listeners may have in any particular communicative situation will relate in part to themselves, in part to the subject matter being considered, and in part to reactions they wish to arouse in the other participants. These three types of purposes are always interrelated; but greater efficiency in communication results when they are considered separately so that specific preparation can be made for each one. The self-centered purposes are called personal purposes; the subject-centered aims are called general purposes; and the goals of securing desired reactions are called responses. Impossible as it is to isolate them from one another in their development or in their effects, it is helpful to think of them separately in planning and preparing for communication.

Personal Purposes

One personal purpose of paramount importance is the maintenance of one's own image of himself. As a speaker and as an evaluative listener, everyone seeks to behave in a manner that accords with his own view of his own true identity. Sincerity, or the determination to be what one seems to be, is a debt owing less to others than to oneself. Another personal purpose is to create, or clarify, or maintain a selective reaction toward oneself by valued associates. In the pursuit of this goal, one naturally behaves differently in different situations and among different people. One may wish to be regarded by his boss as responsible and diligent; by one's comrades as relaxed, unambitious, and devil-may-care; by one's friends as thoughtful and considerate; by one's banker as sober and dependable. Social psychologists sometimes differentiate between the core personality, within which is emphasized the integrity of trying to be precisely what an individual thinks he most truly is; and the social personality, which means trying to be what an individual thinks is most properly expected of him in a particular social situation.[14] These are the two sources of the two kinds of personal purposes by which all communicative interchanges are inevitably influenced. Naturally a speaker or listener can increase his efficiency by giving thought to just what manner of impression he wishes to effect in a particular situation.

General Purposes

However complex and interrelated are the views which are held toward any subject matter by both speakers and listeners, it is helpful

[14] For a fruitful development of this concept, see Erving Goffman, *The Presentation of Self in Everyday Life,* New York: Doubleday & Company, Inc., 1959.

to clear and responsive communication for both speaker and listener to decide whether his aim is primarily to inform (be informed), to persuade (to evaluate), or to enhance sociability (through speaking or responsive listening). When the aim is basically to inform, the speaker should take care to leave open for his listener all available options as to evaluative responses that may be made. He will not load the dice favorably for either the Democrats or the Republicans if his purpose is to inform concerning differences between the two parties. This does not at all mean that he should seek to conceal unfavorable materials which he may know concerning one or the other, or that he should refuse to exercise judgment concerning the merits of historic stands taken by the two parties. His duty, rather, is to tell "the truth, the whole truth, and nothing but the truth," as he sees it. Also, since he is not acting as an advocate for either side, but rather as an impartial referee fairly presenting the relevant data so that listeners may themselves reach their own conclusions, the emphasis is upon a fair, balanced, and sympathetic account of what properly may be said about party differences. The response he aims for will not be, "I agree" but "I understand." Similarly, if the aim is to persuade, or to please, the speaker will select and present his materials with the clear intent of securing the response of, "I do agree," or "This is indeed interesting."

Responses

If an individual is angry (and there are occasions when anger is justified), his purpose in a communicative situation might be to insult or to humiliate his listeners. More often, of course, his purpose is to help them attain a right view of the subject matter under discussion and, concurrently, to heighten their respect and affection for himself. As Henry Ward Beecher discovered in his own early experiences as a preacher (as indicated in a quotation earlier in this chapter), he failed when his purpose was to produce good sermons, however scholarly, factual, and earnest they were. He succeeded when he began to ask himself what his parishioners already knew and believed about the subject he selected to preach about, and then built what he had to say upon the basis of what they knew, with a precise aim toward the result he wanted to achieve. His advice to the young men at Yale who were preparing for the ministry was: "Take men as it has pleased God to make them; and let your preaching, so far as it concerns the selection of material, and the mode and method by which you are presenting the truth, follow the wants of the persons themselves, and not simply the measure of your own minds."[15] The aim to secure a specific audience-response is a purpose developed not only from the subject matter and from the speaker's wishes, but also from the nature of his listeners. A desired response may most surely be secured by preparation in terms of the knowledge, the interests, and the mood of the people who will be listening to the speaker's presentation.

Immediate and Long-Range Goals

Generally a communicant has an immediate goal in any communicative situation, and also a long-range goal. A merchant may wish to sell some particular article, but he also wants to create good will and lasting confidence. A lawyer wants to win a particular case, and he also wants to establish a general reputation for honesty and respect for justice. A listener may feel impelled to reveal his boredom or disgust while listening to a particularly ineffective talk, but may decide that his long-range association with the speaker or with other listeners may be improved if he maintains a respectful attitude.

Only a few people place a distinctly high emphasis upon becoming good speakers. What most people do value is to become known as thoughtful, dependable, considerate, and capable members of their communities. Not many people seek a reputation as eager listeners—though many value being known for their appreciative and sympathetic natures. Long-range goals usually relate less to communicative skill as such than to one's general ambitions and aspirations, vocationally and socially. It would be a mistake to endanger long-term respect and affection for the satisfaction of winning an argument by unfair means or of expressing anger or contempt, which undermines friendly relations, however tempting the immediate goal may seem. Fortunately, it is generally true that careful and honest concentration upon the immediate communicative goal is also constructively helpful toward the attainment of long-range objectives. The kind of speaking and listening that wins enduring respect is normally the kind that also wins a favorable reaction in the immediate situation. On some occasions, however, it is wise to lose a communicative battle in order to win the long-range campaign of friendly relations. A merchant, a lawyer, a politician, or anyone else may gain in the long run by frankly saying, "After listening to your remarks, I can see that my thinking on this subject was wrong."

[15] Henry Ward Beecher, p. 58.

And a listener who endures boredom graciously on occasion may find that he learns something, after all, to his lasting benefit.

The Specific Purpose

Our discussion thus far has been generalized, to describe principles that apply as broadly as possible to all or at least to most communicative situations. However, every time an individual confronts a specific need for communication, it is particular, not general. This is the time when he should do his own best thinking to utilize the general guidance in terms of the immediate need.

When an invitation is accepted to give a talk, whether at the downtown Rotary Club or in the speech class, the problem of preparation focuses upon the precise situation that will be confronted. What is known about personal and general purposes and about audience responses, considered in terms of immediate and long-range goals, becomes of value precisely to the degree that this understanding may help in the formulation of a specific purpose that will fit the needs of the anticipated particular occasion. This problem is generally best solved by deciding on a definite answer to the question: what is it that I want these listeners to do?

The answer to this question will be determined by several considerations. One of them is what the speaker believes and desires. If his attitude toward war is that of a pacifist, naturally his aim in speaking about war will be to persuade his listeners of its evil and futility. But another limiting factor in deciding on a specific purpose is consideration of what the anticipated listeners think about the subject. Are they already pacifists? If so, the specific purpose might become a statement of what "we pacifists" can and should do about a particular military situation. Are the prospective listeners definitely and perhaps even defiantly anti-pacifistic? If so the specific purpose might be realistically limited, to try to convince them that whether or not pacifists might be misguided, they are at least sincere. Again, the specific purpose must be determined in part by the time limitations. If the talk is to be limited to five minutes, the speaker should consider carefully what he might hope to accomplish in that time. Could he sketch the history of pacifism? Could he explain its philosophic foundations? Could he cite instances in which it has proved effective? Could he indicate what a pacifist attitude would require of true believers in the current international circumstances? Could he make explicit what agreement with his principles would demand in terms of action by his individual listeners? These are sample questions the speaker would need to consider. They apply, of course, both to his own beliefs and to the reaction-possibilities of his listeners; but they apply also very realistically to the amount of time he will have available. Not everything can be accomplished at once. For any particular discourse, the topic should be limited to what the circumstances demand, what the audience will receive, and what the time permits.

Criteria Governing the Specific Purpose

For a speaker who is undertaking to formulate a specific purpose for a particular talk, the following guidelines or criteria will be helpful:

1. Is the statement really specific? "I want my listeners to understand permissiveness in child rearing" is less well focused than "I want my listeners to understand the differences among permissiveness, discipline, and neglect in child rearing."

2. Is the stated response achievable? It might be possible to explain the meaning of "$E = MC^2$"—but can it be done in five minutes? Can it be done if the listeners have little background in mathematics or physics? Can it be accomplished on the Saturday morning before the big game?

3. Is the contemplated purpose ethically sound? It might be possible to arouse your fellow students to picket the university administration; would it also be desirable? A speaker bears responsibility for the effects of the influence he exerts. The right to speak freely carries with it the responsibility to consider the effects of what may be said.

4. Is the purpose consistent with the general conduct of the speaker? Ralph Waldo Emerson reminded his lecture audience that: "For the most part, what you are stands over you the while and thunders so that I cannot hear what you say to the contrary."[16] Our words should be consistent with our general pattern of acts and beliefs.

5. Is the response desired of value to the listeners? Should you try to teach the proper way of grasping a tennis racket to people who do not play tennis? If you wish to arouse indignation against a certain

[16] Ralph Waldo Emerson, from "Social Aims," a lecture delivered at the Parker Fraternity, Harvard University, in December, 1864; in *Works* of Ralph Waldo Emerson, ed., Edward Waldo Emerson, New York: Wise Book Company, 1929, VIII, p. 96.

foreign policy, do you have a suggestion as to what your listeners may do about it? What might your listeners gain from your remarks, whether it be new information, clarification of their understanding, strengthening of an existing belief, acquiring fresh insight into a problem, or enjoying an occasion of relaxed and pleasant sociability?

6. How is the purpose significant to the speaker? Will preparation for the speech reward the speaker in terms of additional information he will gain, or clarification of his own understanding? Will it enhance his favorable relations with his listeners? Will the methods he will use help him to increase his skill as a speaker?

Conclusion

As speakers and listeners—and on the frequent occasions when we alternate between these roles, as in conversation, discussion, conference, and interviews—we have a pattern of purposes that relate to our own personal aims, the nature of the subject matter, the nature of the other participants, and the occasion. The general purposes may be classified as informative, persuasive, and social. For each discourse, there should also be a specific purpose, which governs the speaking and guides the listening in a manner suitable to the occasion. The way in which a speaker's purpose is and should be affected by all these factors is well depicted by Ralph Waldo Emerson in a lecture on "Eloquence" which he delivered to the Boston Merchantile Library Association in February, 1847:[17]

> The audience is a constant meter of the orator. There are many audiences in every public assembly, each one of which rules in turn. If anything comic and coarse is spoken, you shall see the emergence of the boys and rowdies, so loud and vivacious that you might think the house was filled with them. If new topics are started, graver and higher, these roisterers recede; a more chaste and wise attention takes place. You would think the boys slept, and that the men have any degree of profoundness. If the speaker utter a noble sentiment, the attention deepens, a new and highest audience now listens. . . . Humble persons are conscious of new illumination; narrow brows expand with enlarged affections;—delicate spirits, long unknown to themselves, masked and muffled in coarsest fortunes, who now hear their own native language for the first time, and leap to hear it. But all these several audiences, each above each, which successively appear to greet the variety of style and topic, are really com-

[17] Emerson, *Works,* VII, pp. 66–7.

posed out of the same persons; nay, sometimes the same individual will take active part in them all, in turn.

Exercises

· *Questions for Discussion*

1. In this chapter the purposes which direct human behavior, including communication, are represented as being complex, mixed, sometimes contradictory, and often only partially understood. Does this seem to you to be characteristic of your own conversational talk? Does it characterize the talk you hear from others? Give examples.

2. Do you ever hear talk which appears earnestly to advocate a particular point of view or attitude when the behavior of the speaker rather clearly seems to indicate that he actually means the contrary of what he says? Could you illustrate a circumstance of this kind? How do you explain it?

3. What is meant by *motivational cohesiveness?* Do you find it illustrated in the speaking-listening behavior of the members of your speech class? Does it characterize your own communicative behavior?

4. Why do textbooks in speech generally list three or five general purposes and textbooks in social psychology often list a dozen or a score or more purposes, or goals, or aims which govern human behavior, including communication? Is it merely a difference in methods of classification, or is there a difference in kind between social motives and speech purposes? If it seems to you to be a difference in kind, what is the distinction? What use can be made of the social motives as guides to efficient speaking and listening?

5. The divergence in what was heard of the Kennedy-Nixon television debate by the two letter-writers quoted in this chapter could be matched by divergence in interpretation of what has been read as indicated in "letters to the editor" from almost any issue of *Time* or *Newsweek.* How do you account for this widespread difference? Does it result from differential perception, or interpretation, or merely in the feelings of the letter writers? What does this divergence suggest to you concerning the way you should speak to a group of listeners—and concerning your own listening?

6. Do you agree that the conclusions summarized are rather obvious, or would you question one or several of them? Do you think the resulting implications discussed are properly drawn from those con-

clusions? What effects should these implications have upon your efforts to improve the effectiveness of your own speaking? Of your own listening?

7. If the purpose of a speaker or a listener may not always be clearly indicated to the other communicants, why is it important to have a clear and dominant purpose? Is it more (or less) important for a listener than for a speaker?

8. What seems to you to be the principal reasons for depicting the general purposes in communication as: (1) to inform and be informed; (2) to persuade and evaluate; and (3) to enhance sociability? What objections do you have to this listing? Might such a classification serve as a useful guide in improving the quality of speaking and listening even if these purposes do overlap?

9. What is a personal purpose? How is it affected by the presumed bifurcation of the core personality and the social personality?

10. In what sense is information persuasive? Is entertainment ever persuasive? Is persuasion ever informative—or ever entertaining? How may you test the validity of your own general purpose in speaking? Can you always be sure of the general purpose of a speaker to whom you are listening?

11. How, when, and in what varied ways should a speaker be alert to the responses of his listeners?

12. When long-range and immediate purposes conflict, how should the difference between them be reconciled?

13. What are the factors which govern the formulation of the specific purpose for a talk? How valid are the six criteria, which serve as guidelines, in deciding on a specific purpose? May some of them be ignored, or assigned low priority, for at least some kinds of communicative situations? Explain.

• *Projects for Speaking and Listening*

1. Write down several ideas which you might like to talk about or to hear discussed. Consider what might be an appropriate general, personal, and specific purpose for each, provided you were to discuss the topics with: (1) the members of your speech class; (2) your roommate; (3) a certain professor or counselor; and (4) your parents.

2. For each of the following situations, what might be an appropriate response to be sought, and how would you phrase a specific purpose that might lead toward securing that response? Begin each statement of purpose with the phrase, "I want my listeners to . . ."

a. A group of students gathered casually in a dormitory room begin to discuss American involvement in Southeast Asia.

b. During a holiday visit at home, you meet a group of seniors from your high school who think they might like to come to your college.

c. You prepare for job interviews with representatives of various companies who come to your campus.

d. As a representative of college-age youth, you are invited to participate in a discussion at your church of "open housing" in your community.

3. As you listen to a visiting lecturer on your campus, try to identify his general, personal, and specific purposes. What response does he seek from his auditors? Estimate the degree to which you think he failed or succeeded in securing the desired response and describe and evaluate the means he used which resulted in partial or complete failure or success.

4. Following a session of talk—which might be a round of speeches in your class, a dinner table conversation, or an evening bull session—analyze the mixed purposes, which characterized at least a portion of the discourse. Would the speaking and listening have been more efficient if the purposes had been less mixed? Were the dominant purposes easily identified? If they were not, did you consider the veiling of the purposes to have been deliberate or careless? Criticize the purposive characteristics of the discourse, indicating how in this respect it might have been improved.

5 · *Finding Content and Substance*

This chapter is concerned with the substance of oral discourse and its meaning to both speaker and listener. In most of man's everyday conversation in social and business situations, his subject content is drawn from his background and resources: his formal education, his reading, his experiences, his travels, and his associates. He probably makes no special effort to reinforce these unless the situation he contemplates assumes some degree of significance. He may do so, for example, when he is invited to dinner at the home of a friend whom he knows to be an avid baseball fan. He may want to take particular note of the scores of the games that day, the standing of the clubs, and even the batting and pitching averages of the season to date. He would thus broaden and strengthen his source materials which he could draw upon in conversing and which would make him a better listener when his host is talking.

In the business setting, daily contacts involving informal speech communication deal with the exchange of ideas based on subjects usually well known to speaker and listener. But as a manager plans to visit a work area to check on production and the safety record in his department, he would first want to read the past record and perhaps the company manual on safety regulations to bring his information up to date. When he plans to talk with an employee about his work performance, the manager might first want to look over the employee's personnel file showing his history of work with the company.

Looking forward to a more formal speaking situation, where the speaker will have choice of his subject selection, it is interesting to conjecture whether he picks one on which he has much information and materials or one of more current interest to his listeners on which he must get more information. It is probably some of both if it is a good topic for the occasion; but regardless of how the choice comes about, he will want to supplement his present knowledge in order to make the speech more meaningful.

Similarly, listeners in contemplating a speech will surely derive greater enjoyment and benefit if they increase their knowledge of the subject before the occasion. Typical of this, of course, is the college student who is almost compelled to prepare for a lecture by reading the chapter assignments in the text before he goes to class. While this compulsion may seem like a chore at times, he knows it is essential for better understanding of the instructor's points; and he should realize the value of this practice in later life, where his motivation to reinforce his knowledge must come from his own desire to get the most he can from the words and thoughts of others.

Therefore, all of us, speakers and listeners alike, as we work toward our goal of being most effective in all contacts with others, must strive to become better informed.[1] This of course is not a goal to be considered only on those occasions when one makes a speech, although this might put the challenge in more acute focus. In this age of mass communication and of rapid accumulation of knowledge on old and new subjects, one of our greatest challenges is to try to keep up with information from day to day. The more we do this as a part of daily living, the more we are prepared to draw upon our knowledge and apply it in speaking and listening situations. But whether we gather the necessary information over a period of time or for a specific occasion, it is crucial to effectiveness that we have the best possible content to our messages and, as listeners, that we know enough about a subject to best understand or evaluate what we hear.

[1] The importance of being well informed, and suggestions for accomplishing this objective, are discussed in Robert T. Oliver, *Becoming an Informed Citizen,* New York: Holt, Rinehart and Winston, Inc., 1964.

Approaching the Job Systematically

In order to develop a systematic approach toward insuring adequate substance and content for good communication, this kind of analysis should be useful:

Assessing the communicator's present state of knowledge.
Assessing the situation, subject, and what is called for.
Determining how much material, and what kind, is needed.

As in most things we do, the search for materials needs to progress through several stages. The obvious first step has been to determine what is to be accomplished in the situation. From this as a base, inquiry extends to one's own background related to the topic; the consideration of the situation, subject, and the listener's needs; and the nature of the material needed[2] to do the job.

1. *Assess the communicator's present state of knowledge.* Both speakers and listeners need to take stock of their present knowledge of the subject in relation to the purpose to be accomplished. The question for the speaker is not merely "How much do I know about the subject?" but rather, "What knowledge do I have which will make my main ideas more understandable and believable; that will best motivate listener interest; that will help achieve the response desired?"[3] For the listener, he might ask himself whether his present level of knowledge is sufficient to follow and interpret the speaker's points or to evaluate properly his judgments and conclusions.

It would be unwise to go to either extreme in assessing one's present state of knowledge: the tendency to jump quickly to the conclusion that his knowledge is indeed very low; or the opposite tendency to feel smug and complacent because he knows all he needs to know. The former reaction usually results in a quick decision to go to the library and start reading, as though printed material is the only or best source of knowledge. Some speakers have a feeling of inadequacy

[2] See Chapter 7 for a full consideration of the needs and uses of materials in developing, validating, and supporting ideas.

[3] A. J. Ayer, *The Problem of Knowledge,* London: Macmillan & Co., Ltd., 1956, p. 7, says that a statement is "knowledgeable" only when three conditions are met by it: 1) it is true; 2) the speaker is sure of its truth; and 3) he has the right to be sure of it.

with respect to subject knowledge which they feel can be satisfied only by reading from subject matter sources. Listeners contemplating a situation calling upon them to assay their knowledge of a subject before the speaking event are more apt to think over what they already know.

To ascertain one's present level of knowledge, an inventory should be made, by evaluating one's factual information to determine how much of this is concrete and specific, and then recording this information on paper. Then he might try to recall his prior experiences with the subject, his personal contacts with people and events related to the subject, courses taken in the general area, and specific materials or notes he may have filed away. Usually this will result in a much greater accumulation of information than he had originally thought. It will also show gaps and suggest the need for specific types of further inquiry. Such an inventory should also include an attempt to bring together his present main thoughts about the subject. These should be thought through and then listed on paper, gradually separating those that are factual from those that represent opinions and judgments. These in turn will suggest types of materials needed that will, on the one hand, best help in the development of information objectives and, on the other hand, best support and prove the opinions and judgments when the objective is to persuade.

2 *Assess the situation.* The lawyer in preparing his case must examine every aspect of the situation out of which it arose. His process is that of analysis, and his ability to be analytical may be the major test of his success, for he must never find himself in a position of surprise or of being confronted for the first time with a point when he is in the courtroom. A Clarence Darrow and a Louis Nizer leave no stone unturned in this process of analyzing the total situation, the subject, and what is called for in order to best present the case. The efficient communicator will do likewise.

Each situation in which the communication takes place will make different demands for materials required to develop a subject. Speaking on "Evaluation and Grading of Students" to a PTA group of parents of elementary school students, following a social hour in one of their evening meetings, would be different from treatment of the same subject at a university seminar. The former could deal in general explanations and opinions, with some validation. The latter would need accurate data, expert opinion, and other concrete material. With either or both audiences, a basic test of the validity of our ideas is "to get them accepted by what in each field we regard as the universality of reasonable men."[4] One set of listeners tests ideas by one kind of experience and standards, another set by quite different criteria.

Again, the nature of the subject has to be assessed in relation to one's own knowledge and, more particularly, in the light of our present area of assessment, the purpose to be accomplished, and the level of depth that this requires. One may know quite a bit about electrical circuits, but it makes a big difference whether he is setting out to explain how to hook up a switch or concepts involving principles of voltage, amperage, and resistance.

3. *Determine how much material, and what kind, is needed.* The eventual result of all this analysis is to make this determination. A major point to keep in mind is that preparation for the speaking situation in a total sense is much more important than preparing a speech as such. If all that one says represents the sum total of what he knows, listeners will sense that he lacks authority.[5]

How much material is needed? The answer should be clear: one is unlikely to have too much material. If icebergs were only what they appear to be on the surface, they could have little destructive effects on shipping. Similarly, surface speaking will have little effect upon listeners. What gives icebergs "authority" in the shipping lanes is the seven-eighths of their bulk below the surface. What gives speakers authority in the minds of listeners is the seven-eighths of the material left unused because the one-eighth that was selected was the most effective in the communicative transaction the speaker and listener shared together.

Actually, how much to know about any subject is less important than knowing what is essential for formation of sound judgments. There is no rule of thumb; the decision of when the evidence will support the assertion must be made by the speaker, with the certainty that it will be checked by each listener. "Every thinking person," we are reminded, "is continually brought face to face with the need to discriminate between what is true and what is false, what is probable and what is doubtful or impossible. These decisions rest on a combination of knowledge, skepticism, faith, common sense, and intelligent

[4] Ch. Perelman, *The Idea of Justice and the Problem of Argument,* tr. John Petrie, New York: Humanities Press, Inc., 1963, p. 133.

[5] A suspicion that the speaker does not know fully and dependably what he is talking about leads to communicative resistance. *Cf.* W. J. McGuire, "Inducing Resistance to Persuasion; Some Contemporary Approaches," in L. Berkowitz, ed., *Advances in Experimental Social Psychology,* New York: Academic Press, Inc., 1964, pp. 191–229.

guessing."[6] We know enough when we know that what we are saying (or hearing) makes sense.

Efficiency and judgment are important qualities in determining how much and what kinds of materials are needed. It would indeed be discouraging (and quite unwise) if we were to give the impression that one must seek out all materials relevant to a topic. This would be impossible, and it is far from the point. An efficient communicator has already narrowed down his subject to a specific phase, has narrowed this to a specific purpose-response to be achieved, and has arrived at certain main points he plans to make. It is with these in mind that the speaker makes a judgment about his present knowledge and materials and about how much more and what kinds he should seek. We have pointed out that every step in the preparation process—choosing and narrowing the subject, analyzing the audience, determining the purpose—is designed to help choose efficiently. In later chapters we see how the principles of organization and of proof and development influence judgment in the selection of materials.

Sources of Materials

It is difficult to narrow down the specific suggestions we now wish to make, for the whole world and everything in it is a source of materials. Our chief endeavor throughout this chapter is to indicate directions, guidelines, and steps that will lead first toward proper analysis, then to specific sources. The increased complexity of world affairs; the combination of technology, electronics, space age, and computer emphasis; and the amazingly fast accumulation of new knowledge and information have led us toward a mad race for information retrieval and storage almost beyond imagination. Government agencies, industry, and professional organizations alike are searching for more and more sophisticated methods of putting information into digested form and developing systems for storing it so that it can be instantly retrieved through computers and data analysis.

With all this complexity, we still know that man's own instruments of the mind, memory, nervous system, and multi-channel scanners are far more complex than any technology he has invented. Every one of us has the capacity for systematic scanning, interrelating, and remem-

[6] Jacques Barzun and Henry F. Graff, *The Modern Researcher,* New York: Harcourt, Brace & World, Inc., 1957, p. 88.

bering information and materials. An individual actually can process data from many sources, both within himself and without, as we have pointed out earlier. His own nervous system must be alerted first toward self-analysis and self-inventory. If he is genuinely interested in his subject, his own internal system will be stimulated and his enthusiasm toward this objective will grow. But this remarkably complex human mechanism is also stubborn and may refuse to process data in which it has no interest.

Look Toward Others

When the President of the United States prepares for a speaking situation or for attendance at a meeting where he will listen to others, he is able to call upon an unlimited source of experts to supply him with information. These may range from cabinet officers, agency heads, and special experts in particular subject areas to personal friends or casual acquaintances. His source of materials is vast. Similarly, persons in less important positions, yet with responsibility in organizations as officers or managers or as individuals in their particular walk of life, may have assistants or associates to whom they can turn for advice and for materials.

All of us develop many kinds of associations with others. As college students, the most likely ones are our classmates, friends, fraternity brothers, and professors. Whether or not such persons can supply us with information we need, sources and ideas are multiplied fast by talking with others. Every opportunity should be used to turn conversations with others to the subject on which material is needed. Today, many suggestions are being made in this country toward revising the draft laws for military service. If one is well prepared to speak on this subject and is walking toward class to make the speech, a conversation with a friend on the way might reveal a very late announcement made by the President which the friend heard on the radio a few moments before. By incorporating this into his speech, the speaker would have a most timely way of making his speech more interesting, authoritative, and up-to-date.

Such conversations with others lead to sources of ideas not considered earlier. They may stimulate toward revising one's own ideas, or suggest the use of analogies, examples, or figures, which were not known. They may provide a test of the speaker's ability to achieve understanding or belief with a particular listener, so that he may better judge whether he is sufficiently prepared with the right kind of material for the speech audience. And of course for both speaker and listener, such conversations afford endless opportunities to talk and listen and to test and practice abilities at both ends of the communication process.

Listen to Speeches and Lectures

Most students need to become more effective listeners in the classes they attend. In addition, college students are in an enviable position with regard to the accessibility of prominent lecturers with varied backgrounds and subjects that may be drawn upon for material and testimonials. The free lecture on the campus, so often poorly attended by college students, is frequently the same lecture that people in isolated places would gladly pay money to hear. Whatever the subject treated, the student as a good listener has the opportunity to acquire ideas and materials which he can later use in his own speech preparation.

The speech class itself is a forum for the exchange of ideas and materials, with a wide variety of subjects discussed by students from many backgrounds and fields of study. The history major will listen to the student of architecture discuss the use of the flying buttress in Gothic cathedrals; the student of forestry talk about conservation, soil erosion, tree planting, and insect control; the engineer explain the vacuum tube by comparing its operation to the water faucet; the economics major discuss inflationary factors in the economy; and the science student explain atomic energy. It should be obvious that new ideas and possibly new materials will be suggested by these classmates and that careful listening should pay off.

Listen to All Faculty and Course Discussions

It should be obvious from the above examples that one can often draw considerably from his major course interests and from particular courses for materials in his speaking. The texts and other reading sources are perhaps the most tangible, but the regular instructors daily bring additional material into their lectures and class discussions. The ability to listen carefully and analytically is well worth developing and using in all courses, along with the ability to take notes accurately.

Listen to Radio and Television Programs

This medium of sharing information with the public has grown immensely in recent years. Speeches of leading citizens, broadcasts of news, and forums on which discussions and debates are regularly featured offer a great range of subjects and materials. The growth of educational television stations and networks includes a heavy concentration of programs dealing with instruction of the public on everything from cooking to space travel. In the discussion of current subjects by prominent authorities, such programs as *Meet the Press* and *Face the Nation* are examples of the wealth of ideas and factual material available at the switch of the dial, when the listener is guided by an attitude of conscientious inquiry.

Read

We come now to the method of finding source materials which many regard as the primary method.[7] Although we warned earlier that there are many other sources to be explored before going to the books and periodicals, these probably represent the most abundant and reliable sources of materials. They are also usually the most accessible. Francis Bacon said, "Reading maketh a full man." Although Ralph Waldo Emerson warned against thoughtless reading when he said, "Books are the best of things well used; abused, among the worst," it is unusual to find one who reads too much. The acquisition of the library habit is a great asset to speakers and listeners as well . . . to all of us. A good newspaper should be read every day. Books, periodicals, reports, summaries, digests, and reviews are among the great sources of materials. When Senator Wayne Morse once said of his busy colleagues in the United States Senate that they were an increasingly unread group, he was expressing a disturbing fact in the lives of our public leaders.[8] Indeed, most people read too little and lack both breadth of information and the informed judgment needed for good discourse—both as speakers and as listeners. A balance is desirable between books and periodicals devoted to science, culture, current

[7] Among recently developed sourcebooks particularly useful for speakers are Robert T. Oliver, Carroll C. Arnold, and Eugene E. White, *Speech Preparation Sourcebook,* Boston, Mass.: Allyn and Bacon, Inc., 1966, and Paul D. Brandes and Theodore J. Walwik, *A Research Manual for the Performance Course in Speech,* New York: Harper & Row Publishers, Inc., 1967.

[8] As John Foster Dulles, when he was Secretary of State, phrased it: "We are kept so busy at the front door dealing with urgent problems that we have no time to go out in the quiet of the back yard and study them." *Cf.* John R. Beal, *John Foster Dulles: A Biography,* New York: Harper & Row Publishers, 1957.

events, biography, history, and other aspects of life in general and those devoted to particular professional or vocational interests. Special interests of all of us will naturally influence our selection of reading matter.

In reading for particular information for a speaking or listening assignment, the practice of finding one article which we offer as our own or as the completed speech is obviously both unethical and unrewarding. The student who attempted to pass off as his own material a printed column, which had appeared in a prominent newspaper (which his professor had also read), deserved the severe reprimand given him for doing an essentially dishonest thing.

The habit of persistent, selective, and discriminating reading stimulates one's growth as a person while he makes a systematic attempt to digest and excerpt from it what will be useful. Even the habit of browsing in the reading room of a library or through one's own book collection leads to more specific values. As one reads for speech materials as well as for interest and enjoyment, he will nearly always discover that it becomes increasingly profitable. Reading makes the fuller man and the better communicator.

Standard Reference Works

Certain standard reference works are in every good library. These sources can be used for condensed factual information and for more substantial material on almost every conceivable subject. A complete list would be too lengthy to provide here, but the following sources are some of the major library reference works.

Indexes and Reference Works

Winchell's Guide to Reference Books. A comprehensive listing of reference works, both English and foreign, with annual supplements.

The *card catalogue* in the library. This index is by author, title, and subject of all books in the library.

Readers' Guide to Periodical Literature, 1900 to date. An author and subject index to current general periodicals.

Poole's Index to Periodical Literature, 1802–1906. The earliest general magazine index.

Nineteenth Century Readers' Guide, 1890–1899. An author and subject index to 51 leading periodicals of the nineteenth century.

New York Times Index, with supplements. This lists alphabetically by subject the news stories published in *The New York Times.*

Cumulative Book Index, with supplements. These volumes list every book published in the English language according to author, title, and subject.

Engineering Index, 1844 to date. Guide to engineering literature of the world.

Encyclopedia: *Britannica, Americana,* and others.

Encyclopedia of World Travel, 1967. Information on all countries of the world.

Encyclopedia of the Social Sciences, 1930–37.

U.S. Superintendent of Documents. Monthly catalogue of federal publications.

Essay and General Literature Index, 1900 to date. Index to essays and articles in collections and various works.

Book Review Digest, 1905 to date. Excerpts from reviews of current books published in the United States.

Annual Magazine Subject Index, 1907–49. A subject index to a selected list of American and English periodicals and society publications.

International Index, 1907 to date. A quarterly guide to periodical literature in the fields of business, finance, and technology.

Public Affairs Information Service, 1915 to date. A monthly index to books, periodicals, and materials pertaining to economics and public affairs.

Agricultural Index, 1916 to date. Guide to periodicals in agriculture, including pamphlets, bulletins, and reports by agricultural agencies.

Education Index, 1929 to date. A cumulative author and subject index to selected educational periodicals, books, and pamphlets.

Art Index, 1929 to date. Author and subject index to art journals and museum publications.

Music Index, 1949 to date. The key to current music periodical literature.

Applied Science and Technology Index, 1958 to date. A cumulative subject index to periodicals in fields including aeronautics, automation, chemistry, electricity, engineering, industrial arts, transportation, and related subjects.

Business Periodicals Index, 1958 to date. A cumulative subject index to periodicals in the fields of accounting, advertising, banking, business, marketing, management, taxation, and public administration.

World Almanac and Book of Facts, 1868 to date. Data and factual information.

Familiar Quotations, John Bartlett, 13th ed., 1955. Contains a variety of quotations from famous persons and sources.
Reference Shelf Series. Volumes containing varied materials, each devoted to a particular subject.
Debaters Annual and *Intercollegiate Debates.* Two separate series of annual volumes containing full texts of debates held each year.

In view of the availability of a vast number of facts provided in clearly organized and alphabetical order in such works as those listed above, there seems to be little excuse for the communicator who satisfies himself with a thin, superficial knowledge or who abandons a promising subject with the excuse, "I don't know enough," or "I don't know where I can get information on that subject. . . ." Facts in abundance—specific, dependable, exact—are ready and waiting to be found and used.

Using and Testing Sources

There are some more important general factors in the handling of materials which must be considered, for they make a difference in how one records and talks about them. The communicator has certain obligations to meet in his goal of developing speaking and listening effectiveness to serve throughout a lifetime.

"Where did you learn that President Johnson favors an expanded program of urban development?" a student speaker was asked. "I read it some place," was the response, which later was indicated as "in some magazine." For want of the desire to use his sources properly, effectiveness was lost in this situation. But that is not all. The speaker lowered his standing as an authority for future speaking. And related to this loss was the inevitable reflection upon his honesty, because of his willingness to present ideas or opinions from a source he could not verify.

Listeners should and do want to know the answers to these questions about the speaker's materials:

1. How do you know?
2. Is this an accurate report or statement?
3. Does this agree with other sources?
4. What does this have to do with the subject?
5. What does this have to do with me?

Crediting the Source Accurately

Honesty dictates that the exact source be indicated. Further, it is dangerous not to do so if such failure arouses doubts about you or your points. In most cases, if the listener knows and respects your sources, he is more likely to respond in the right direction.

Listeners also want to be assured that the quotation is accurate, not out of context, and used fully where necessary to give correct meaning. "Eat, drink, and be merry," is hardly appropriately attributed to the Bible, where this sentiment is followed by, "But God said unto him, 'Thou fool.' "

It is also dishonest to attribute a source to someone who does not actually hold this opinion, by distorting, editing, or otherwise inaccurately quoting. This can lead to both immediate and long-range ineffectiveness. If a speaker reveals dishonesty even on an unimportant point, listener suspicion of dishonesty may be applied to anything else he has to say.

Corroborating the Source

Human perception is determined largely by what a person wants to perceive. We experience this when we have misconstrued a teacher's instruction, the report of the outcome of a game, or the attitude of a parent on a certain issue. Scientists know this and insist on confirming results through repeated experiments and checking of results of other scientists. Listeners are similarly wary of single, unconfirmed reports. The effective speaker, then, must present confirming materials from varied sources rather than just one or two, whenever this might occur.

What Bearing Does This Have on the Subject?

Materials, which have been selected for the support of an idea, will frequently not be effective in the same form in which they were found. The speaker must adapt his materials to the ideas which they support and point out the particular relationships of materials to ideas.

The effective speaker selects materials, including stories, which are related to and lend support to his main ideas. The all too common practice of beginning with a story that does get desired laughter but is unrelated to the subject is of far less value than using one that is related to a point or theme in the speech. Again, he must realize that his listeners may not readily see the relationship. Then he must explain how the relationship exists, depending, of course, on many factors, such as the degree of complexity of the subject or point, level of audience ability, and clarity of his presentation.

Relationship to the Listener

The question "What does this have to do with me?" is certain to be in the listener's mind and must constantly be considered by the speaker. Since listeners demand that both ideas and materials have some degree of importance to them, it behooves the speaker to show this. The astute speaker will see how materials can be made effective by properly adapting them to his particular listeners' interests, experiences, and wants. Even death on the highway or on the battlefield is remote to listeners until they are forced to see and feel that this might affect them. Large sums, such as the national debt of a third of a trillion dollars, have some meaning in themselves but become more meaningful when related to what this costs each of us.

Some Cautions in Searching for Materials

A speaker is sometimes led into one of two traps in looking for materials. One is the single source which he is tempted to use as a base for his speech. The other is the possible discovery that his subject or purpose is not worthwhile or appropriate after all.

Beware of the Single Predigested Source

The student of speech, under pressure of many courses, may easily be lured into a false goal in meeting assignments. The goal is not only to make good speeches but to learn, through speaking, how to improve as a communicator through a lifetime. Yet some may be tempted to try to present what seems to be a ready-made speech, such as a magazine article or digest of articles, newspaper stories, published speech, or one found in a fraternity file. There may be nothing wrong with any of these sources for stimulating ideas or for providing material to be used. They may often suggest additional sources. But there is little that is either right or educational about paraphrasing, or memorizing, or even extemporizing from a single predigested source.

Listeners can easily detect this kind of speaking. The vocabulary and style are not the speaker's; the adaptation is usually to some other audience. More important, the speaker learns little in his aim to become an effective communicator. He must learn originality in selecting, integrating, and adapting to both his and his listeners' experiences and needs.

Be Willing to Change

Gathering materials for effective communication is a process of inquiry. It is quite possible, as an inquirer, that you sometimes will not find what you want or expect to find. You should then be able and willing to consider the possibilty that you are seeking an inappropriate goal. Maybe you can not find ways to get a particular group of listeners to understand the concept underlying atomic energy applied to space craft. Or maybe you are led to the conclusion that these listeners have no need to understand this. In either case, you should be willing to backtrack, re-examine, and re-plan your subject and purpose, arriving at another that is meaningful and communicable in this situation.

This warning is even more applicable in persuasive speaking. Before you come to the conclusion that your listeners should condone capital punishment (or do away with it), you must make sure they understand the problem that is meant to be solved. As you gather materials you should be fully prepared to discover that you no longer believe your proposition and that, therefore, neither your classmates nor anyone else should be led to believe it through your speaking. You of course would then change the purpose you seek to accomplish.

Suggestions for Recording

Whether preparing for a specific speaking or listening engagement, or for general self-enlightenment, it is well to adopt a systematic method of recording concepts, convictions, beliefs, and facts as these develop out of reading or other kinds of experiences. All of these will aid in the choice of subjects and purposes for speeches, as well as provide a basis for more meaningful conversational speaking and listening. An ever expanding file of material on which to draw is invaluable.

Techniques of Recording

A notebook is standard equipment for the college student. Many items in it may be used for material for speeches. It is well to go through your daily notes from all your courses and pick out or underline, or rearrange important items. A section of the notebook should be arranged and reserved for the course in speech. In this there should be a continuing growth of materials drawn from other courses and outside sources, as well as a method of recording principles learned in the Speech class. Another method is to develop a card index file. This is almost a necessity for the well-organized individual. By carrying a few small cards with you at all times, you can record materials of many kinds and then insert them in proper categories in your permanent file.

Your memory is not good enough to enable you to recall precisely what you heard or read a week or more ago. The exact method you use for recording is relatively unimportant; what is important is that you devise a method suitable to yourself, so that you will have the materials readily available.[9]

Suggested Categories for Recording

Everyone should develop his own categories for keeping things in organized fashion. The following may be of practical use, although it is not an all-inclusive list:

1. *List subjects which might be developed into speeches.* Often an event you attend or observe suggests ideas for speeches or conversation. Jot down the ideas at once and add them to your file of topics. The list will grow surprisingly fast. Some topics will be discarded after thought and reflection, but others will be retained and new ones added.

2. *Make recordings of significant facts.* Information in the form of specific facts is indispensable in speeches, as in all communication. As you come upon them in reading the newspaper or hearing a radio broadcast, make a habit of recording those that seem significant. Sometimes they are of a statistical nature; again they may include historic dates, events, incidents, or subjects of current interest. If a fact or item of information strikes you at the time as important and worth remembering, jot it down and file it for possible future use.

3. *Record striking and significant ideas.* The power and force of an idea sometimes strikes us forcefully. It may be a different and unique expression of a familiar thought, or it may be a powerful new concept. It should be recorded for your files. The very act of recording it will plant the idea more firmly in your mind and will cause you to weigh its significance. It may lose some of its importance after a

[9] Many methods for recording materials are described in Jacques Barzun and Henry F. Graff, *The Modern Researcher,* New York: Harcourt, Brace & World, Inc., 1957, pp. 22–36.

time or prove less vital than your first thought; or it may grow in value and in turn stimulate other ideas.

4. *Record examples, illustrations, and specific instances.* When developing ideas for a speech or in conversation, we frequently wish we could think of an actual example or comparison, for these can provide the highlights of good development. They serve to make vital and concrete the material which may otherwise be vague and abstract. Comparisons and examples are needed for most good speech development. A file of these will be invaluable.

5. *Record quotations, testimonials, and provocative sayings.* You may work very hard at wording your ideas yet find that the thought was better expressed by another speaker or writer. Shakespeare, the Bible, Ralph Waldo Emerson, and many other great writers may be drawn upon and quoted if you can find their statements. Usually such a quotation is used as a more colorful, a clearer, or an emphatic way of supporting what you also say in ordinary language. Again, experts and famous people are quoted in testimony of your own point, to support and add proof. Whether your quotation is used chiefly for reasons of style, such as epigrams, figures of speech, or poetic phrasings; or whether it is to corroborate your position, it will add considerably to the point.

6. *Record jokes and anecdotes.* There is a place for jokes and humorous stories in many speaking situations. Adlai Stevenson made much use of these in serious speeches. Perhaps for the average person they are more useful in informal conversation. Most of us forget the jokes we hear and occasionally would like to remember. Being able to find them in a file may prove of real help.

7. *Record human interest stories.* Daily experiences and reading give rise to situations or stories with unusual examples of basic human qualities of courage, sacrifice, affection, and virtue. A good conversationalist will be able to weave these into a discussion to explain or demonstrate a point, or simply to hold listener interest and attention. He may find one of them especially fitting in a speech to persuade or to enhance sociability. And a listener may derive great stimulation and reward in attending to such a story.

Conclusion

The mere statement of an idea does not communicate it. There must be a continuing search and inquiry for materials that will help develop existing ideas and be the source of new understanding, belief, or action. Properly selected and adapted to the communication situation, these materials provide the content for speaking and listening. Discovering materials for effectiveness in speaking is a process interwoven with most other activities. Likewise, the listener who anticipates a speech or social situation on particular subjects will be more motivated and have better ability to understand or evaluate what he hears if he has done research on the subject. Materials are found everywhere if an alert speaker's and listener's perceptions are operating: in himself, in other people, in mass media, in course content, and in general reading. They must be used honestly and wisely, and when discovered they must be recorded and stored systematically.

Gathering materials should not be narrowly construed as merely a process of gathering support and proof. It is, rather, a process of learning and of storing for future use. It adds to one's total development as an effective communicator in all situations.

Exercises

· *Questions for Discussion*

1. Why is the statement of an ideal usually inadequate to communicate it?
2. How do you decide what kinds of materials you will need?
3. What is the iceberg technique? Why is it important?
4. How can you make easier your job of gathering materials for a speech? What can you learn from yourself? From discussions with others? From your other courses? From newspapers, magazines, radio and television? From general reading?
5. What library reference sources are available to you for your speaking? Which ones are you personally familiar with? Which among those listed have you never used? Which sources that have been unused by you in the past could be of most value?
6. What are the five questions concerning your use of sources?
7. What is wrong with using a single source, or a predigested source? What proper use could you make from even a speech outline in a fraternity file?
8. To what extent should a listener gather materials in preparing for communication?
9. What are the seven categories suggested for a speech file? Which of these seem likely to be of most use to you? Are there other

categories you would add? What kind of filing system do you find most helpful?

· *Projects for Speaking and Listening*

1. Make a list of at least five topics on which you would like to talk. Jot down several main ideas for each topic by which you could gain some specific response from your classroom listeners. Note what areas of ignorance must be illuminated with fresh information before speaking on these topics.

2. Take one of these five topics and note, in writing, some ideas or facts seemingly unrelated to it that might serve you well in clarifying it for your listeners, or in making it more interesting for them, or in persuading them to believe, feel, or do something specific about it.

3. In your daily conversations, and also in the talks you present in class or elsewhere, make a habit of identifying the sources of the information you present, and of evaluating the dependability of those sources. Note the reactions of your listeners to try to determine whether by this means you are not acquiring more authority and arousing more confidence in your declared opinions.

4. Prepare a five-minute talk for delivery in class in which you reinforce the outline handed to your instructor with an appended note on the sources you have used, from all the kinds of sources discussed in this chapter. Be sure your preparation covers the subject so thoroughly that your own convictions will be supported by a much larger accumulation of data than you have time to present to your listeners. Be prepared to answer questions that may probe into the depth and breadth of your understanding of the topic.

5. Plan to attend a speech as a listener. Make an analysis of how you can profitably reinforce your knowledge of the subject in order to be a better listener. After you have done this, plan to speak in class about the value of this special preparation in improving your listening in the actual situation.

6 · *Programing for Response: Organization*

Communication begins not at the first utterance but—for both listeners and speakers—at the moment that a confrontation is anticipated. The listener at that first moment begins to respond to what he knows about the speaker, the subject, and the occasion. He is a preparing listener. He is an effective preparing listener to the extent that he goes beyond his first impressions and alerts himself to relevant materials, experiences, and other sources of pertinent information. The speaker at that first moment begins to respond to what he knows about the listener, the subject, and the occasion. He is a preparing speaker. To be effective he must do more than gather content appropriate to his purpose, subject, audience, and the anticipated social context. A mind filled to capacity with appropriate materials does not necessarily signify that one is ready for communicative speaking and listening. In order to serve communicative purposes, the content must be organized. This does not mean that it must be merely classified and sorted. It means much more. Organization is a structuring process: a way of first examining ideas in relation to their supporting ideas and, second, of arranging a sequence of ideas for step-by-step responses.

The organizing process, then, is really not one but two important mental processes: (1) testing the validity of ideas and (2) programing for response. Validation of ideas provides the building blocks for effective communication. This is the thought process of developing ideas, the subject of the next chapter. Programing, which provides the structure for effective communication, is the concern of the present chapter.

The Idea of Programing

High school and college students are old hands at making effective listener contributions to their own education, sometimes against great odds.[1] They know, however, that they are able to contribute more, and more easily, when instructors and lectures are well organized. Some methods of educational communication require the instructor to be organized. Programed instruction—with which most students are familiar—is a case in point; the program must be organized (sequenced) in certain ways. It is not the machine (or "hardware") that succeeds in teaching; it is the program (or "software") that determines the step-by-step progression of the learner.

Francis Cartier has commented that such educational technologies are not necessarily, in themselves, superior to lecture methods, though some research may suggest their superiority. He points out that the programer is forced, by the very nature of his medium, to program for response; the lecturer is not.[2] However, we would point out here that any speaker who is predominantly motivated to communicate rather than to express is forced by this intention to program for response.

By programing, then, we refer to nothing different from the step-by-step ordering of ideas and their support, which is essential to almost any communication, whether it be a simple declarative sentence or a textbook; a simple arithmetic statement (two times two equals four)

[1] Recent research reveals that "as students increase in mean academic aptitude they grow in another way too; in the ability to extract substantial amounts of information from very bad oral messages. . . . Sometimes this requires a perceptiveness which verges on clairvoyance, but in order to survive the system the student must develop the ability to listen so as to get at the facts, however badly they are presented." Theodore Clevenger, Jr., "The Model and the Problem in the Educational Setting," in Paul E. Reid, ed., *The Frontiers in Experimental Speech-Communication Research,* Syracuse, N.Y.: Syracuse University Press, 1966, p. 38.

[2] See "After the Programming Fad Fades, Then What?" *Audio-Visual Communication Review* (January, 1963), pp. 3–9.

or an extended derivation of a new equation; a few "frames" for programed instruction or a lecture.

Except possibly in the simpler tasks, the programer does not arrive quickly and intuitively at an effective sequence. He must take some prior steps. So it is with the preparing speaker.

A necessary preliminary to programing is determination of the purpose or behavioral goal or goals to be achieved. Chapter 4 states the necessity for establishing general and specific purposes—or responses desired—early in the process of preparing for speech communication. Thus, whatever mental structuring takes place must be motivated by the desire to achieve the stated listener responses. To accomplish his stated purpose, the effective preparing speaker engages in the outlining process before he is ready for programing.

Outlining

A preparing speaker engages in the thinking–writing process of outlining in a sequence different from his ultimate programing. He focuses on three purposes—in the following order:

1. Outlining for support of the central idea.
2. Outlining for listener commitment to participate in the communication.
3. Outlining for listener commitment to remember.

In traditional terms, the speaker outlines for support of the central idea for the body of his speech, for listener commitment to participate for the introduction, and for listener commitment to remember for the conclusion. Ultimately, of course, it is the first purpose which must be served, for without it the other two have little meaning.

A written outline is not the end goal of the process. The outline is something left over from the experience of outlining, which is what helps a speaker prepare himself. The outline itself may serve later to help a speaker or listener evaluate a communication transaction. This is especially true in a speech course where speaker and teacher, having evaluated the effects of an attempted communication, may look to the outline to see what the *thinking processes* were during preparation for speaking and how they are related to the speech evaluation.

The outline, then, is neither script nor notes but, rather, a study and structuring of the ideas and materials. Readers are urged not to by-pass this valuable experience by somehow composing a speech and afterwards casting it into outline form. This serves neither educational nor speech purposes.

To aid the student in grasping the essential ideas that can help him prepare effectively, this chapter is organized from the parts to the whole; from outlining processes to over-all programing.

The Listener's Focus: the Remembered Idea

The preparing speaker properly focuses on his specific purpose. But in any speaker–listener interaction, what does the speaker wish the listener to focus on? Everything said? Whatever he wants to listen to? Or as much as he can? None of these is realistic. It is true that ultimately the listener decides what he will remember. But the preparing speaker outlines and programs in order to influence that decision. The communicative speaker must determine—as focal point for the listener—the idea to be remembered: an idea which, when embraced and understood and believed, will lead the listener to the specific response desired by the speaker.

Outlining, then, begins with what should be the remembered—or central—idea.

Students sometimes confuse idea and topic, creating unnecessary confusion for themselves. Topics or subjects for speaking may be "American Women" or "The *Playboy* Philosophy" or "Architecture as Expression." If topics are selected as the listener focus, the preparing speaker may easily select his ideas for their relevance alone and not necessarily in support of a central idea. Listeners may be asked, "What did the speaker talk about?" and respond easily enough, "American Women." But if asked, "What did he say?", the listener may be at a loss or he may pick any of a variety of ideas that he himself elected to focus on. Thus one listener may report, "He said that women have all the money." But another may declare, "He said that women have more influence on future generations than do men." A third listener may remember a third idea that appealed to him. However, when a speaker outlines effectively for listener focus on a clear and complete idea, such as, "American women are the stronger sex," his listeners are apt to remember the idea that he selected, are apt to remember their new understanding or belief about it, and are apt to remember some of the ideas as support for the central idea.

Outlining for Support: the Main Ideas

Students may confuse the kind of outlining presented here with another kind, for the structures are similar. Outlining is sometimes used as an analytic tool, delineating the parts of written discourse, often in English courses. However, the outlining of the preparing speaker is not analysis—which would be study by breakdown of a whole into its constituent parts. It is the opposite: it is a *building* rather than a separating process.

We may have as the central idea, for instance:

> Our mental hospitals must be enlarged and improved.

It could be divided into two parts regarding enlargement and improvement. But this would be an exercise of little value to the preparing speaker. In outlining he is not looking for the parts. He is, rather, looking for supporting ideas—ideas which, if grasped by his listeners, will lead those listeners to new understanding or new belief. The test of a main idea is, "Does it make the central idea more understandable or more believable?" In this example, then, main ideas might be stated:

I. The frequency of occurrence of mental illness is rising.
II. Present practices are not providing adequate treatment.
III. With proper treatment patients would spend less time in the hospitals.

Where do these ideas come from? In gathering materials—speech content—certain data and patterns of data emerge. In the example here, the preparing speaker is apt to find data on increasing rates of hospital admissions, both in percentages and in actual numbers. The discovery of several such items might suggest the first main idea. Also in his memory and in his notes he is apt to have many items testifying to crowded conditions, shortages of professional psychiatric personnel, or poor records of successful treatment (as, for instance, a report that of 250,000 persons who enter a hospital for the first time, 150,000 never leave alive). These would seem to suggest and support the second idea. Another set of materials might include data on the numbers of patients retained in hospitals even after recovery because they are not wanted at home and have no rehabilitation services available; on examples of the effects of adequate care (as in the case of one hospital with 80 percent of its patients returning to normal living as compared with a national average of about 45 percent); on the situation in one state where the availability of psychiatrists is six times greater than the national average. From such findings might the third idea emerge.

Thus, the preparing speaker in his mental structuring discovers the support relationships of ideas and speech content. The outline[3] begins to fill out.

BODY

Central Idea: Our mental hospitals must be enlarged and improved.

I. The frequency of occurrence of mental illness is rising.

A. Every tenth child born this year will some day be admitted to a mental hospital, a rate double that of twenty years ago.

B. More than 300,000 people will be admitted for the first time this year and over 125,000 former patients will be going back.

C. Demand for practicing psychiatrists is outstripping the supply.

II. Present practices are not providing adequate treatment.

A. Living conditions are very poor.

B. Three out of every five patients entering mental hospitals are never returned to normal living.

C. For minimal treatment, state hospitals presently need twice as many doctors, five times as many graduate nurses, and four times as many social workers as they now have.

III. With proper treatment patients would spend less time in the hospitals.

A. Studies show that 70 percent of all patients could leave within six months and 80 percent within one year if they had proper care.

B. The state of Kansas provides an example of what enough well-trained doctors working in the right environment can do.

C. Proper treatment includes help in readjustment to home and job.

[3] This developing outline is adapted from one prepared by Miss Joyce Bedrava while a student in the basic speech course at The Pennsylvania State University.

How many main ideas should there be? The proper answer is enough to assure listener grasp of the central idea and not so many as to confuse the listener.

How many subordinate ideas should there be? If there is an *A* must there be a *B*? In analytic outlining the answer is yes, because if an idea has separable parts, there are at least two. In the building outlining of a preparing speaker the answer is likely to be the same—but for a different reason. *A* may represent adequate support for some listeners but not for others, so a preparing speaker seeks a *B* and *C* and *D*, etc., in building an ample reserve of support. Thus, in the very unlikely event that *A* would support thoroughly (make thoroughly understandable or believable to all listeners)—only in such a case—could it be said that a second subordinate idea is not necessary. However, the preparing speaker can never be sure that the one supporting idea will do the job; and so, again, he builds his reserve of content by thinking through to the discovery of other ideas for support.

Further, it should be remembered that the outlined ideas must be developed in detail (see next chapter) in order to find the means of validating them in the minds of listeners. For example, the first section of the outline above might read:

I. The frequency of occurrence of mental illness is rising.

  A. Every tenth child born this year will someday be admitted to a mental hospital, a rate double that of twenty years ago.

    1. This is supported by available statistics.

      a. According to *U.S. Statistical Abstracts,* in 1967 there were . . . .

      b. This compares with a figure in 1947 of . . . .

      c. The difference is accentuated by the growth of the population.

        (1) Per capita difference is . . . .
        (2) Actual difference is . . . .

    2. This increase means that no one will escape some contact with mental illness.

      a. Distribution studies show that mental illness can strike anywhere.

(1) It is increasing at all socioeconomic levels.
   (a) A statistical breakdown shows . . . .
   (b) The Surgeon-General of the United States recently reported . . . .

(2) It is no respecter of family histories.
   (a) The pertinent statistics show . . . .
   (b) In one state hospital, persons with no family history of mental illness accounted for . . . .

b. Case studies dramatize the indiscriminate occurrences.
   (1) The case of . . . .
   (2) The case of . . .
   (3) The case of . . . .
   (4) Thirty-seven other cases reviewed showed equally unexpected occurrences.

B.

It should be noted, as the outlining goes on, that it deals with the preparing speaker's concern for the support relationships of his ideas and does not necessarily predict the sequence in which he will later talk about the ideas. The ordering—or programing—comes later in the preparation process. Often it is effective to have listeners arrive at the ideas themselves by presenting the supporting data first and then, perhaps, confirming what the listeners have already concluded.

Outlining for Listener Commitment to Participate: Introductory Ideas

When the preparing speaker has structured the central idea and main ideas which will effectively support it—only then is he ready to think of introductory ideas, for only then does he know specifically to what line of thinking his listeners are to be introduced. Basically there is one purpose of introductory ideas: to invite listeners to participate in the transaction. But other purposes should be noted.

One of these purposes is traditionally stated as gaining attention. Yet in most situations speakers already have the attention of their listeners when they begin. It is true that that attention may soon be lost, unless principles discussed in Chapter 8 are applied. But the outlining, preparing speaker must seek main introductory ideas that, more than inviting attention, capture listener interest and commitment to discover and to come to grips with the speaker's idea. In the outlining process, the preparing speaker's mind must turn to what he knows about his expected listeners, especially their experiences, knowledge, and beliefs. If our hypothetical speaker on "improving care for the mentally ill" knows that many of his listeners have seen a recent film or television feature involving psychiatric treatment or mental hospitals, this will suggest a means of adaptation and evocation of interest. On the other hand, he may find that he can only assume that most of his listeners have had at least some contact with someone who is or has been mentally ill. The preparing speaker is searching for the best means of involving his listeners and must, therefore, select introductory ideas in which his listeners are already involved and which are relevant to the direction of thought in which he believes his listeners should move.

This suggests a second introductory purpose which the preparing speaker must ponder at this point: getting the listener to want to listen. The preparing speaker knows that people by being present are not necessarily going to listen; for listening is an active process. Listening is activated when listeners anticipate that what they might hear concerns them or things that they are interested in. The job of the preparing speaker is to discover how his idea is relevant and important to his audience-to-be. He must find ways to develop that relevance so as to persuade his listeners that what he has to say is worthwhile.

In our continuing example, the preparing speaker may select as one introductory idea:

No one escapes mental illness.

He may plan to clarify this idea with data on the probability that all Americans, at one time or another, must come to grips with mental illness, either in themselves or in those with whom they live. For another introductory idea the preparing speaker may remember:

Mental illness strikes 25 times more people than polio
ever did in the years before vaccines were developed.

Here he may have in mind involving his listeners in a memory of massive efforts to dispel a numerically lesser disease. Here, too, he may be discovering the common premise, which is essential to persuasion (see Chapter 11).

The developing outline now might read:

INTRODUCTION

I. No one escapes mental illness.

  A. Over one million persons in the United States suffer from serious mental disorders.

  B. A friend, a relative, a loved one or perhaps we ourselves can be included in that million.

  C. A recent White House conference concluded that mental illness is the greatest single problem in the nation's health picture.

II. Mental disease deserves at least as much effort as we have given to the treatment and eradication of less frequently occurring diseases.

  A. Mental illness strikes more than 25 times more people than polio ever did in the years of epidemics.

  B. The frequency of tuberculosis has dwindled in the face of massive efforts that still continue today.

III. No one really tolerates the conditions some of us saw in the television documentary, *The Greatest Ill.*

  A. Some viewers were shocked, others disgusted, and a few quite depressed.

  B. Each of us must have wanted to do something about those conditions . . . and probably still do.

One or more of these ideas may—when properly developed (see next chapter)—capture listener involvement, get him to want to listen.

An important third introductory purpose is what might be called "cueing perception," or alerting the listener about what to watch for. Everyone has had the experience of failing to find an unfamiliar article, only to have someone who knows what to look for walk directly to it and pick it up; or has been unable to spot a book until someone said, "It's the orange one." Teachers know that for effective use of a film they must tell their students what, specifically, to look for. Similarly, any listener who is so alerted or "cued" is better prepared and less likely to miss the speaker's idea.

In our continuing example, the appropriate introductory idea might be:

IV. There is a way that something can and should be done about mental illness.

Or a speaker may plan to cue the perception of his listeners by use of the "initial summary," thus:

A. It is necessary to know if mental disease is increasing or decreasing.

B. It is necessary to see how effective present treatment is.

C. Finally, it is necessary to learn what increased effectiveness is possible.

In summary, introductory ideas include those selected to capture listener attention, those which will invite listeners to listen actively and constructively, and those which would alert listeners to what, specifically, to listen *for*.

Outlining for Commitment to Remember: Concluding Ideas

The preparing speaker knows that he has one more task after he succeeds in inviting his audience to listen and in evoking the desired response. That task is to make the effect lasting, to make the central idea memorable and, therefore, remembered. Sometimes, too, he must organize for commitment to act.

These are usual purposes of concluding ideas. They challenge the preparing speaker to careful thought; for communication that appears to be successful without having a lasting effect is, as Bolivar once observed, "but plowing in the seas."

In our example of the preparing speaker structuring his ideas on mental hospitals, his concluding ideas might be:

I. The urgency of the problem is summed up in a statement from the Menninger Clinic.

II. In doing research for this speech I have become convinced that I should change my professional goal.

Students are frequently advised that an effective conclusion is a final summary. This may be appropriate in situations where listeners are highly motivated to remember—as for an examination, or when the listeners are delegates who must report to others. On other occasions motivation to remember must come from the speaker's concluding ideas. Commitment to remember may be aroused by appropriate stories, anecdotes, or pithy quotations, such as the reminder of Pogo: "I have seen the enemy and he is us." As in the case of the introduction, the more the listener becomes involved as a result of the conclusion, the more lasting will be the effects.

Commitment to act does not follow automatically from a new attitude. A recent experimental study revealed little correlation between speech-induced attitudes and subsequent actions. The preparing speaker whose goal is listener action cannot depend, therefore, on mere acceptance of his idea without commitment. Speeches to persuade classmates to donate a pint of their blood are common occurrences in basic speech courses—with effects that seldom last until the next campus visit of the Bloodmobile. One speaker, however, succeeded where so many have failed. His concluding idea was:

I. I am circulating among you a sign-up sheet for appointments at the Bloodmobile, which will be on campus tomorrow.

Outlining Processes

It has been noted that outlining by the preparing speaker is a building process, rather than an analytical one. The building materials are the main ideas in support of the central idea, the introductory ideas, the concluding ideas, and all of the supporting ideas. The preparing speaker does not merely compose an outline. Rather, he arranges and rearranges all the pertinent ideas according to their support relationships. Some speakers find it advantageous to put each idea on a separate piece of paper or file card and to spread them out on desk or table and then construct an outline by arranging them according to the supporting relationships of ideas and materials and according to the purposes discussed above.

This juxtaposing of the building materials is only a part of the organizing outlining-programing process. It is not the ideas that do the communicating. It is their development that does so: the supporting and validating statistics, stories, analogies, and examples, which have not been included in our examples above. These so-called subordinate points are really the parts of the building materials that do the job; that hold the structure together or make the ideas more binding; that involve listeners in the ideas. The next chapter is devoted to the problems and means of bringing the preparing speaker's ideas within the experiences and knowledge and perceptions and realities of his listeners-to-be: the development of ideas.

The outlining thought processes must include the forms and methods of development discussed in the next chapter. They are, after all, the nails and mortar that make the building hang together. Thus, not only the ideas but the materials that will support or validate them should be noted in the cards or building blocks.

The Complete-Sentence Outline

Speech students engaged in the outlining process are tempted to "build" with topics rather than with ideas. That is, they apparently find it easier to think of topics, while feeling that they are coming to grips with ideas. The danger here is that the building materials are apt to be selected for mere relevance rather than for the special relevance of support.

If our hypothetical speaker on mental hospitals were to select three main topics, rather than three main ideas, they might be:

I. Frequency of occurrence

II. Present practices

III. Proper treatment

The search among available data might then lead to a variety of relevant but not necessarily supporting materials, such as information on the frequency of occurrence of certain illnesses, or current statistics which, by themselves, give no picture of current trends. The merely topical outliner might continue by selecting—as relevant to topic II, "present practices"—details of psychotherapeutic techniques, without information on the outcomes of such practices. Similarly, selection of the topic, "proper treatment," may invite inclusion of materials not necessary to focusing listeners on the central idea. The preparing speaker would be tempted to include materials he had discovered about new proposals for psychotherapy, without regard for the matter of shortening treatment.

There is a further drawback to the experience of topical outlining. This is the fact that a topical outline does not record the preparing speaker's thought processes: his search for support relationships of ideas and materials. This information is likely to be lost, then, when we are trying to recreate the preparing process in order to understand and to learn from the actual communication outcome. It is probably true that an experienced preparing speaker can think sentences and write topics; and doubtless many do. But the *beginner* in speech is apt to deceive himself and, at the same time, deprive himself of valuable instructor feedback if he simply records topical notations.

There is a third kind of outline that offers even less than the topical outline. This is the *key-word* outline. It has all the limitations of the topical outline, plus the danger that even the topic may not be clear. A key-word outline derived from a complete-sentence outline can serve as a kind of mental summary of the outlining process. This is sometimes a valuable practice in the transition from outlining to programing. But it offers little aid in the thought-structuring process of outlining.

Outlining Suggestions

Each part of an outline must meet a single test: does each subordinate idea or each bit of subordinate material make the idea to which it is subordinate understandable or believable or compelling or enjoyable (depending upon the purpose)? Thus, the proper test of outline items is the test for support. When the preparing speaker finds that two items do not meet this test, he knows that one or the other is inappropriate. One item in this developed section of an outline does not pass this test:

C. The eardrum converts air vibrations into mechanical vibrations.
  1. This starts with sympathetic vibration of the eardrum itself.
    a. Sympathetic vibration is what causes windows to rattle because of planes and other sound sources.
    b. It is sympathetic vibration which causes the visible vibrations of a bass drum on the side opposite the hammer.
    c. The eardrum is an important protection against infection.

Thus item c., though true and chosen for its relevance, would be found to offer no clarification of item 1., and would be put aside in favor of some other material that would support the idea to which it is subordinate. Sometimes the failure of an item to pass the test of support will reveal that the idea being supported is not appropriate or is misstated, thus leading to revision of the idea rather than of the supporting item.

The preparing speaker will do well to have before him always—though subject to change as he engages in outlining—complete statements of his purpose (desired response) and the central idea that he wants his listeners to focus on and remember. So these items, at least, should head the outline.

It must be remembered that outlining is not preparing the speech but preparing for speaking; that it is a structuring and arranging of thought; that when the outlining is done there is programing yet to come. It should be remembered, too, that in the outlining process the preparing speaker comes to grips with and probably records more material than he can possibly use in the speaking situation and in the time he will have for speaking. But, because he has engaged in the experience, he is prepared for listener feedback of puzzlement or disbelief or apathy, because he has in reserve other means of support to apply. A speaker who knows only what he plans to say carries little authority and loses even that when confronted with a question from a listener.

One sign that students have engaged in speech composition rather than in outlining—that is, programing without prior planning—is the use of questions in the outlines they submit. The crusader for better mental hospitals, for instance, on the basis of his preparation, might properly and effectively ask his listeners, "Do you know how many of us will be affected in one way or another by mental illness?" But he will not put it down in his outline, for it is neither idea nor support. He cannot test it to see if it supports a main idea or is supported by subordinate material. The preparing, outlining speaker at his desk will often find, when he feels a question coming on, that he is imagining himself speaking to an audience rather than engaging in the thinking process of outlining. Further, he will often discover that the idea he is seeking is the answer to his question.

In determining how far he should go in development of ideas—of sub-sub-sub-subpoints—the preparing speaker must remember that it is these basic points which touch the experience and realities and involvement of his listener, and that they, therefore, determine his communicative effectiveness.

From Outlining to Programing

It was pointed out at the beginning of this chapter that programing is the process of ordering what will be said, step by step, to assure maximum effectiveness. Though outlining is a prerequisite to effective programing, the programing sequence does not follow that of outlining. However, a pattern emerges from the outlining which, with some rearrangement, begins the programing process.

The programed order of purposes would usually become:

INTRODUCTION	Step 1.	**Secure listener attention (if not already demanded by the situation).**
	Step 2.	**Secure listener commitment to find out what the speaker has to say.**
	Step 3.	**Alert the listener to what, specifically, to listen for.**
BODY	Step 4.	**Focus listener on the central idea through development and adaptation of main supporting ideas.**
CONCLUSION	Step 5.	**Secure listener commitment to remember the central idea.**
	Step 6.	**Secure listener commitment to act, or secure the action itself (if an overt response is desired).**

This is not unlike other statements of communication and thought patterns.[4] Yet there may be situations which call for different patterns. The most compelling introduction may be a statement of the central idea. In other situations it would be dangerous for the central idea to emerge before the conclusion. The preparing speaker must always remember that he should not follow a standardized program or a set formula but should engage in creative programing for response for each communication task.

In programing the order of developed ideas and materials, the speaker who has done his outlining with each item on a card can rearrange those cards, keeping in mind his expected listeners and his communicative purpose. Ideas and their support will still be kept together in most instances, but the ordering may be changed to suit

[4] See, for instance, Alan Monroe and Douglas Ehninger, "Monroe's Motivated Speech Sequence," *Principles of Speech,* 6th ed., Glenview, Ill.: Scott, Foresman and Company, 1967; John Dewey, "Dewey's Thought Pattern," *How We Think,* rev. ed., Boston: D.C. Heath and Company, 1933; Richard C. Borden, "Borden's Formula," *Public Speaking—as Listeners Like it!,* New York: Harper & Row, Publishers, Inc., 1935. Also for a plan of audience adaptation during speaking, see Robert T. Oliver, *The Psychology of Persuasive Speech,* Chapter 15, New York: David McKay Company, Inc., 1957.

specific purposes. Several programing methods are discussed in the chapters on Sharing Understanding and Persuasion.

Programing Practice

The preparing speaker has, to this point, engaged in no programed oral behavior, though he is preparing for a speaking situation. He needs experience in talking about the developed ideas and materials he has been thinking about. This is very different from saying he needs to practice what words he will say. Practice—with or without listeners—is not total programing but preparation for final programing; not speech composition, but preparation for final speech composition in the speaking situation.[5]

Thus, the practicing speaker talks about his ideas in the programed order. The first time he may note that he has taken more than the amount of time allotted for his speaking. This may lead to programing alterations. He is hearing his ideas for the first time. This feedback may suggest changes. If there is a listener—a roommate or other friend—his responses will suggest further needs to re-program.

As the speaker continues to practice, he should talk about each idea in different ways each time. He is not necessarily seeking the best way to talk about his ideas, not trying to commit to memory the best words. Instead, he is building experience in talking about these matters in a wide variety of ways so that the best way can emerge in the speaking situation itself; for the prepared, practiced speaker is free to concentrate on his listeners and on his communicative goal. The rest can come automatically. The programing is completed only at the moment of utterance.

After much practice, then, the preparing speaker is apt to have firmly in mind the sequence of ideas. He may want the additional mnemonic support of a "key-word outline," which is really a key-word program, for it reflects the ordering rather than the outlining experience.

Conclusion

Outlining has been discussed as a thinking process—prerequisite to programing—whose value lies in the experience and not so much in the outline which results. Outlining is a process of testing the sup-

[5] For appropriate occasions final programing may take place before confrontation, as in the case of a manuscript speech. See Chapter 14.

porting relationship of ideas and content. The preparing speaker assembles and arranges the ideas that, first, will focus listeners on his central idea; second, will invite listeners to listen; and, third, will influence listeners to remember and, if appropriate, to act. Conversion of the outline into a program begins with reordering to serve appropriate successive purposes in the speaking situation. Programing continues through the practice and testing of various ways of talking about and sequencing ideas and their support. Final programing usually takes place in the speaking situation itself, influenced by the interaction of speaker and listener as the speaker focuses on his purpose while focusing listeners on his idea.

Outlining and programing phases of organizing must also include the thought processes involved in developing ideas, the subject of the next chapter.

Exercises

Questions for Discussion

1. How are outlining and programing different? How are they related?
2. What is the purpose of outlining? Of programing?
3. Are you like the students who were reported to listen with equal effectiveness to teachers who program both well and poorly? As a speaker, do you need to program effectively? Why?
4. Are you familiar with programed instruction? How does that programing differ from programing for speaking? How are they the same?
5. Is it true that the communicative speaker "is forced by this intention to program for response?" Explain.
6. Why do the authors suggest that outlining in support of the central idea should precede outlining for introductory ideas? Can you make a case for outlining introductory ideas last?
7. What is meant by "the outline is not the program?" Explain. Why is the experience of outlining more important than the outline itself?
8. Explain why the authors suggest that a key-word outline is really a key-word program.
9. Why are "sub-sub-sub-subpoints" so important? Aren't they apt to be trivial? Explain.

10. Why would a speaker want to reverse parts of his outline when converting it into a program? Is this more likely to happen in sharing understanding or in persuasion? Why?

11. Explain why outlining by a preparing speaker is not analysis.

· *Projects for Speaking and Listening*

1. Select a broad subject and phrase five specific purposes and related central ideas for five different speeches on it. Under each central idea, list three main ideas that support it.

2. Engage in complete-sentence outlining in preparation for your next speaking assignment in class.

3. Engage in complete-sentence outlining using individual cards for each idea. Rearrange the cards in a variety of sequences. Assess the effectiveness of each sequence.

4. For an impromptu exercise, have someone describe a speaking situation in which you might find yourself (examples: "You have been stopped for speeding on the outskirts of town," "You are scheduled for an interview with the personnel director of a company you want to enter."). Determine what might be your specific purpose, the central idea, and some main ideas in support.

5. In listening to your classmates, try to discriminate between those who are programing as they speak and those who seem to be remembering a program. Indicate which you perceive in each category on listener feedback cards.

Part Three

Factors of Support and Presentation

7 · *Development and Proof*

Listeners and speakers alike are concerned with the question of the validity of whatever is being discussed. Speakers try to select and use the most effective materials and methods available in order to achieve their intended meaning and response. Listeners seek to analyze and evaluate the speaker's methods and materials in order to understand and to determine whether to accept what they hear. For both speakers and listeners, the final outcome of the communication is likely to be determined more by the substance of the supporting data and the methods of reasoning used than by any other factors. The purpose of this chapter is to present methods by which ideas may be developed and supported with effective proof.

An alert speaker might warn his listeners: "I know that you think you understand what I said. But I'm sure you realize, too, that your understanding is not precisely the same as mine." The problem is to attain a mutuality of understanding. Chapter 5 discussed the search for materials and standards governing their selection to prepare for an adequate development of the subject matter. This chapter considers the selection and use of materials for their probable effects upon listeners.

The Objectives of Idea Development

Commenting on the success of a recent Summit Conference of heads of state in the Western Hemisphere, Secretary of State Dean Rusk said, "there was very little empty rhetoric at this conference."[1] He was saying, in effect, that most of the speaking at the conference had substance and was thus meaningful. Empty rhetoric is the probable result of failure to find and include the kinds of materials for development of ideas that make them worthwhile. A less polite term for such speaking is *hot air*. The less one knows about a subject, the easier it is to speak about it in vague generalities and abstract ideas. President John F. Kennedy once said that anyone can talk about a subject in generalities, but that it is necessary to bring it down to specifics to convey real meaning and obtain specific responses.

The development of an idea or point is the expansion of the point in order to accomplish one or possibly a variety of objectives. Among the chief types of responses desired from the point are:

To gain interest and attention
To clarify and achieve understanding
To gain or strengthen acceptance and belief

1. *To gain interest and attention.*[2] This is the initial and basic objective of all communication, for if the listener is not interested and not attending, he will find it very difficult to respond to the substance of the point. The primary factor in listener attention is probably that of concreteness, which is the quality of being specific, real, factual, vivid, and precise in the use of material to develop the point. Listeners attend to the specific and find themselves wandering from the speaker's point when it is general, vague, and abstract. With this principle in mind, effective speech communicators strive for the concrete even when the following more specific responses are desired.

2. *To clarify and achieve understanding.* This is the goal of all communication, even when acceptance and belief are involved. The communicator must consider the way he develops any point from the standpoint of whether the method of development is going to enhance

[1] *Meet the Press* television panel, National Broadcasting Company, Washington, D.C., April 15, 1967.

[2] See Chapter 8 for fuller discussion of this principle.

the understanding and clarity of it. When his over-all desired response is learning on the part of the listener, such as achieving greater knowledge, more information, or the ability to do something physically, his developmental methods and forms will be selected for this purpose.

3. *To gain or strengthen acceptance and belief.* For the speaker, the objective in developing his ideas with this purpose in mind will be to use the most effective supporting forms for the *proof, validation,* and *support* most acceptable to the listener. For the listener, his objective will be to evaluate the kinds and degrees of proof and support in order to determine whether to accept (and to what degree) the speaker's point.

Proof is used here as a term embracing the sum total of the support, evidence, validation, and reasoning processes used to develop the point.[3]

Support and *evidence* are terms used to encompass the specific materials in the form of facts, information, testimony, and others, which are used to validate and prove the point. Traditionally, the "Forms of Support" is the typical heading for these devices,[4] usually treated as all-inclusive of the devices and forms used to develop ideas for any purpose. *Evidence* is a term borrowed from the law and thus means the support used to prove a point or establish facts. In using this term as a meaningful factor in the communication process, it should tend to have this meaning. There have been attempts in recent years to examine and study the relative values of logical evidence as proof (in relation to other factors), and some would shed some doubt over the long-felt agreement of the value of evidence in gaining listener acceptance and belief, particularly of controversial points. Studies have compared the relative effects of evidence and the speaker's *ethos* (the ethical and personal proof values of the speaker as an individual) and found a tendency for listeners to want more evidence when the speaker's

[3] While "proof" usually implies the logical development of the point, it has a broader meaning to include all methods of influence or persuasion, as in the well-known trilogy of logical, emotional, and ethical proofs first advanced in Aristotle's *Rhetoric.* Cf. Lane Cooper, *The Rhetoric of Aristotle,* New York: Appleton-Century-Crofts, 1932. See also Douglas Ehninger and Wayne Brockriede, *Decision by Debate,* New York: Dodd, Mead & Co., 1963.

[4] See Eugene E. White, *Practical Speech Fundamentals,* Chapter 13, New York: Crowell-Collier and Macmillan, Inc., 1960.

ethos was to them low, and to need less evidence when they regarded the speaker highly in terms of his ethical and personal proof value.[5]

Validation is another essential in idea development, including as a term many of the principles suggested in the others. It is a combined process of the speaker's validating the worthiness of his ideas to himself through a combination of research in gathering materials and analysis. It is thus a process of proving to himself that his ideas are sound and then proceeding to prove this to his listener. All education, in a sense, is directed toward this goal. Logic and scientific method are two approaches to it. One may not think of himself as "research-minded," yet he does not want to come to wrong conclusions or be responsible for others doing so. Since he wants to think soundly and not contribute to faulty thinking by his listeners, the validation of ideas is a daily necessity. The means may be rigorous, but they are reasonably clear and are available to anyone willing to take the trouble to use them with precision.

The Process of Idea Development

In working toward the best methods and forms of idea development, it is necessary to go through some systematic steps or processes to achieve maximum effective use of ideas and materials. Listener analysis, topic selection, narrowing this to a specific purpose and response desired, and organization of the points or ideas are the steps preceding this. In considering idea development, the speech communicator has additional analysis to consider: he has to determine the methods of development to be used; he must select the most effective supporting forms; and he must synthesize all into a coherent whole.

If it is determined that the listener knows little about the subject or point, more factual and informational material will be needed. If

[5] James C. McCroskey, "Experimental Studies of the Effects of Ethos and Evidence in Persuasive Communication," unpublished PhD dissertation, The Pennsylvania State University, University Park, 1966; James C. McCroskey and Robert E. Dunham, "Ethos: A Confounding Element in Communication Research"; and Paul D. Holtzman, "Confirmation of Ethos as a Confounding Element in Communication Research," both in *Speech Monographs,* 33 (November, 1966), pp. 456–63, and 464–6.

his degree of belief is low or unfavorable, more of the supporting material must be validated and have qualities of logical proof value.

Determining the best methods to be used involves a careful consideration of the methods available and an evaluation of what will be most useful in the development of the point. Where the purpose of the speech or point at hand is to achieve clarity and understanding, explanation and perhaps description would obviously be used. But just how much explanation and what kind will probably depend on the evaluation of the listener's present knowledge as well as his background of education and experience on the subject or particular point. In a speech involving three main points, the listener may be well informed on two of them but have no knowledge at all on the third. In addition to explanation, demonstration and visual aids may be necessary for real clarity. In another instance, in exchanging ideas on a controversial subject, one communicator may have made a point using a generalization from just one fact. The other, now changing from listener to speaker, would immediately realize the method of reasoning involved. In his own reply, he would have to use clear reasoning, well supported in the opinion of his listener. He may have to consider whether he should introduce his point directly and then support it or indirectly, by first presenting evidence and then drawing his conclusion. Similarly, in a speech where the desired response is to get support for labor unions from an audience of conservative business owners, his method might wisely be to use the indirect method.

Selecting the most effective supporting forms brings the communicator to the heart of his effort for good idea development. At this point, he will have made the maximum effort to find materials that have added to his fund of knowledge and helped shape his opinions and conclusions. He will have analyzed these in relation to the response desired and the objective of each of his main ideas. Now he is ready to consider the relative value of the use of specific examples to support a point, as compared with the use of illustration in the form of comparison or story, or the use of one extended example in great detail, or the use of testimonials. He will give thought to which of these would make the point more clear, and which would do more to hold interest and attention, and which might be more useful in influencing belief and attitudes.

Much of the effort in this direction will consist of research and reading to find the kinds of supporting forms needed. The effective communicator will never be quite satisfied that what he has is the best, and he will continue his search through reading and other methods.[6]

Synthesis of all the ideas and developmental methods and forms will follow the kind of analysis and selection factors we have just indicated. This is the process of bringing all the ideas, supports and developmental materials together into the best coherence and order. This involves factors of re-evaluating the organization and sequence of the ideas, again assessing the methods of development, and working toward a unified theme and central idea, which had been first determined in the initial phases of preparation.

Forms and Methods of Development and Proof

In the discussions that follow, remember that what is said about listeners must first be said of speakers. What listeners question, the speaker must first have questioned; what listeners need to know, the speaker will first have needed to know; what will move listeners to feel, or believe, or do, will often be what has first moved the speaker himself to feel, or believe, or to conclude what must be done.

The means of development, proof, and validation of ideas usually fall into two categories: the forms of support, which include the kinds of materials and tools that clarify, prove, and validate; and the methods of development, which are processes and devices that include the use of the forms. A cardinal principle to keep in mind always is that it is usually not the statement of the idea or point, in itself, that gives it power with the listener; it is the development and proof of the point.

The Forms of Support

Examples
Illustrations and Comparisons
Statistics
Testimony and Quotations

[6] Helpful suggestions for methods and sources are found in: William M. Salter, "The Library Survey"; Gregg Phifer, "The Historical Approach"; Elton S. Carter and Iline Fife, "The Critical Approach," in Clyde W. Dow, ed., *An Introduction to Graduate Study in Speech and Theatre,* Chapters 3, 4, 5, Ann Arbor, Mich.: University of Michigan Press, 1961.

The example. This is said to be the most basic and useful tool for the development of ideas. Some would say that if every point made in oral communication could be developed by an example, the speaker would have more likelihood of success than with any other single form. The example may be defined broadly as reference to a happening, event, situation, place, person, or thing. It is the first step toward concreteness, toward going from the general to the specific. It is the "for instance" tool which makes the listener now attend to the reality of the point. This would suggest that of all the forms of the example, the specific instance, or real example of something that actually happened and can be mentioned by name, date, and place, is its most effective form. Examples may be general, specific, or hypothetical; and in their use by the speaker they may be detailed or undetailed.

Using the example as the basis for drawing generalizations or conclusions is basically the inductive process of reasoning from the specific to the general. In speaking, the communicator is usually making the generalization as a main point, and he should obviously support it so that his listeners will themselves reason toward the acceptance of the conclusion as he did. He would usually do this by using specific examples, sufficient in number and detail to warrant the conclusion. Examples should be truly representative of the general conclusion being drawn. In preparing speeches, one can be selective and careful to choose the examples he wishes. In social conversation the listener may cite examples which counter those of the speaker. In either case it is wise to give careful attention to validating both the authenticity and the representativeness of examples used.

The general example is the least effective of the various forms and is usually used as a basis for more specific examples to follow. In an expository speech on the subject of airplanes, the point might be made that airplanes have many uses: ". . . for example, airplanes play an important part in our commercial life, in travel for pleasure, and as instruments of war. For commerce, in carrying express cargoes, in California alone there have been three companies formed in the last year, the X Company in San Francisco, the Y Company in Fresno, and the Z Company in Los Angeles. For general travel and for pleasure, the major airlines, such as Eastern, Pan American, and Trans-World, are constantly expanding their facilities to serve the public. Just in the past week, Eastern Airlines announced increased services. . . ."

Thus the development of this point gets more and more concrete and the specific or real example plays a major part as the speaker brings his subject down to the actual. In the one instance, the examples are undetailed in series, and in another the speaker selects one specific example and expands it in greater detail. In the expansion he adds factual and vivid material that may both make the point clearer and validate it for his listeners.

In explaining through demonstration, it is both more interesting and clearer to use specific examples than to demonstrate abstractly. The principles and movements of batting a baseball can be explained and demonstrated in general, but they become more meaningful when the speaker goes on to say that "Roger Maris, in breaking Babe Ruth's home run record, rather consistently gripped the bat this way. . . ; Roberto Clemente, one of the most consistent batters in modern baseball, who aims for the base hit rather than the home run, uses this kind of a grip and stance at the plate. . . ."

The example as proof, as pointed out above, is one of the primary tools for supporting a generalization or conclusion. In attempting to convince listeners that government control of banks is sound, examples of countries A, B, and C, where this has been done successfully, would support the speaker's conclusion. He of course would have to define clearly what he means by "control" and show that the examples represent this kind of control.

The hypothetical example is an imaginary specific example cited to show how an idea would work in a hypothetical situation which is assumed and described by the speaker. From the listener's standpoint, his reaction to the hypothetical example may depend on whether the situation depicted relates to his interests and background, and whether he thinks it could possibly happen. In our current increased interest in highway safety, an example of a tragic wreck in which the driver was saved because he used a fastened seat belt becomes vital to the listener when the speaker adds, "Imagine yourself in this driver's seat without your seat belt fastened." Again, developing a point dealing with the increased use of airplanes by private persons, one might say, "When airplanes are as common as automobiles, the Sunday afternoon drive may then take the family to Niagara Falls several hundred miles away. And we might even have traffic police in the sky." A minister may request increased support for the church by asking his listeners to imagine what a community without churches would be like.

Illustrations and comparisons. These are considered together because most forms of the illustration are used as comparisons of some sort, usually with the point of the speaker. Actually, the term *to illustrate* means to many the same as "to develop," "to prove," or "to clarify," thus encompassing all the forms of support, used in the same sense as "to develop an idea."[7] The term itself comes from the Latin, *illustrare*, meaning "to shed light upon." We often hear a speaker say, "let me illustrate this," followed by a story, an analogy, a quotation from an expert, an example, a history of the point, or even statistical data.

The more specific meaning of the illustration is: a device or form usually used to make an idea clearer, or more attractive, or even more acceptable to the listener. The primary principle is to compare the unfamiliar (speaker's point) with the familiar (the form of the illustration used). The basic forms are the analogy or comparison, the simile and metaphor, and the story or anecdote.

The analogy is an extended comparison.[8] It may start with the use of an example, as when one wishes to make clear certain features of a university, such as The Ohio State University, with which the listener is not familiar. He draws upon the example of The Pennsylvania State University, with which the listener is familiar. He points out that both are state universities and compares the operation of the one to that of the other. This, in the form of a literal analogy, compares two things quite alike and transposes the characteristics of the known to the unknown. Another use of literal analogy would be to liken the United Nations to the League of Nations, both world bodies, yet with some differences. When the literal analogy is used as logical proof, to get the listener to accept a point with which he did not initially agree, the degree of likeness or differences between the two things being compared would be a vital factor in the soundness of the speaker's conclusion. A figurative analogy is the comparison of two things in different realms of being to allow the listener to visualize; such as to liken the United Nations to a flight of sparrows: the birds fly together only when it suits their convenience, but they separate to go their individual ways whenever they wish.

The simile is a brief comparison, using the word "like" or "as," such as, "He eats like a pig," or "Hitler was like a rat." Using the

[7] For practical guidance, see Lionel Crocker, "Make the Illustration Linger," *Today's Speech,* 4 (January, 1956), pp. 3–5; and J. H. Baccus, "Building A Stock of Illustrations," *The Quarterly Journal of Speech,* 21 (June, 1935), pp. 373–5.

[8] See Gladys Murphy Graham, "Analogy—A Study in Proof and Persuasion Values," *Quarterly Journal of Speech,* 14 (November, 1928), pp. 534–42.

figurative analogy himself, Adolf Hitler once said, "I take my words and throw them like burning torches into the crowd—and they burn."

The metaphor is a brief comparison in which one thing is named or labeled or treated like something that it obviously is not.[9] The metaphor is an invitation to the listener to apply his connotative meaning of one thing to another; to feel about one thing as he does about the other. The simile cited above, "He eats like a pig" denotes or refers to certain behaviors while, "That pig!" is vague in reference but generally clear in connotation. One says of a person, "He is a diamond in the rough," not so much to refer to his need of the niceties of behavior as to evoke a feeling about that person.

The *story, anecdote,* and *parable* are all forms of the illustration that involve narrative in telling the details, these being compared with the point of the speaker. In this way, the story is used chiefly to clarify a point and make it vivid, although it is of course frequently used just for sociability or for pleasing the listener, without any other point being made. Jesus used the parable frequently and Lincoln the anecdote to make their speaking more effective. The parable is usually a somewhat extended story. Russell Conwell used these to build one of the most famous lectures of all time, "Acres of Diamonds," some of such length as to occupy several pages of print. Each story in this unusual speech made the point, which was the central theme of the speaker, that one's happiness may be found close to home.

Storytelling for validation requires two elements. First, the anecdote must be told with sufficient interest—building toward an unexpected climax—to hold the absorbed attention of the listeners. And, second, it must be selected because it reinforces the idea which it illustrates. The listener cannot be left in doubt as to the point being made.

An example may be used to illustrate when it is extended, described, narrated, compared, or contrasted. Let us assume one is considering the point that African nations are ready for self-government. An example of gross inefficiency might be placed in proper perspective by comparing it with a similar instance from American history; or it might be contrasted with a more successful example of how another African nation dealt with a similar problem. Cramming for a final exam may be shown to be bad by comparing it with the disaster follow-

[9] See Michael M. Osborn and Douglas Ehninger, "The Metaphor in Public Address," *Speech Monographs,* 29 (August, 1962), pp. 223–34.

ing the hurried and unplanned building of a house. Comparison and contrast help the listener see the speaker's point more clearly, to understand it, and perhaps to evaluate its acceptability to him.

Statistics. Statistics are the extended or repeated use of figures or numerical summaries to support, clarify, or prove a point.[10] Often, the use of example or testimony or other forms of support is accompanied by statistics in order to lend more concreteness, accuracy, and proof value in developing the point. Statistics do not usually speak for themselves. In using them, care should be taken to interpret precisely what they mean to the particular listeners. And if there is any doubt about their credibility, the source should be cited to strengthen their use as proof. Further, if listeners understand how the statistics were determined, additional credibility is likely.

When reminded that the Department of Labor announced that the cost of living had risen by one-tenth of one percent during the preceding month, listeners may not be much impressed unless this is interpreted in terms of specific prices. Franklin Roosevelt and Winston Churchill combined the use of statistics with figurative analogy and vividness in these examples: "The box score when the Democratic Administration came to bat in 1933 showed a net deficit in our national accounts of about $3,000,000,000," said Roosevelt on assuming office. And on the famous occasion of Dunkirk in World War II, Churchill said, "The navy, using nearly 1000 ships of all kinds, carried over 350,000 men out of the jaws of death and shame to their native land and to the tasks which lie ahead."

Bob Hope used statistics for humorous effect as follows: "Today my heart beat 103,000 times, my blood traveled 168,000,000 miles, I breathed 23,000 times, I inhaled 438 cubic feet of air, I spoke 4,800 words, moved 750 major muscles, and I exercised 7,000,000 brain cells. I'm tired."

In using statistics, keep these principles in mind: Do not overuse them in the development of any one point or speech. Make them specific and accurate, but use round numbers, such as, "approximately $100,000" for the figure "$99,999.85." Keep them up to date. Quote the source whenever there can be any doubt of their acceptance. Apply them to the particular listeners.

[10] The use and abuse of statistics are presented interestingly in Darrell Huff, *How to Lie with Statistics,* New York: W. W. Norton & Company, Inc., 1954.

Testimony and quotations. In listening to a speaker, we frequently wonder, "How much weight should I give to what he says? I wonder what the real experts have to say on this point?" Listening requires an evaluation of the source, credibility, and status of the person making the point. Because it is difficult to become truly expert on a subject, speakers find themselves in need of the support of those whose business it is to know about it. Expert testimony is used in this way for proof rather than for clarification. A number of suggestions and cautions should be observed in the use of testimony:

—The person quoted should be truly established as expert by being shown to be knowledgeable, fair-minded, and experienced.

—Make known the qualifications of the expert to the group, particularly when the point is controversial.

—If there is a doubt of his impartiality or acceptability by the listeners, cite facts that show his lack of prejudice.

—Use the testimony of another expert to corroborate this one.

—Make sure the testimony is recent enough to apply to present conditions and to the point being made.

—Show that the statement is accurate by reading it from a card or from the original source when this is feasible.

—Keep the quotation within a reasonable length and read only the comment that applies directly to the point it supports, so that irrelevant material is not included. But be sure that what is selected genuinely represents the expert's true opinion and is not distorted or taken out of context.

—Be familiar with the testimony so that it can be read well while keeping good directness and rapport.

The quotation used to make the speaker's point more vivid and attractive is usually drawn from literature or from the saying of some famous person who is known to the audience. It is thus called the literary or historic quotation. In the development of the thought of the greatness of American liberty, these types of quotations might be effective: Lincoln has said of America that it is "the last, best hope on earth." Patrick Henry laid a cornerstone for American freedom when he said, "Give me liberty, or give me death!"

In summarizing the uses of the forms of support, we might say that when the objective is to clarify and achieve understanding, the example, illustration, and comparison are probably the most useful. When the objective is to prove and validate to gain belief and acceptance, examples, testimony, and statistics may be most effective, with statistics obviously of use for informative purposes as well.

Methods of Idea Development

In determining the best way to develop an idea, there are a number of methods and processes available, and the careful speech communicator will know which he can best use at the given time and what the particular method will accomplish. Although these are not all mutually separate and distinct processes and more often several are being used at the same time, we will list them separately as follows:

Explanation	Description
Classification	Historical perspective
Discrimination	Reasoning
Qualification	Questions
Definition	Summation techniques
Narration	Visual aids and demonstration

Explanation includes many other methods as well as the use of supporting forms for its accomplishment. When one explains, he may go into detail in describing the various components making up the point at hand; he may classify, define, and qualify. And while doing these he may use specific examples or analogies or comparisons, all for the purpose of making the point more clear and understandable. The process of explaining, then, will be better understood as we consider the many other methods and processes which contribute to its accomplishment.

Classification is a grouping or regrouping of items or parts of the whole according to their similarities. In discussing history, one could classify historians as primarily descriptive, evaluative, or prophetic; their subject matter as primarily political, military, economic, or social. Painting might be classified as impressionistic or representative; wars as defensive or offensive. Yet all of these may not be clear-cut classifications, as it may be necessary to define "defensive" and "offensive" and also to point out that one can become the other.

Reliable classification depends upon the definition of key characteristics, which are invariable for all the items in the class being considered. Mathematicians can dependably catalogue all numbers as cardinal or ordinal. Anthropologists, on the other hand, have difficulty categorizing implicit and explicit cultural traits. We roughly classify some subjects as being liberal arts (literature, philosophy, speech) and others as being vocational (engineering, agronomy, accounting); yet it is obvious that the distinction is not definitive.

We try to classify acts of human conduct as legal or illegal, but this can only be done accurately when the acts in question fit directly into the legal statement of the law. It is even more difficult to classify acts of social conduct as moral or immoral, as this may depend on the standards of the speaker and listener, which may be quite different from their respective frames of reference.

Classification becomes helpful to communication when listeners are called upon to remember many related items or to keep many distinctions in mind. The mind often boggles at remembering all the details of a history, for instance, but it is helped by grouping or classifying, whether by chronological periods, political movements, or other devices. This is the process, which the psychologist George A. Miller calls "chunking," that people use to manage multiple ideas, labels, and distinctions.[11]

Discrimination is the ability to recognize differences. If a parent, listening to a jukebox rendition of rock-and-roll, remarks, "This jazz is terrible," he should be told some facts concerning differences in types of popular music. When someone says he thinks a certain congressional committee is unfair for charging a witness with contempt for refusing to answer questions, he might be asked to discriminate among the kinds of questions that are involved.

Listening to a discussion of Riesman's book, *The Lonely Crowd,* one may mentally make a discriminatory analysis of his own personality, trying to decide in what way he may be "tradition-directed," "inner-directed," "other-directed" or "autonomous." As a matter of convenience, we depend a great deal upon labels or stereotypes, making such comments as, "John is not progressive; he is a Republican;" or, "He's a radical Democrat." This kind of labeling results in half-truths, while claiming to be discriminatory. Another fault under the guise of discrimination is the tendency to make broad categories of an "allness" nature, when everything we are including does not belong in the category. We say that the Japanese are imitative (implying that all of

[11] See "The Magic Number Seven, Plus or Minus Two: Some Limits on Our Capacity for Processing Information," in David C. Beardslee and Michael Wertheimer, eds., *Readings in Perception,* Princeton, N.J.: D. Van Nostrand Company, Inc., 1958.

them are), that all detective novels are exciting (while some may be boring), and that there is no good in modern art. Discrimination, then, is another step toward clear and accurate thinking.

Qualification is related to discrimination and classification in that it strives to avoid sweeping statements by qualifying what is said or claimed. A speaker's judgment will deserve and receive higher confidence and respect from his listeners if he does not claim more knowledge than he possesses. It is one thing to say, "The current administration in Washington is popular"; and quite another to say, "The current administration seems to be popular among college students, but even some of them complain about the policies that affect them." The latter is a qualified statement, claiming far less than the seeming "allness" of the first statement. Qualified thinking includes the difference between knowing and assuming. In commenting on "What kind of a teacher is Professor Jones?", a qualified answer might be, "In the course I had with him, I liked his lectures, but he seldom made clear assignments." Qualification, then, depends upon discriminative judgment. In informal relations with others, if one occasionally uses such phrases as, "To some extent," or "So far as I know," he will indicate to listeners that they are invited to modify what is said in the light of their thinking and experience, which the speaker indicates he respects.

Definition is usually the process of trying to explain the exact meaning of a word or group of words. Both listeners and speakers need to come to the closest possible mutual understanding of language used to accomplish the meaning intended. We, therefore, strive to define whenever there is doubt whether the listener may know the speaker's meaning or may have one different from that of the speaker. In using the word "disarmament," does he mean complete elimination of all types of weapons? Or a partial retention of some for police purposes? Then, if the word "immediate" is placed before it, does this mean at once, or in a reasonable time? And what is a reasonable time to one person surely is not considered the same by another. Speakers, then, should always stop to consider whether their words or terms need defining; and listeners should strive to interpret meaning with the speaker's frame of reference in mind.

Narration as a process is similar to explanation in that it must make use of other processes and forms and is thus a broad method of development. The term itself suggests discourse unfolding a succession of events or happenings, probably in chronological order, or as a story. It would thus include description and perhaps explanation and definition, as well as the use of examples or forms of the illustration.

The typical story involving characters and a plot would be a narrative, as would the development of a point where history of a subject is included.

Description points to the thing itself to be defined and then made more real by expansion into greater detail for clarity and vividness. The process should be distinguished from definition, which primarily uses words or phrases to clarify the meaning of the word being defined. Description attempts to focus on the thing being described, with effort to arouse the senses and utilize the principle of imagery. Happiness might be defined by using pleasure as a synonym. But it can be described in terms of contentment and the combination of pleasures one might experience by being happy. Asia, by definition, is a continent. But, by description, "Asia is a great land mass of endless plains, sky-towering mountains, and river valleys bulging with peasants toiling and crowding together like ants in an ant hill."

It is usually much more meaningful to describe when the factor of listener involvement in the speaker's point, thoughts, and feelings is important. In most instances, it is easier to describe something physical, such as a building, a table, a chair, or the appearance of a person, than it is to describe an idea or concept. The chief qualities of good description are precision and vividness of language that will create the imagery desired.

Historical perspective is the consideration of whatever degree of the historical development of the subject will be valuable to bring the listeners to the best understanding of the present point being made. In trying to convince listeners that labor unions have not gained too much power, it may be necessary to explain the history of labor union organization, to show why they were organized, what obstacles they had to overcome, and what they have accomplished. Similarly, many topics for conversation, discussion, or speeches may need to be examined in the light of their origin and background, thus placing a responsibility on the speaker and listener to learn this kind of information as well as the present status of the subject.

Reasoning is a process employing many of the other forms of development. It is the ability to draw inferences and conclusions from facts, information, observation, or prior conclusions. Through his reasoning ability, man can make generalizations from specifics, make deductions about specifics from generalizations, establish cause and effect relationships, and draw conclusions about the unfamiliar by analogy with the familiar.

The astute listener is constantly alert to detect what reasoning process the speaker is using and to what extent it is sound and to be accepted. He looks for the number and quality of examples or facts the speaker is using to support a generalization; for whether what the speaker claims is a causal relationship actually may have been interrupted by an intervening event known to the listener but which the speaker is ignoring. In many other ways, the listener's reasoning process is helping shape his total response to the speaker's point.

Questions should be used chiefly to draw the listener more actively into involvement with the speaker's point. They indicate that the speaker is concerned about his listener's reaction, and the speaker should always pause briefly after raising a question, even though the answer is unspoken. The chief forms of questions are rhetorical, direct, leading, and hypothetical.

The rhetorical question is perhaps the most common form used in a speech, as it does not anticipate a spoken answer but rather a mental response from the listener. It should be so phrased that the mental answer will be in the direction of the speaker's point, chiefly to emphasize and highlight points of view that are held in common. Sometimes a series of such questions, all seeking a yes-response, will build up a favorable receptivity to the speaker's theme, such as Patrick Henry did in his famous "Give me liberty or give me death" speech. This abounds with questions, often as the chief or only form for developing a point, such as:

> They tell us, sir, that we are weak; unable to cope with so formidable an adversary. But when shall we be stronger? Will it be the next week, or the next year? Will it be when we are totally disarmed, and when a British guard shall be stationed in every house? Shall we gather strength by irresolution and inaction?

It can be noted that these questions are phrased mostly for a "no" answer in the minds of the listener, in order to get a favorable response to the speaker's point of making immediate war on the British.

The direct question does call for an overt answer. This should be used with caution. In a speech on auto safety, asking a question such as, "How many of you had an accident last year?" might get a number of responses that require quick thinking and adaptation on the part of the speaker in using the responses as further development of his point.

Leading questions suggest the answer in their own wording, such as, "Aren't we all agreed that war should be eliminated?"; "Haven't you seen many people on relief who should be working?"; "Is there anyone here who would not want to see his taxes lowered?" This is a method of getting the audience to affirm a conclusion which they might not agree to as readily if the same point were stated as an assertion by the speaker, and it allows them to participate in the conclusion themselves.

Hypothetical questions have several uses, one of which is to try to project the listener's thinking toward the possibility of the point applying to him in a situation not yet developed. It is similar to the use of the hypothetical example. An obvious type of this might be, "What would you do if you found yourself in this situation?" Or again, "Assuming that the cost of living continues to go up at the same rate for several more years, what measures should be taken to counteract this?" In this latter question, the use might also be for transitional purposes, assuming that the speaker has just finished developing the problem, that the cost of living has risen steadily in the past year, and he is now turning to the solution phase of his speech. The question asks the listeners to think along with him toward trying to find the best solution to this problem.

Summation techniques can be incorporated into any of the above processes, methods, and forms, to help accomplish one's desired response or reinforce his points. These are the use of *restatement, internal summaries, and cumulation.*

Restatement is primarily for clarity and greater emphasis. It embraces several methods by which a speaker may repeat in the same way or in another way what he has said before. In a sense, one does this in applying supporting forms and methods whose primary value is to impress the point. A good story restates the point it supports, as do examples, historical narrative, or testimony. The chief consideration of the speaker is the extent to which he finds it valuable to keep repeating the point he started to make as he goes into more and more development of it. The value of repetition has been well established in securing the desired response, both in informing and persuading listeners.[12]

This may be done by identical restatement of what has been said

[12] A. T. Jersild, "Modes of Emphasis in Public Speaking," *Journal of Applied Psychology,* XII (December, 1928), pp. 611–20.

before, by giving the point in different language, by reference to points or material brought out earlier in the speech, or by *internal summaries* which go back over what has been said and then move to the next point by transition. It must be remembered that the spoken word must supply a sufficient number of repetitions within the speaker's discourse so that the listener has the same opportunity to hear the point again as he might by reading again and again a written message.

Cumulation is the building up of validating evidence and support in using the same form of support in a series. This can be done by using a succession of specific examples, or of statistics from many sources, or a series of testimonials. This method of development of an idea is extremely valuable to impress the listener with the depth of knowledge of the speaker, as well as to prove a point more effectively. Obviously, the more controversial the point the more valuable will be the cumulation of one form of support. Sometimes one example in very vivid detail will clarify or impress the point, but for logical proof a series of them will be more useful. One testimonial may have some effect, but it will add weight if a speaker can say, "This is not the thought of just one U.S. senator. Leaders from all walks of life have spoken similarly. Governor X had this to say . . . ; Ambassador Y said . . . ; a leading economist, Mr. Z, recently wrote . . . ; etc. . . . .

Visual Aids and Demonstration

The effective communicator will want to consider the use of visual aids to supplement and make more effective any of the processes, forms, and methods of development. Psychologists and educators agree with speech and communication experts that more learning is achieved through the eyes than through the ears. The Army, Navy, and Air Force training experts have conducted research to confirm that up to 85 percent of learning is through the eyes. H. E. Nelson and A. W. VanderMeer conducted research using instructional films with and without verbal exposition and found that, "The proportion of learning that is attributable solely to listening is significantly smaller than that which is attained when viewing the picture and sound."[13]

[13] *Speech Monographs,* XX (November, 1953), p. 7.

Specifically, the values of visual aids are:

—*Understanding* is increased by both reinforcing the explanation or other development process and by making clearer the point or material being explained. Oral discourse depends on words given one at a time to build up meaning; the visual symbol, on the other hand, may be shown and perceived all at once.[14] A graph can show at a glance the relationship between the cost of living and buying power; whereas the verbal explanation of these same statistics could be comprehended only slowly and might even prove confusing.

—General speech effectiveness is increased by adding the extra degree of concreteness and clarity, as is the proof value suggested by the axiom that "Seeing is believing."

—The analogical use of visual aids is sometimes more effective than the direct showing of the object itself or the data; and sometimes an object would be too big and cumbersome to bring to the speaking situation. If one uses a rolling pin and a pile of dough to show how steel is flattened into sheets, or some colored water with both cube sugar and loose sugar to demonstrate differences of absorption while making an explanation of proper cultivation related to soil erosion, these will vividly be transferred to the point he is making.

—More positive use of nervous energy is also accomplished through the use and demonstration of visual aids, as this focuses attention on the aid by the listener and thus makes the speaker feel less self-conscious. Also the movement involved in showing the aid helps relax the speaker while generating his own animation. He should be careful, of course, not to concentrate on his aid by looking at it when he should be establishing direct rapport with his listeners.

—The *memory value* is also an important one to the speaker who would be inclined to overuse notes, for the aids may well serve to help guide him and his listeners through the speech.

—The visual impact of the speaker contributes greatly to his listeners' reaction to his message. If he slouches onto the platform dressed inappropriately and not properly groomed, an unfavorable impression may be formed at the outset. If he continues to twist, stand on one leg, and look at the floor or window, the negative effect of all these is apparent. It should be remembered that the speaker is usually

[14] For a full treatment of this interesting difference see Susanne Langer, "Discursive and Presentational Forms," *Philosophy in a New Key,* Chapter 3, Cambridge, Mass.: Harvard University Press, 1942.

his own best visual aid, and that his appearance, manner, and enthusiasm contribute greatly to his effectiveness.

Types of Visual Aids

Many types of aids are available: the blackboard or easel pad, charts, and actual objects are perhaps the most common. The following are the major types of visual aids:[15]

Blackboard or easel pad. The blackboard is most commonly available and may still be the most used form. Far too frequently it is used in impromptu fashion, with the speaker suddenly deciding to put some figure or point on it. And he may find that he has to erase it. The board should always be erased cleanly *before* starting to speak lest materials there be distracting. The material to be put on it should be well planned in advance, both as to selection and space to be used. The material should be coordinated with the spoken word; the speaker should strive to retain eye contact with the audience as much as possible and position his back toward them only when absolutely necessary. The voice projection should be kept up higher than usual, and it is best to keep talking while working at the board. If the material is quite complex, perhaps it should be put up before the talk; but in this case a prepared chart would be better, so that it could be introduced at the appropriate time. Sometimes it is well to practice handling the visual material with the speech in advance.

The easel pad presents a smaller area than most blackboards, but it has the advantage of permitting the speaker to flip one chart and then start on a clean one, while being able to retain all of them. Such charts can also more readily be prepared in advance and integrated with the speech at the proper time.

Prepared charts, graphs, and drawings. There are many ways that material can be attractively prepared on pad paper or cardboard. The size is important in relation to the size of the room, number of listeners, and amount of material to be presented. If they cannot be clearly seen, there is no point using them at all. And in actually showing them, holding them in the hands is usually very cumbersome and awk-

[15] Among the many books devoted to this subject, see Edgar Dale, *Audio-visual Methods in Teaching,* New York: Holt, Rinehart and Winston, Inc., 1963; and Jerold E. Kemp, *Planning and Producing Audio-visual Materials,* San Francisco: Chandler Publishing Co., 1963.

ward and results in ineffective use, and also ties down the speaker's hands. Whether to stand them on the table in front of the podium or tape them to the wall behind the speaker are considerations to be thought out in advance.

Objects, models, and samples. The actual object itself may be used, such as a baseball when demonstrating how to pitch. Again, objects should be clearly shown or displayed and integrated with the spoken word at the appropriate time. It is well always to face the audience, look at them, and show them while explaining.

Handout materials. Handout material is usually used to supplement points being made by the speaker, perhaps as a summary or as data, graph, or diagram which each listener may keep. When such is used to help develop a point being made while the listener looks at it or reads it, care should be taken to focus his attention on what is being said and not to let him read ahead on the handout material. If pictures are being used in quantity, it is hazardous to start handing these to listeners one at a time, for in a short while each will be looking at one or anticipating the next one rather than attending to the message.

Demonstration. Many subjects call for the speaker to demonstrate physically his message, such as the talk on pitching mentioned above. The chief cautions here are that this be done in good sight of the listeners, that it be well coordinated with the spoken word, that speaking be continued while demonstrating, that steps be indicated clearly as the subject progresses, and that frequent repetition, restatement, and internal summaries be used.

Projected visual and audio-visual methods. The chief methods of projecting materials are slides and films, with slides being the more common for the average speaker. In using *slides,* careful planning should include proper positioning of the projector, preferably with a remote control switch which the speaker can operate; or he should make arrangements for the operator to respond to a signal. The room should be sufficiently darkened, yet the speaker must retain a commanding position for proper projection of voice and for ability to point to the slide with a pointer. His remarks related to each slide should be prepared as to timing and substance, with special emphasis on transitions. There should always be an appropriate introduction before showing the slides, and concluding remarks as well.

In showing films, it is important to preface the showing with explanation of the film, its theme, what should be looked for, and any special areas of emphasis for the discussion period to follow. Sometimes a handout sheet of information and questions to be raised may be helpful in advance of the showing. If the film is used as a basis for developing a theme or specific points, these should be summarized at the conclusion of the discussion period.

The overhead projector is a useful method of throwing charts or other prepared materials on a screen or wall in back of the speaker while he stands facing the audience and controls the use of the machine. Such materials are prepared in advance and sometimes a series of data or parts of a diagram may be shown one at a time and in series, gradually building up the total visual impression by the viewer-listener. The chief advantage of this method is that it allows the speaker to stand facing the audience while the visual material may be shown in more attractive manner than it could be on a blackboard or chart easel.

Conclusion

This chapter stresses the importance, objectives, processes, methods, and forms of idea development and proof, all aimed toward giving the message of the speech communicator more substance and concreteness, greater interest and attention value, greater clarity and understanding, more likelihood of acceptance and belief, and more validity. To do this, one must systematically analyze, select methods and forms, and synthesize toward a coherent whole. He must consider the various developmental methods of explanation, narration, description, classification, definition, qualification, discrimination, and summation. In the vital step of selection of the best forms of support as evidence, proof, and validation of his points, he should carefully weigh the various forms of support and determine which will be most useful among those available: examples in their various forms, illustrations, testimony, and statistics. Then the possible values of visual aids should be considered to supplement the oral communication. All of this represents a most challenging and rewarding aspect both in the development of speeches and in the use of oral communication in conversation, conferences, and discussions.

Exercises

Questions for Discussion

1. How do the various principles in this chapter relate to the quality of your thinking? How would you use some of the processes, such as definition, discrimination, and qualification, in your study of

history or chemistry, or in your choice of friends or hobbies? In what ways do you judge the intellectual level of the speaking you hear?

2. What are some of the tests for using testimony? Statistics? Why are they important, and which is the most important to you?

3. What are the qualities of good specific examples? Distinguish between this form and the hypothetical example.

4. Discuss and distinguish between the use of restatement and cumulation, between definition and description, between simile and metaphor.

5. How do you illustrate an idea?

6. Distinguish and show the relationship among the terms *support, development, proof, validation, evidence, explanation*, and *reasoning*.

7. In using visual aids, what methods and cautions should be observed in the use of the blackboard, handout materials, and the speaker as "his own best visual aid?"

Projects for Speaking and Listening

1. Listen to a speech on your campus, or on the radio or television, and evaluate the development of it in the light of principles in this chapter. Determine as many different processes, methods, and forms of support as you can. Take one of the main ideas and show how it could have been better developed and supported.

2. Plan to discuss social conversation with others in class, showing some common faults and how these could be remedied by better use of developmental methods and forms.

3. Take one idea and plan for the development of it in several different ways: first, by using all specific examples; then, by using statistics and testimony; finally, by illustration. Show how the processes of explanation, description, definition, reasoning, or others are used in the development.

4. In planning to present an instructional talk, include the use of visual aids by using the blackboard, prepared charts, or an object during the presentation. When using the blackboard, show on paper, in advance of the talk, what this will look like when you are finished.

8 · *Factors of Listener Interest*

Communication fails when the listener offers neither attention nor interest. Consequently, this chapter discusses the interacting factors which are most basic to interpersonal contact—the determiners of both listener and speaker desire to communicate. An effective speaker must establish, maintain, and invite continuing listener interest in his subject and his idea.

Establishing Initial Interest

In certain circumstances, initial interest, or attention, is established for the speaker. This is true for the celebrity—whether his name and fame be local or international. This is also true for the speaker who—in social gathering or on public platform—has been effectively introduced. Initial interest is available also to the speaker who may not be well known but who is speaking on a topic or issue of great importance to the listener.

But even in such instances of built-in initial interest, the effective speaker will often give thought to ways of arousing listener curiosity and establishing that what he has to say is of real significance to the listener.[1] From the outset of any communication, listeners are asking, in essence, "What has this got to do with me?"

Title

The title of a public speech may or may not capture the interest of a prospective listener. And it may determine whether he will be there to listen. The title of a speech may serve several functions: (1) to indicate the subject but not necessarily the purpose; (2) to sound sufficiently appealing to attract; (3) to set or suggest a tone or mood; and (4) to offer a subtle key to the central idea that will be satisfying to the listener during speaking and a reminder afterward.

Not all titles can achieve these diverse purposes, nor are all of them equally important in all situations. But these are useful guidelines to apply in situations when speech titles are called for.

What about conversational speech? Would or should a speaker think of a title at the outset of a story or a report or an inquiry? The listener response is necessarily different if his conversant begins, "How's this for the Department of Understatement?", than if he launches directly into a quotation by a speech teacher that "improving one's effectiveness isn't easy." In a sense, titles can be applied to more than just formal public speaking.

When appropriate, then, a title should be short, should "name" the speech, and should provide an abbreviated, attention-getting statement of the theme in order to capture and hold listener interest.

Introduction

Several functions of introductory programing have already been discussed in Chapter 6. Here we are concerned primarily with what the speaker may do to achieve or strengthen initial interest and to focus that interest on his introductory ideas. In general, there are two methods: the striking and the adaptive.

A striking beginning is one which is both unexpected and forceful.

[1] Interest, significance, and curiosity have been cited as closely related factors among fourteen factors found to significantly influence listening comprehension. See discussion of "Maintaining Interest" in Jon Eisenson, J. Jeffery Auer, and John V. Irwin, *The Psychology of Communication,* New York: Appleton-Century-Crofts, 1963, pp. 291–3. For a report on the fourteen factors, see Ralph G. Nichols, "Factors in Listening Comprehension," *Speech Monographs,* XV (1948), pp. 154–63.

A Johnson administration spokesman in the sixties might have forestalled some of the heckling with a beginning statement such as, "Let's get out of Vietnam!" This would have provided an unexpected, forceful and yet thematic beginning to a speech on the government's hopes to gain an honorable peace and withdrawal. Listeners poised to demonstrate might have become interested in learning how the government hoped to accomplish the very thing which they hoped for—and dared not expect from the speaker. In similar vein, speakers begin with a striking or challenging statement such as, "Half of you will be dead, mentally ill, invalided, imprisoned, or impoverished within thirty years," or, "Never underestimate the political power of a song-and-dance man."

To be effective, the striking beginning must not only be unexpected and compelling, it must also lead listeners to an introductory idea or to the main idea. Many speakers who succeed in stimulating strong feeling and interest in an irrelevant idea lose their listeners, who continue to think about the introductory idea while the speakers move on to their subjects, which are quite different. Further, a beginning can be too striking. An example of this is the student who began a talk on how to replace a window pane by shattering a classroom window. Many of his classmates failed to recover in time to learn what the student was trying to teach.

The warning that the striking beginning must have clear relevance to the speech subject is especially appropriate to the method of starting with one or more humorous stories, intended both to capture initial interest and to create a receptive attitude. Often a speaker has undermined his ultimate purpose by using what he thinks is the easy means of getting attention with humor, and then attempting to shift quickly to a serious note. In such an instance he may arouse interest that changes to resentment or, at best, he may arouse initial interest but not continuing interest when he needs it most—while developing his central idea and attempting to achieve the purpose of his speech. Humorous beginnings must be used with caution and used chiefly to make the point carry over into a main idea of the speech.

Advantages of the striking beginning are that it can be programed in advance and that it can move listeners quickly and forcefully to the thinking that the speaker has in mind for them. Disadvantages of the striking start are that it may overshoot its mark and distract listeners from the thinking the speaker is trying to induce, that it requires considerable dramatic skill lest it fall flat, and that it may not be well adapted to the social context of the speaking situation when the moment arrives. For most speaking, therefore, it is likely that speakers should be prepared for a perhaps less immediately compelling but a surer start: an adaptive opening statement.

The adaptive introduction begins with an awareness of what the listener or listeners may be thinking or feeling or expecting at the moment. The speaker links his beginning idea with his listeners' thinking.

A speaker may say, "Thank you, Mr. Chairman. It's true that I am as busy as you suggest, but it is only because I am seriously concerned about what we came here to discuss." In conversation one often relates an experience to one just reported as, for example, "Your experience with the book club is a little like an experience I had with a broken slot machine that kept repeatedly paying off." In a speech class a speaker may begin by noting, "Bill has just gotten us worked up over dangerous and unfair traffic laws. There are other unfair laws plaguing us. Take for instance the military draft laws." Whether listeners are responding to the situation, to a "happening" that has just taken place, or to a chairman's introduction, a speaker can find a sure and effective way to link his interest with that of his listeners.

In a public speaking situation, the adaptive beginning does something else as well. It diverts the attention of the listeners from the idea that the speaker is engaged in oratory or trying to make a good speech, and enhances the probability that listeners will know that the speaker is inviting them to consider a subject or problem of mutual speaker–listener interest.

Communication of Speaker Interest

Speaker interest and enthusiasm—both in his subject and in his listeners—is a potent source of listener interest in the subject and in the speaker. Interest begets interest in the speech–communication situation. People usually find themselves attracted to animated, interested speakers like some of the current civil rights spokesmen and like teachers who clearly care about their students. Likewise, many have quickly lost interest in listening to a lackadaisical speaker who has gone through obviously pre-programed, robot-like motions of speaking without seeming to care much what he is talking about or what his listeners are thinking about.

Listeners respond with interest to signs of speaker preparation, to signs of speaker concern for his listeners, to signs that the speaker is responding to feedback, and to signs that the speaker is dealing in realities.

Signs of speaker preparation are many: the confidence that comes from being prepared for the situation; the adaptability that comes from having prepared oneself for speaking rather than having written a script; the related ease of speaking with a purpose in mind rather than straining to remember the words one planned to utter; the reserve of materials and ways of developing ideas that also lend authority to the speaker; in cases where a manuscript is appropriate, the communicative writing and the communicative manner of the speaker who does not seem bound to his paper. All of these communicate the interest that begets interest, the speaker concern that captures and maintains listener participation in interaction with the speaker.

Signs of speaker concern for his listeners are readily available in both content and manner of speaking. The speaker who adapts to the experiences and knowledge of his listeners communicates such concern. Listeners who say that someone speaks over their heads are commenting not on the subject but on this lack of adaptation; not on the difficulties of comprehending the speaker's idea but on the fact that the speaker does not care enough to help the listener comprehend.

Listeners see speaker concern in a lively, sincere manner of speaking that is clear enough and loud enough so as not to tax their concentration. It is easy for any listener to decide—whether rightly or wrongly—that a barely audible and therefore unintelligible speaker really doesn't care enough to be heard; that he doesn't care enough about his subject or how his listener responds.

Signs that the speaker is responding to feedback include all those speaker behaviors that result directly from speaker–listener interaction during speaking: engaging in new attempts at clarity after noting, "I can see that this is a difficult concept for some of you"; acknowledging and perhaps capitalizing upon unexpected laughter or applause; seeming to engage more in conversation than in merely reproducing a message. Speaker response, then, is another sign of the kind of interest that invites listener interest in what is going on.

A speaker who is not responding to feedback does not seem—to his would-be listeners—to be really engaging in communication. He seems to be engaging in a kind of social gesture with little reality behind it.

Signs that the speaker is dealing in realities are seen in the feasibility of his purpose, in his apparent "sense of communication," and in the development of his ideas.

A speaker who is seeking approval of a proposition to which his listener is unalterably opposed is being unrealistic and is risking loss of interest in what he has to say, or, worse still, is risking a hostile response. In neither case does he communicate interest to his listener. Similarly unrealistic is a speaker who attempts to teach beyond his listener's ability to comprehend. It is not uncommon to say that *anyone* is out of his head who would try, in one communicative attempt, to persuade us to reject a strong commitment to a religious or political belief, or a strong attitude toward modern art or flag-burning. The prime characteristic of one who is, literally, out of his head is that he has withdrawn from reality. The beginning speaker who attempts to teach an entire new "dialect" of Fortran in five minutes, for instance, is similarly removed from reality, if only momentarily. His listeners are very apt to perceive the unfeasibility of purpose—and to lose interest.

Related to feasibility of purpose is any speaker's sense of communication. For many students, long years of concentration on proper English in writing and in speaking dulls their sense of communication. That is, they develop the sense that a communication is judged by its correctness or accuracy rather than by the response it elicits from reader or listener. Any speaker who seems to be concentrating on his own behavior more than on his listeners' behaviors is not apt to be perceived as operating from a real sense of communication. If such a performance elicits any interest in the listeners, it is an interest in the performance more than in the ideas of the speaker.

Reality in the development of ideas—as noted in the previous chapter and below—depends upon the extent to which a speaker's supporting or validating materials tap the experiences, knowledge, and beliefs of his listener. Unless the listener feels that what the speaker is saying is down to earth, his interest is apt to lag. It is important, therefore, for the preparing speaker to recognize the listener realities, the keys to tapping listeners' experiences, knowledge, and beliefs.

Listener Realities

The effective speaker has available for his use a wide variety of devices for tapping listener realities. To do the job of communication he has in mind, in most instances he must have listener involvement or no real interaction takes place. His listeners will maintain their interest so long as they feel that what is being discussed has something to do with them, with what they know, and with how they see their worlds. (See Chapter 10.) Each individual perceives the world about him in his own way and on the basis of his own experiences and memories. The devices for maintaining listener interest and involvement are those that recall to the listener relevant experiences and memories. These include use of the concrete and the vivid, the specific and the general, the familiar and the novel, change and suspense, and conflict and its resolution.

The Concrete and the Vivid

Marshall McLuhan has observed that reading from the printed page involves only the visual sense, but that listening—whether in the pre-Gutenberg era or in the present age of electronic media—involves all of the senses.[2] Interest is maintained when listeners are made to see, taste, hear, smell and feel; when the speaker's abstractions are supported by these realities of experience. In these days of growing international exchange and of the Peace Corps, one hears frequently of cultural shock. What does it mean? No one can know just from hearing the two words, cultural shock. But if one is reminded of experienced dizziness or disorientation in some new situation; of revulsion from strange, fetid odors; of an introduction to an unappetizing food; of a time of trouble, with apparently no one to turn to—these concrete, remembered examples can convert an unsensed abstraction into a vivid, interesting, and compelling reality. What does loyalty look like? How does teamwork sound? How does failure taste? These may seem nonsensical questions. But they are all answerable—and to communicative effect—in the sight of a weary precinct worker, in the rhythm and buzz of an editorial office, and in the bitterness of disappointment. Once again, it is the sensed, the concrete, which is vivid and, therefore, interesting.

The concrete and, therefore, vivid development of ideas is no less important for maintaining interest in teaching than it is in persuading. A speech scientist may tell his students that the tongue serves a more vital purpose than the articulation of speech sounds; that it is needed to place food between the grinding surfaces of the teeth. He may stop there or he may recognize the communicative need for more concreteness and go on to say, "Imagine what it would be like

[2] *Understanding Media: The Extensions of Man,* New York: McGraw Hill, Inc., 1964 (paperback edition, New York: Signet Books, 1966).

if you had no tongue and were to bite into a peanut-butter sandwich. Your jaw would go up and down and that sticky wad would merely glue itself to the roof of your mouth."

It should be noted from the foregoing examples that concreteness does more than maintain listener interest. Concreteness also communicates more effectively than does unsupported or undeveloped abstraction. This can be said, too, for all the factors of interest which follow.

The Specific and the General

Similarly, unsupported or undeveloped generalizations, unless startling in themselves, rarely capture and hold listener interest. It is details that lend interest and communicative effect. Thus, it is not enough to generalize that bird watching and bird banding contribute to conservation of natural resources. Listeners may nod and think, "So what else is new?" Specific ways in which the activities are carried out and specific statements of the knowledge and conservation that accrue are much more apt to spark genuine interest. So it is with many "ho-hum" generalizations which are made interesting by making them specific and meaningful. "Life expectancy is on the increase." What are the specifics? Where? By how much? What does this mean for my generation? The speaker who answers such questions is apt to have an interested listener.

The Familiar and the Novel

Psychologist–philosopher William James observed that "It is an odd circumstance that neither the old nor the new, by itself, is interesting: the absolutely old is insipid; the absolutely new makes no appeal at all. The old in the new is what claims attention—the old with a slightly new turn."

Every speaker is inviting his listener to new perceptions. He cannot maintain listener interest unless this is so. And he is not likely to maintain interest unless he deals with the new in relation to the old. The perception process, with its dependence upon previously established categories of "perceptual expectancies,"[3] demands that the effective speaker know and adapt to what is familiar to his listener, for every

[3] See, for instance, Jerome S. Bruner, "On Perceptual Readiness," David C. Beardslee and Michael Wertheimer, eds., *Readings in Perception,* Chapter 52, Princeton, N.J.: D. Van Nostrand Company, Inc., 1958, pp. 686–729.

listener asks, in turn, "What is this like (of all the relevant things that I have experienced and know and believe)?" It is easy to see, for instance, that for some audiences a speaker favoring medicare might affect listener interest differently when noting that medicare is like national compulsory health insurance than when comparing it to socialized medicine. Similarly, the use of apt analogies helps bridge the gap between the unfamiliar and the familiar in making many points both clear and interesting.

Change and Suspense

It is proverbial that variety is the spice of life. Change in itself is interesting. So is the anticipation of change—if we are not sure what is coming. Thus, as we listen to a good narrative or anecdote, we are held in suspense to the end. However, a joke loses its savor—and listener interest—if we know the punch line. Speakers can maintain listener interest by planning for change and suspense.

Chapter 11 presents several methods of indirect development in persuasion, methods of moving from problem to solution which, when properly paced, can build listeners' suspense as they wonder how best to solve the problem. In teaching, inductive methods, in which one wonders about and then discovers general rules, are usually more interesting than didactic or direct methods (and generally more effective in providing both understanding and long-run retention).

Humor is a special kind of change and suspense which, when effective, is interesting to everyone—even to those who habitually groan or complain at an unexpected pun. Laughter is prompted by the unexpected, by reminders of shared human foibles, by a suspense-building narrative with a surprise ending. An important lesson for speakers—learned from professional comedians—is that the joke must not be on the audience. The joke must be on somebody else and usually, for greatest humorous effect, on the speaker.

In our earlier discussion of humor as a factor of initial interest, the point was made that humorous material must focus listeners on the speaker's idea—not divert them from it. This is no less true in maintaining interest through the use of humor.

Conflict and Its Resolution

In the dramatic arts, regardless of medium—whether theatre, television, film, or radio—the prime goal is listener interest or entertainment and the prime method is conflict. Even when the outcome is well known, listeners find themselves attracted, interested, and identifying with one side or the other, and, as the case may be, fearing or hoping that the conflict will be resolved as they know it must. It is clear that the interest of professional historians is drawn almost constantly to conflict. Managers of the news media, concerned not only with reporting the news but with maintaining reader or viewer interest, know that they must headline conflict and that harmony or cooperation are interesting and newsworthy only as resolution of long-standing conflict.

The lesson for speakers, then, is that conflict attracts listener interest; that a steady diet of milk and honey, of sweetness and light soon palls. The separate television appearances of John F. Kennedy and Richard M. Nixon in their 1960 race for the Presidency were not nearly as attractive to television audiences as the so-called great debates in which they appeared jointly. Just over one hundred years earlier, Abraham Lincoln, in his debates with Stephen A. Douglas, utilized conflict effectively by his practice of giving in his opening remarks a sympathetic summary of the views stated by his opponent. Interest was heightened as his audiences wondered how he would combat opinions that appeared to be so strongly supported. Again, in our time, militant pacifism has attracted far more public interest and support than did earlier versions, when there was little confrontation between the pacifist minority and the war-supporting majority.

To maintain listener interest, then, speakers should not necessarily soft-pedal conflict but often should expose it. A speaker who honestly confides to his listeners, "There is much to be said for both sides," and soundly presents the evidence for each point of view, is making effective use of the interest-generating principle of conflict.[4] So is a teacher who points to conflicting theories.

Adaptation to all of the listener realities presented in the paragraphs above does not provide mere ornaments to speaking; it provides the basic component. For without listener interest there can be no interaction. Where there is interaction, the language used and the language listeners expect combine in another important set of factors of interest.

[4] It is not intended that one should present in all situations both sides of a controversy for maximum effectiveness. Other factors must be considered in each case. See Herbert I. Abelson "How To Present the Issues," *Persuasion,* Chapter 1, Berlin: Springer-Verlag, 1959, pp. 1–18. Also see Chapter 11, "Persuasion Processes."

Language Expectancies and Interest

As the interesting speaker adapts to the experiences of his listener, so does he adapt to the language expectancies of his listener. This is the matter of style—but not style in the sense of something put on for show. Every speaker has not one style but an automatically available repertoire of styles: different modes of talking depending upon the formality of the situation, the intimacy of the communicators, certain group variables, and the medium of message transmission.

Levels of Style

The now historic Berkeley uprisings came in two waves. First there was the student drive for free speech in the sense discussed in Chapter 11: freedom to listen to a free competition of persuasion. There followed a second drive for free speech in the sense discussed in Chapter 1: freedom of *expression* without regard for listener (or reader) responses. Our language of expression is necessarily different from our language of communication, for in the one we are dealing only with our own language expectancies, and in the other we are dealing with both our own and others' listening expectancies. What happens when a campus activist uses the pithy and slangy (even dirty) language of expression in a communication situation—as when he commands a president or the trustees to honor the requests (or demands) of his organization? The listeners are very likely "turned off." Thus, the petitioner succeeds in exercising his freedom of expression but fails in his attempt at communication. His mistaken version may be, of course, that the opposite has occurred: that he has communicated but has been denied freedom of expression.

Such expressive levels of style are not necessarily inappropriate to all communication situations. While inappropriate to the formality of the board room or the public platform, such language, it is usually assumed, is acceptable—even enjoyed—in the intimacy of locker room, the dormitory bull session, and in some kinds of psychotherapy.

Language style, levels of formality, and good taste are inextricably bound to variations in communication situations. Education generally, and speech education specifically, is aimed at equipping one to interact with others effectively, at appropriate levels, in all situations. As civil rights leaders attempt to spread the benefits of democracy to all citizens, it is worth noting that one, Martin Luther King, seems to have but one style regardless of audience, while another, Stokely Carmichael, speaks at different levels for different occasions and for different audiences. As observers, we may admire the single style of the one and deplore the chameleon quality of the other. But, as students of speech communication, we are forced to note that Mr. Carmichael interests a wider variety of listeners. Further, before we may be critical of one for speaking with different styles, we must first be critical of our own natural tendencies to address the boss in one way in his office and in another on the golf course; to speak with a librarian differently than we do with a brother or sister; to speak with one style in a parliamentary debate and in another at a "jammy."

Listeners do—rightly or wrongly—tend to withdraw their interest from the ideas of a speaker who uses unexpected or inappropriate style. It is true that they may then become interested in the style itself as a source of curiosity or of hostility. But this is rarely a speaker's purpose. As listeners, on the other hand, we need to learn to overcome this natural prejudice, to ward off distractions from ideas to style.

Each of us has at least three levels of language expectancy:[5] the formal, the casual, and the expressive. The latter label may be misleading to some readers for, in another sense, all speaking must be expressive to maintain interest. This usage, however, refers to a vitality of utterance, a quality of style that can be sensed as much in the measured rhythm, force, and imagery of a Martin Luther King as in the exhortations of a volatile football coach at halftime.

Group Variables

Somewhat related to levels of style are what are known as the sociolinguistic variations of style. Different socioeconomic groups have different styles and distinctive dialects. Each vocation, profession and avocation has its own "expertese." Language styles vary also with social groups. These variations have been noted by linguists and sociologists.[6] More important for speech students, these variations have been found to block communication when they draw attention to themselves. The

[5] For a more detailed treatment of levels of style, see Charles C. Fries, "Usage Levels and Dialect Distribution," *The American College Dictionary,* New York: Random House, Inc., 1963, pp. xxix–xxx.

[6] See for instance, Joyce O. Hertzler, "Social Differentiation and Linguistic Specialization in the Language Community: II The Special Group and Technical Language," *A Sociology of Language,* Chapter XIII, New York: Random House, Inc., 1965, pp. 317–64.

members of one racial group from a low socioeconomic level found that they could not find employment after training in secretarial skills. When they added to their repertoires the language characteristics of the middle-class group, they were offered employment.

There are two very important implications for the student of oral communication. One is that the language styles expected by listeners for given situations evoke interest in the content of communication, and that unexpected language styles evoke interest in the styles themselves. The other implication is that, again, as listeners, we should not let sociolinguistic variations of style block communication.

No one should recommend rejection of any language which one has learned to use in communicative situations in his home, neighborhood, and school. As a person moves into a new socioeconomic level, meets new communication situations, and enters new fields of endeavor, he has a need not to replace his original styles and dialects but to add new ones to his repertoire. No communicatively effective style and dialect is better than any other. But one style and dialect is usually better than others for given people in given situations. There is no logical reason why a person from one socioeconomic group should be rebuffed for his dialect in his communication attempts with members of another group. But it happens, and is avoidable.

Written and Spoken Style

Sometimes confused with levels of style are the written and the spoken, or colloquial, styles. In most situations when listeners expect spoken style and hear written style, they find it to be dull. Those who write out their speeches—thinking, perhaps, to attain a better style—are likely to make the speeches stilted and to drain from them the direct communicativeness that should always link speakers and listeners. Thus, for almost all oral communication situations, spoken style helps to maintain listener interest; written style to reduce it.

Even when a manuscript is called for, it should usually be prepared in the same manner described in previous chapters and composed in spoken rather than written style.

It is possible to describe some of the differences between written and spoken styles.[7] Normally, in speaking, we use shorter sentences

[7] For discussion of research on the differences, see John B. Newman and Milton W. Horowitz, "Writing and Speaking," *College Composition and Communication,* XVI (October, 1965), pp. 160–4.

and often incomplete and disjointed sentences (although they seldom sound as disjointed to a listener as they appear in a transcript), simpler language, more personal pronouns, more repetition of words and phrases. It should be noted, however, that neither speakers nor listeners consciously analyze style for such written or spoken characteristics. Each of us has learned a "set" for putting words on paper that is different from our "set" for talking. Without knowing how, we can almost always tell when a speaker meets our expectancy for spoken language and when he does not.

By way of summary, factors which influence maintenance of listener interest include all of the signs that the speaker is interested in his subject and in his listeners; all of the means of tapping listener realities of experience, knowledge, and beliefs; and all of the language expectancies that listeners have for the speaker in the situation.

Invitation to Continuing Interest

Having initiated and maintained listener interest, the effective speaker faces one more problem: how to invite listeners to continue their interest in what he has been saying—even after the speaking is over and after days and weeks have passed. On some occasions, of course, this problem does not exist, when only an immediate response is needed—as when the goal is some parliamentary action or some immediate use of new information or just listener entertainment.

In Chapter 6 it was pointed out that, in concluding, a speaker usually seeks ways to make his idea memorable. When some subsequent act or some thinking-through of an idea is called for, continuing interest is an additional goal. The speaker must discover strong appeals for eliciting commitment to action. (See pp. 252–3, Programing for Action).

Something should be said here that may not apply to speaking in the classroom but which has great importance for personal effectiveness in one's professional and social affairs. In thinking about establishing continuing interest in his subject, a speaker is apt to recognize that one speaking attempt is not enough; that interest can quickly fade when contact is over. This should lead him to think of ways of being in contact again, of follow-up either through later speaking with the same group or through telephone contact or through the mail. Persistence is a potent factor, both of continuing interest and of persuasive effectiveness.

Conclusion

We have noted that listener interest is essential to effective communication. It is the sign that channels of interaction are open. Speakers must keep in mind the need and means of establishing initial interest, or attention; of maintaining that interest; and, where appropriate, of inviting continuing interest in his ideas.

The prime sources of listener interest are (1) the speaker's own genuine interest in his subject and in his listeners, for interest begets interest; (2) the speaker's adaptation to his listeners' realities of experience, knowledge, and beliefs; and (3) the interaction of the speaker's style of language and his listeners' language expectancies.

In addition, special note has been taken that listeners, to improve their communicative effectiveness, must be prepared to overcome certain natural distractions from speakers' ideas and intentions in certain situations, especially those involving sociolinguistic and other stylistic variables which may violate listener expectancies.

In one sense there is a further important factor of listener interest to add to the information here on speaker attitudes, materials, and language choice. This is in the *way* he speaks—the subject of the next chapter.

Exercises

Questions for Discussion

1. What are the functions of the factors of interest—that is, what do they accomplish?

2. Turn back to Chapter 6 to review what is said there about the varied purposes of the introduction. Discuss striking and adaptive introductions and their relations to the factors of interest. What type of introductions do you generally prefer? What factors help you decide which type to use?

3. Consider each of the factors of interest in relation to topics that have been discussed in class. What factors of interest have been used? What additional ones might the speakers have applied?

4. Discuss the effects of dialects on listener interest. Why is dialect so important to many people? Should other people learn your dialect? Should you learn theirs?

5. Can you tell when speakers have composed their speeches in written language? How do you respond to the speaking of written language? What is the dictionary meaning of *colloquial?* Should colloquial language be avoided?

6. Discuss the signs of speaker interest. Among the people that you know and who know you, think of the one you consider most interesting. Is he someone who is interested in you?

· *Projects for Speaking and Listening*

1. Select a well-known speaker whom you have heard in person or on television and present to your class a brief report in which you analyze his methods of inviting interest. Evaluate his speech on the basis of the factors presented in this chapter.

2. Review a speech that you have already made in your class. Find how you might have made it more interesting. Take the speech outline and note in the margins all of the ways you might develop the ideas to invite listener interest.

3. Prepare to speak for five minutes with the general purpose to enhance sociability. See how many of the factors of interest you can apply in preparing and in speaking. Team up with another member of the class so that you can report to each other how much interest you seemed to elicit.

4. Study the titles in a collection of speeches (see, for instance, Carroll C. Arnold, Douglas Ehninger and John C. Gerber, *The Speaker's Resource Book,* Chicago: Scott, Foresman, 1966), to see which of the titles serve which of the four functions discussed in this chapter.

5. Note the classroom speeches which interest you most and those which interest you least. What are the significant differences? What can you learn from this analysis to help improve your own speaking? Your listening?

9 · *Communicative Behavior: Delivery*

Communication occurs not only through words but also through physical behavior and appearance and through the qualities of the voice. When messages are being exchanged and evaluated, the intention is to refer to facts and ideas. But a vast amount of meaningful communication contains an overlay of attitude—attitudes that signal such messages as: "This is significant (or unimportant)" or "I like you (or don't care about you)" or "please pay attention (or don't bother)." Such exposed attitudes are exceedingly influential in human relationships. And attitudes are more largely and also more accurately communicated through bodily bearings and vocal nuances than through words. Even when the words might seem to bear the crucial message—as in such an emphatic statement as "You thieving scoundrel!"—it is well known that the manner of speaking, including the bearing and the vocal intonations, determine wholly and unmistakably whether this form of words is a denunciation or a declaration of affectionate regard. Well known also is the effect upon a speaker whose communication is discouraged by a cold, expressionless response. All oral communication involves a complex pattern of behavior that includes words, appearance, bearing, and voice, all of which make decisive contributions to the interactions that take place.

Actually, communicative speaking and listening involve three different channels: the linguistic, the auditory, and the visual. In other words, meanings are conveyed in ordinary discourse by what is said, by how the voice sounds, and by the way speakers and listeners interpret one another's appearance. These three modes of communication may be designated as the linguistic code, the auditory code, and the visual code. The aim of this chapter is to depict the nature and the uses of the visual and auditory codes.

Functions of Codes

Code means a "system of symbols with agreed-upon or conventionalized meanings." The English language is a code, as is French or any other language. So is algebra, the cries of crows, and the secret cryptographs used to smuggle information through enemy territory.

Codes have five different communicative functions: (1) to represent meaning; (2) to group people into different types of code-users; (3) to serve special and limited communication needs; (4) to serve needs of varying levels of complexity; and (5) to convey meaning to selected receivers while simultaneously concealing it from others.

To Represent Meaning

It seems a truism to declare that codes are formulated for the purpose of representing meaning. Nevertheless, this is the absolutely essential principle, which must be dominant at all times while a code is in use if confusion and misunderstanding are to be prevented. A code is used to convey a message, which means to provide information.

But if meaningless elements are interjected, the message is distorted. It is obvious that the linguistic code would lose effectiveness if the speaker were to say, "I do not quirkly guw gehinkmud believe it." It should be equally obvious that meaning is distorted if a speaker interrupts the succession of his words by inserting a frequent "uh, er, hmmn," or if he uses words that seem to indicate an important message while his voice maintains a flat and expressionless quality, such as is commonly intended to signal boredom or indifference. Random bodily movements, or downcast eyes, or gestures unrelated to the message being linguistically coded are also irrelevant codes that thwart communication. A listener who slumps in his seat or who stares at the speaker with a dull, uncomprehending expression is conveying a kind of meaning, though not perhaps what he intends—and surely not what the situation requires in order to heighten the effectiveness of the communication.

What speakers and listeners need to keep in mind is that while they are communicating they can not engage in meaningless behavioral code transmittals. Everything not enhancing the effectiveness of their exchange of meanings must detract from it.

To Group Code-users According to Type

No one knows how or why different languages developed. But it is well known that the principal function of the differences is to group people into separate language communities. Those who speak a common language (English, for example) form an in-group, as contrasted with everyone else, all over the world. No other factor is so influential in making a people feel bound to one another as their use of a common code. This is what chiefly identifies them as belonging in a cooperating community. This feeling is well illustrated by the tendency of each succeeding generation of teen-agers to adopt a new type of clothing, of hair styles, of music and dancing, and of slang—all of which signal their feeling that they form a special, distinctive group.

Among the slum youngsters of Pittsburgh, for example (according to an Associated Press dispatch of August 25, 1966), there is a special vocabulary amounting to some 3,200 words, with which they communicate among themselves. The "hip frogs and foxes" (boys and girls) may seem way out to "Smokey Bear" (teacher). In a "knuckle drill" (fight) it is important to them to know "what key you are in" (whose side you are on) and to avoid trouble with "Rays" (parents), "Fine Peelers" (magistrates), and "mink jobs" (people in authority). Such special languages are developed by men in the armed forces, by crooks, by every vocational group, and by other groups that feel a need to signify they belong together and are different from others.

When a professor talks like a professor to his students, part of the message that is conveyed, aside from the coded information, is the fact of his different status and different function. When a speaker wishes to strengthen the bonds that unite him with his listeners, one crucial element in his presentation must be care in using a level of style, a type of illustrations, and other grammatical and vocabulary characteristics that resemble as closely as his role permits the kind of speech used and valued by his listeners. "He's not our type" is a judgment listeners are likely to make upon the basis of the code used by the speaker more quickly and surely than for almost any other reason.

To Serve Special and Limiting Communication Needs

A picture, according to the old Chinese proverb, is worth a thousand words. So it might be—to depict the misery of a child starving to death, or the happiness of a young couple in love. But to show the abstract relationship of one quantity to another, an algebraic formula is worth a thousand pictures. And to explain the meaning of the term *epistemological,* an explanatory passage in words would be worth any number of pictures.

Bodily bearing, the amount and kind of tension exhibited, the quality of a hand gesture, the tilt of the head, a pursing of the lips—any or all of these in conjunction might say far more to listeners about the sincerity of the speaker, or his depth of feeling, than his words could ever effectively either affirm or deny. The rate at which he speaks, either slowly and deliberately or with tumultuous speed, signals a great deal about his temperament. His dialect (Brooklyn, Pennsylvania Dutch, Southern, Midwestern, or New England) is a code that indicates where he is from. The precision of his articulation, along with his pronunciation and choice of words, indicates something of his social standing and level of education. As these examples suggest, in any communicative situation many communicative codes are used.

Listeners employ them as surely as do speakers, for the nature of the response they make (by facial expressions, bodily presence, degree of alertness) reveals not only their comprehension and interest but also their attitude toward the speaker and their polite awareness, or indifference, to their own responsibility in the situation. Oral communication is vastly more than the utterance and reception of spoken words.

Many codes are used and interpreted simultaneously, each with its own limited and specialized communicative function. When all the codes unite in delivering a coherent message, the results are far more satisfactory than when the codes partly or directly contradict one another.

To Serve Needs of Varying Levels of Complexity

If someone is about to step absent-mindedly in front of an oncoming automobile, the simple word, "Stop!" shouted with appropriate urgency may be all the code required to serve the needs of the occasion.

If someone should ask you, "What is your opinion of American involvement in Southeastern Asia?" your response would probably be vastly more complex. Some communication is brief, clear-cut, and emphatic; but there is also a need for explanations that are analytical, evaluative, and carefully qualified. Similarly, in some situations only minimal listening will suffice—enough, perhaps, to let the listener know whether the speaker is still talking or has stopped. Other messages are of such importance and perhaps of such complexity that adequate listening requires not only the utmost in attention but also frequent summaries and requests for repetition or further explanation of some portions.

Both speakers and listeners need to educate themselves to use their communicative codes appropriately, varying their complexity in terms of the function currently to be performed. The polite conversational inquiry, "How are you today?" seldom is intended to invite a detailed clinical report. The question, "How do you think racial integration may best be achieved?" requires more than a grunt and shrug in response. The ability to perceive the level of complexity that will best serve the ideational and social demands of a particular communicative situation is one of the cardinal skills of effective speech.

To Represent Meaning for Some While Concealing It from Others

This function is the principal reason for the development of such cryptographs as are used by spies or in the transmission of important diplomatic messages. It also is a common practice among lovers, who wish to signal their affection to one another without being obvious to their associates. In many social situations, a speaker is aware of one or several special members among the listeners. Perhaps his boss may be present and, while entertaining the company with an account of a trip he has recently taken, he wishes simultaneously to impress upon the boss that he was specially attentive to the business opportunities that exist in the areas visited. Or a husband may want to have his wife notice how carefully he avoids a subject she has asked him not to discuss, while the others present may be wholly unaware of his skirting of certain aspects of the topic under discussion. If an expert sanitary engineer is speaking to a community audience on a new sewage disposal plant and knows that another expert is in the audience, he may make several comments, which these two and these two alone will recognize, as an acknowledgement of their special knowledge of the subject.

According to a story in *The New York Times* for Sunday, April 16, 1967, those teen-agers and young adults in Boston's East Village (below 14th street) who habitually take hashish, marijuana, or such drugs as L.S.D., heroin, and cocaine, have developed a language of their own to signal their recognition of one another. An Acid Head may greet a newcomer by saying: "This is the real bag. The scene here is where it's at and we don't need any outsiders. We've all seen shrinks and they couldn't help us. We have to find out ourselves where our head is and then we're O.K." When a common identity has been established, the newcomer may be invited in to "trip off an onion." Those who don't understand don't belong.

Whenever more than two people are engaged in discourse, it is likely that some of the codes used will deliberately be intended to deliver to one or more of the participants a special message not intended for the others. Similarly, it is a commonplace of experience that listeners may choose to ignore much of what is being said, on the ground that it is for others, while becoming especially alert to certain parts they feel are meaningful to them.

Intentional and Unintentional Uses of the Codes

Signals are sometimes given that are not intended. In fact, what is communicated may fall into any one of four distinctly different classes:

1. What is meant to be communicated and is understood by the listener precisely as the speaker intends. An example might be: "The Globe theatre is one block down the street, on the right-hand side."

2. What is meant to be communicated but is misunderstood by the listener. An example might be: "I will let you have my book if you promise to return it the first thing in the morning"—when the speaker intends the emphasis to rest upon the conditional clause; whereas the listener is so delighted to get the book that he pays virtually no attention to the condition of the loan.

3. What is not intended to be communicated but, nevertheless, the listener gets as an unintended message. This might be illustrated by the signs that communicate to the listener that the speaker has stage fright, or that communicate to the speaker that the listener is bored.

4. What is intended to be withheld from communication, but, nevertheless, the listener gets the very message the speaker meant to

conceal. An example might be a verbal slip by which a speaker reveals a dislike for the listener, which he was trying to conceal.[1]

These four ways in which codes are used (and misused) are analyzed by Erving Goffman in the two categories of "signs given" and "signs given off."[2] He points out that whenever two or more people are engaged in discourse, they deliberately try to secure certain reactions by what they say and do. These deliberate communicative efforts he calls "signs given." But simultaneously they also reveal some things about themselves or their attitudes toward the listener, or perhaps toward the subject matter, or the occasion, which they do not mean to communicate. These "signs given off" are interpreted by listeners just as surely as they interpret the "signs given." Just as we read between the lines, so do we listen between the words and watch between the gestures. It is a commonplace of the communicative process that several different messages may be sent simultaneously, either intentionally or unintentionally. A listener may reveal that: (a) I hear what you say; (b) I don't like it; but (c) however reluctantly, I guess I have to agree. A speaker may reveal that: (a) I believe earnestly in what I am saying; (b) but I really don't know very much about the subject; and (c) I don't care what you think just so long as you let me have my way. Of course, the complex of codes being communicated both by speaker and by listener could be even more involved and perhaps even more contradictory than these brief examples illustrate. And unless extreme care and attentiveness are exercised by both parties to the discourse, misunderstandings are almost inevitable.[3]

The Visual Code

Everyone is more of an expert than he realizes about the nature and uses of the visual code. Infants start learning it even before they can use language; and everyone continues throughout life to study it

[1] Sigmund Freud, in his *Psychopathology of Everyday Life,* cites many examples of both unintended and nonintended communication. See *The Basic Writings of Sigmund Freud,* A. A. Brill, ed., New York: Modern Library, Inc., 1938, pp. 35–178.

[2] Erving Goffman, *Presentation of the Self in Everyday Life,* New York: Doubleday & Company, Inc., 1959, pp. 2–4.

[3] Gustav Ichheiser, "Misunderstandings in Human Relations," supplement to *The American Journal of Sociology,* 55 (September, 1949), pp. 6–7.

closely. But most learning about the visual code is unconscious and unintended. Through visual cues within the family, children learn to evaluate the moods of their parents, brothers, and sisters—to tell whether they are happy or unhappy, confident or ill at ease, worried or content, nervous or calm, affectionate or irritated, gay or serious, alert or tired, eager to talk or reluctant to communicate. All this and more is revealed through the visual code.

Similarly, individuals everywhere respond easily and naturally to visual perception of cues indicating approval or disapproval, enthusiasm or boredom, assertiveness or submission, interest or apathy. A great deal of meaning is suggested and interpreted merely through the sense of sight: by gestures, such as looking at or motioning toward the salt when it is desired; by an inquiring glance, which asks as clearly as words could do where you have been or what you are up to now; by dress and manner, as when a father appears in slippers and smoking jacket and settles wearily into his favorite chair, indicating as surely as if he said so that if the lawn is to be mowed he is not the one who will do it. A vast amount of what people communicate to one another is conveyed wholly by appearance, manner, and behavior.

Friends feel that an indication of their friendship is the ability to understand one another without explanations. Even in dealing with strangers or casual acquaintances, attitudes of friendliness, indifference, or antagonism are easily communicated without words. So are fear, anger, joy, enthusiasm, unhappiness, worry, and many more feelings. Smiles and frowns, gestures of acceptance or rejection, coy glances or cold stares—these and many other elements of the visual code shape a large portion of our relations with other people.

Students of gesture have estimated that there are at least 700,000 different symbolic physical manifestations (gestures) that are capable of conveying fairly precise meanings.[4] It has also been ascertained that different cultural groups (races, nations, social classes) have their own fairly distinct types of gestures.[5] A Frenchman is likely to be demonstrative, an Oriental decorously restrained. A professional man bears himself so differently from a day laborer that if we happen to see a coarsely

[4] Richard Paget, *Human Speech,* London: Routledge and Kegan Paul Ltd., 1930. See also R. L. Birdwhistell, "Body Behavior and Communication," *International Encyclopedia of Social Sciences,* New York: Crowell-Collier and Macmillan, 1968.

[5] Charles D. Hockett, "The Origin of Speech," *Scientific American,* 203 (March, 1960), pp. 88–96.

dressed man whose posture suggests dignity and self-esteem, we are likely to assume he is well educated and well-to-do. This is not to say that our judgments from such cues are necessarily correct. On the contrary, we form many false impressions, both of the character or personality of strangers and of the emotional reactions of our associates. The visual cues upon which we depend are often misinterpreted.[6]

But because they are often wrongly used does not mean that visual communicative cues should be ignored. The opposite conclusion is more meaningful. As listeners we should by all means do what we can to sharpen the keenness with which we appraise the behavioral signs given off by speakers to whom we attend; and as speakers we should make an effort to suggest with our bodily posture, facial expressions, and gestures what we concurrently say, or want to say, with our words. The two points of consequence are: (1) that the visual code is of tremendous consequence in oral discourse; and (2) that because of carelessness and inattention by both speakers and listeners, the visual cues are often and widely misunderstood.

Empathy

Empathy refers to the intuitive or unconscious experiencing of the feelings of another person by a neuromuscular imitation of his actions. A common experience of this sort is the straining of spectators at a football game to help their team gain vital yardage at the goal line. Social psychologists make much of the process of "taking the role of the other person" as a means of understanding him. Through a process called *psychodrama* individuals are helped to understand the position of another person by pretending to be him. For example, a disobedient child may be helped to understand and accept parental discipline by taking the role of the father.

In a less formal way, even in ordinary conversational and public speaking situations, understanding depends to a high degree on the ability to "empathize" with the other participants. "A person, by imagining or actually using the gestures, postures, words and intonations of someone else and by drawing upon his understanding of that person

[6] See S. E. Asch, "Forming Impressions of Personality," *Journal of Abnormal and Social Psychology,* 41 (1946), pp. 258–90; and V. B. Cline and J. M. Richards, Jr., "Accuracy of Interpersonal Perception—a General Trait?" *Journal of Abnormal and Social Psychology,* 60 (1960), pp. 1–7.

from past experience, evokes in himself responses which approximate those of the other person. He thus 'feels' his way into the other's views . . ."[7] This is why speakers use vigorous gestures when they wish to arouse an active, emotional response. This is why listeners who alertly follow with their eyes the movements—even the minute changes in bodily tension and posture—of a speaker get more from his message than do those who loll back, with eyes half closed, and simply listen to his voice.

How much our communication is neuromuscular is indicated by our tendency to reply to a smile with a smile, a frown with a frown. If the speaker slumps limply, because he himself is largely indifferent to what he is saying, his listeners slump also—and feel a comparable indifference. If the speaker is physically alert and reveals through his bodily bearing the deep concern he feels for what he is talking about, his listeners tend to imitate his physical alertness and, concurrently, are far more readily receptive to his attitude of serious concern than they would be if they somehow avoided the influence of empathy in their reactions. Thus speakers help listeners to get in the mood for their remarks, just as listeners may help or hinder speakers by physical manifestations of either interest or apathy.

When we imitate, or empathize, in response to certain elements in the behavior of another person, our own behavior strengthens those same tendencies in his. This is very evident when a mild argument between two individuals develops into a violent quarrel, each one imitating the heightened vocal volume and enlarged gestures of the other, thereby stimulating both himself and the other to more violent feelings. But it is equally true that a quarrel may be diverted if a third person intervenes to present a pattern of relaxed pleasantness and makes his presence so dominant that the other two will tend to imitate his smiles, chuckles, and gentle mannerisms. It is well known that we can change the mood and behavior of our associates significantly by presenting for them a pattern to which they respond empathically. This is precisely what happens when one person cheers up a downcast friend by behaving toward him in a cheerful manner.

Empathy is a mode of communication, which operates physically in order to achieve a mental and emotional response. Its operation is largely unconscious in the sense that riding a bicycle is unconscious. The rider, of course, deliberately decides to ride the bicycle, mounts

[7] Alfred R. Lindesmith and Anselm L. Strauss, *Social Psychology,* rev., New York: Holt, Rinehart and Winston, Inc., 1956, p. 386.

it, and takes off with conscious purpose. However, if he should try to give conscious attention to his balance, his pedaling motions, and his guidance, his riding would be exceedingly awkward and he might well tumble. We skate, bicycle, swim, play tennis, and indeed engage in most habitual physical activities most successfully when we have learned them well enough so that we do them without deliberate thought about the process. So it is that empathy may be utilized best by a speaker who has learned how to establish a clear and meaningful pattern for the responses of his listeners and has learned so well how to do it that he does it spontaneously and naturally, without conscious manipulation. Similarly, empathy is effective as a communication device precisely because the listener does not feel that he is being consciously guided in his responses. This is one of the tremendous advantages that actions have over words. If one should say to a despondent friend, "Snap out of it! You have nothing to worry about!" he would probably get a growl or an argument in response. But if the despondent one is greeted with sympathetic awareness of his troubles, then with a general aura of cheerfulness, it is remarkable how influential the empathic process is likely to be.

In oral communication empathy is important because the speaker is seen as well as heard. If the listeners droop wearily and look sleepy, the speaker finds his enthusiasm or desire to communicate evaporating. If the speaker looks absently out the window, his listeners find it difficult to feel that his message is significant for them. The words may say this is vital, but the manner denies it. Two contradictory messages are being relayed by the linguistic and the visual codes. Since, generally, seeing is believing, the message displayed by the visual code is the one likely to be accepted.

There is a tendency to trust empathic reactions precisely because it is more difficult to pretend with the whole body than with words alone. This is a major reason why bodily action is an important aspect of delivery in public speaking. This is why Demosthenes, when asked to name three cardinal attributes of good speech, said: "Action! Action! Action!"

Principles of Delivery

There is no single pattern of effective communicative speech. If there were, everyone should be trained to speak the same way. As a matter of fact, there are as many ways of speaking effectively as there are personality types. Each person has to find and develop the kinds of delivery that best fits his own purposes, his own convictions, and his own conception of his relationship with his listeners. This does not mean that the habitual ways in which everyone speaks and listens are their own best ways. There are bad habits of communication just as there are bad habits of posture, of eating, and of general behavior. Different as people are, the following principles serve as general guides, which all may profitably follow.

Develop the Urge to Communicate

People vary greatly in their generalized desire for leadership. But even those who usually do not seek to influence others should avoid wasting their time and their listeners' if they have nothing they consider worth saying. When there is a message to be delivered, the essential consideration is not its mere statement but its delivery. Thoughts may be entertained privately, but when they are made public the speaker has an acute responsibility to phrase them and reinforce them with an urgency of voice and manner. The fact that man is a social being demands that each of us be attentive to the ideas of others; and it similarly requires that from time to time each individual must contribute his own ideas and convictions to his associates. Social living requires a sharing of viewpoints. It is only sensible that after a speaker has prepared a message worthy of being heard, he should pour his energies emotionally as well as intellectually into the process of communicating it so urgently and forcefully that his listeners will be emphatically drawn to give it full consideration.

Speak Extempore

As is pointed out in Chapter 14, there are occasions when speeches should be written out and read. Yet young and inexperienced speakers should neither read their talks nor recite them from memory. The quality of genuine oral communication requires a responsiveness between speaker and listeners that can only be attained when the speaker has his ideas and supporting facts thoroughly mastered and when he presents them to his listeners with spontaneous adaptation to the circumstances of the moment.

Extempore speaking should never be confused with *impromptu* speaking—meaning to speak on the spur of the moment, unexpectedly, with no opportunity for preparation. There is no limit to the amount of preparation for a speech that is delivered extemporaneously. In using the extempore method the speaker knows, through preliminary thinking and research, what he will talk about and the probable order in which he will do so; but the precise wording and perhaps even the choice of examples and proof he will use depends on his interpretation of the needs of his listeners while he is speaking. It may be that his first point will need more elaboration, more support, or more pointed adaptation to his audience than he had planned. It may be that he will have to make a lightning-fast decision to condense his second or third point into a mere summary sentence, in order to provide time for sufficient development of the first. It should be obvious, then, that the extempore method demands that the speaker be both alert to the responses of his listeners and very thoroughly prepared concerning the subject he is discussing. Only when both these requirements are met is it possible to speak extemporaneously. A memorized or a manuscript speech is completed in substance and form before the delivery commences. But an extemporized speech is created during its presentation. This can only be accomplished when the substance is exceptionally sound and when the basic form or outline is unshakably strong.

Extempore speaking demands the utmost in preparation, in intellectual agility, and in sound thinking about the real meanings of the subject and of its bearing upon the listeners. No matter what other kinds of speaking may appropriately be done on occasion (impromptu, memorized, or manuscript reading) the extempore is the method which above all others is useful for those who are trying to learn and master the communicative principles. Because it calls for the best qualities of both speakers and listeners, it provides the standards by which all oral communication may be judged.

Be Genuine

Naturalness is advised as the median position between random awkwardness and formalized artificiality. Natural delivery means that you should walk confidently to the front of the room, encompass your listeners with a glance of genuine recognition and fellowship, and say what you have to say with the maximum communicativeness of words, voice, and bodily expressiveness. Meaningless gestures, the nervous twisting of the hands, or the shifting of one's weight back and forth from one foot to another with pendulum-like regularity may for some be habitual, but they surely are not natural parts of oral communication.

Behavior is genuine when it is appropriate, when it is relevant to the situation, and when it contributes helpfully to attainment of the goal toward which it is aimed. One reason for undertaking the study of speech is to unlearn unnatural habits that interfere with communication and to relearn the genuine ones.

Be Conversational

The circular-response feature of conversation is its chief characteristic. The speakers are also listeners. Each one fits his comments to what the others say. There is an immediacy and a constancy of response by each participant to what is revealed from the minds and feelings of the others. The whole process is an exchange of feelings and ideas, with the understanding and convictions of each member of the group being modified by the contributions of the others. Another important characteristic of good conversation is that it is an honest communication and interrelating of ideas and feelings, and not at all a performance in which successive speakers seek to win admiration for their skill as speakers.

Public speaking presents problems that are also present but less evident in conversation. It is more difficult for the public speaker than for the conversationalist to tailor what he is saying to the immediate reactions of listeners. However, he should never forget that their feelings and ideas are fully as real and significant to them as his are to him. They respond with doubt to some statements, with antagonism to others, with misunderstanding to some, and with willing acceptance to some. If the speaker is talking with his listeners, not making statements at or toward them, he will be alert to detect and interpret their responses and will shift and adjust his modes of presentation in accordance with their reactions.

The conversational mode requires special efforts by the speaker. He will be able to detect the responsive reactions of his audience if he invites and induces them to make their responses overt and clear. He should indicate that he is trying to think with them, rather than to dictate their thoughts, by use of such expressions as, "You yourselves have probably observed . . . ," and "If you will judge this from your own experience . . ." He should intersperse questions through his presentation and make clear that he is watching alertly to learn their responses to the questions. He should use illustrations drawn from their experiences as well as his own. He should make it clear that he is trying to find a solution for a problem that is as much theirs as his. He should indicate his need to know their doubts and perplexities so that he may try to deal with them. And he should communicate that he is seeking a basis of mutual understanding, rather than trying to impose his own. These are qualities of conversation that should be retained, so far as possible, in platform speaking. They unite speaker and listeners in a mutual quest.

Use Approved Forms of Etiquette

Speech has its own rules of etiquette, most of which are comprised within the principle of manifesting self-respect and respect for the others present. In conversation this means sharing the opportunity for talk rather than engaging in monologues; not interrupting others; bearing one's own responsibility for the development of topics under discussion; maintaining the sociable tone; showing a live interest in the remarks of others; and being alert to invite comments from participants who may be eager to speak but slow to interject themselves into the flow of talk. As listeners, in all kinds of situations, etiquette requires that one not only attend carefully to what others are saying but that he also provide visible cues that demonstrate beyond question the reality of his interest. Listening etiquette also requires that even when the listener may strongly disagree with what is being said, he should at least make it clear that he is listening and that he is giving consideration to the real meaning of the speaker, before expressing distaste for his sentiments. In public speaking, since the situation is more formalized than in conversation, the rules of etiquette are more detailed.

a. When there are several speakers for an occasion, good taste dictates that they should listen to one another and that those about to speak should not distract the audience's attention by openly scanning their own notes.

b. Normally the speaker's attire should be a bit more formal than that worn by most of his listeners, since he will be the focus of attention.

c. In opening his talk, the speaker should acknowledge the chairman and the audience. Often a smile and a nod will suffice. A simple "Mr. Chairman, Ladies, and Gentleman," or "Friends," usually is preferable to more detailed acknowledgement; but if there is a distinguished guest present it is proper to include his name in the salutation.

d. Since everyone present is part of the audience, it is polite for the speaker to distribute his remarks fairly evenly around the group. He should of course, avoid systematically turning from one side to another, like a weathercock swinging in the breeze.

Use Your Body to Contribute to the Message

Bodily bearing is a major cue to the real meanings, often unintended, that are aroused by the speaker even when he does not wish to communicate them. If the speaker's body is squeezed into a cringe and his eyes shift uneasily, it would be hard for the listeners to believe he really has an urge to communicate his ideas to them. When the speaker's bearing suggests confident poise and an eagerness to get his message accepted, then his signs given off and his signs given carry the same message and thus reinforce one another.

Gestures are the natural physical evidence of the speaker's desire to use all his resources to aid his communication.[8] In conversation, where the participants feel little strain, many gestures are used spontaneously to support what is said. Whenever people really mean to communicate, they do it with their whole bodies. But in delivering a public speech, the speaker may be talking in part to himself—asking himself whether he is doing well, whether the listeners are pleased with him, whether he really has surveyed the facts and done the careful thinking required to insure confidence in the validity of what he is saying. These inner questions are communicated vaguely to the listeners by jerkily random or unnaturally stiff movements, or by gestures that have little relationship with the mood or the ideas indicated by the speaker's words. Effective gesturing requires that the speaker not only have his ideas prepared but that he also prepare himself—to feel confident of what he has to say and eager to say it because he has thought through the significance of his message for his listeners.

The number and kinds of gestures a speaker uses will depend on his own personality, on the nature of the subject, and on the occasion. An exuberant, extroverted individual will tend to be vitally expressive. An introverted speaker may generate an air of thoughtfulness by reserve in action, although one of his goals in his study of speech may be to develop habits of more effective communicativeness. Of course, the topic has its own influence. An appeal for students to take a stand on a controversial issue requires a more vigorous delivery than the explanation of an intricate structure, such as the pattern of an

[8] Maurice H. Krout believes that the human hand is 20,000 times as versatile as the human mouth in producing understandable signs. See his *Introduction to Social Psychology,* New York: Harper & Row, Publishers, 1942, p. 323.

enzyme molecule. The situation also makes its own demands. An indifferent audience requires more action from the speaker to arouse their interest. A large auditorium demands more sweeping gestures than a small room, if only in order that distant listeners may observe them.

Use Appropriate Facial Expressions

The face, especially around the eyes and mouth, is wonderfully expressive. Tilts of the head, smiles, frowns, furrowing of the brow, puzzled expressions, pursing of the lips, firming the muscles of the jaw: these are among hundreds of small but significant variations of facial expression that convey significant meanings. The poker face should be reserved for occasions when meaning is meant to be concealed. It is well known that when a person makes an odd or incomprehensible comment, his companions will quickly glance at his face, expecting to find there a real clue to his meaning. Effective oral discourse requires that the entire visual code correspond with and support the linguistic and vocal components of the communicative process.

The Auditory Code

Listeners are wonderfully discriminating in their interpretation of vocal qualities. One expert estimate is that the human ear normally discriminates some ten thousand qualities of the human voice.[9] Friends recognize one another's voices over the telephone even when the call is wholly unexpected and even when the one speaking may have a cold or may try to disguise his voice. Emotional states of excitement, suggesting fear, or pleasure, or bewilderment, are about as readily and accurately identified from vocal tones as from facial expressions.[10] Dialectal differences label the speaker as being from a particular section of the country, and such elements of the auditory codes as articulation and pronunciation strongly suggest the speaker's level of education and social standing. It is not only words and physical appearance that communicate meaning, but also the various qualities of the voice.

[9] Giles Wilkeson Gray and Claude Merton Wise, *The Bases of Speech,* 3rd ed., New York: Harper and Row, Publishers, Inc., 1959, p. 12.

[10] Delwin Dusenberry and Franklin Knower, "Experimental Studies of the Symbolism of Action and Voice: II," *Quarterly Journal of Speech,* 25 (February, 1939), pp. 67–75.

Whether a speaker's voice conveys a quietly confident impression to his listeners or one of anxiety and uneasiness will depend in part on such situational factors as his own self-confidence, his feeling of preparedness, his relationship with the listeners, and his feelings about the occasion and the subject matter. Other influential factors, however, are based in the neurological and anatomical structure of the speaker's vocal equipment—the environment in which he grew up and the predispositions of his listeners. A girl who grew up on a ranch in Arizona, went to Radcliffe for her education, and returned home speaking a westernized version of the New England dialect might be considered affected by her childhood friends and outlandish by her New England associates. A person (especially a man) who has an unnaturally high pitched voice, especially if accompanied by a slight tremolo, might be considered to be habitually unsure of himself, even though the vocal quality depends partly on physiological as well as social or psychological factors.

As listeners, it is well to listen again when a strong impression results from a first hearing of a speaker's voice; it may be that certain cues to meaning are so exaggerated in importance that others are being missed. If a man lisps or substitutes *w* for *r* he may not be at all effeminate or babyish, despite the first impression to that effect which listeners receive. If his voice sounds rasping, or shrill, or too loud, he nevertheless may not be bombastic, or dogmatic, or irritable. Even if his voice is soft or his words muffled in articulation, he may not be uncertain or stupid. Listeners should learn to be suspicious of their own first reactions to vocal qualities. But speakers should be aware that how they use their voice does convey strong messages, which may be far different from what they want or expect.

It is well known that when an individual listens to a recording of his own voice, he usually is startled and feels definitely that it does not sound like himself. Even when his friends assure him that the recording is genuinely representative of how he talks, he still feels that something is wrong. The reasons are many. For one thing, a person hears himself partly through the bone structure of the head, as well as through the airwaves between his mouth and his ear; and the bones considerably modify the quality of the sound. For another thing, everyone interprets himself, including the sound of his voice, in terms of his own self-image, which is always different—and sometimes widely different—from the way others observe him. It is wise to have one's voice recorded for self-study; and it is wise to study attentively the reactions of friends and strangers to one's vocal qualities; for these factors are constantly conveying a stream of messages concerning the speaker's personality—and not always the message he desires.

A person's character is what he is; his personality is what he is thought to be. And, as Wendell Johnson has acutely pointed out, "Generally speaking, the relationship between speech and personality is so close that the two terms can hardly be disentangled." Then he added an even more striking observation: "Speech is not only the evidence of personality, but it is probably the chief means by which it is molded. It seems hardly possible that either term could have any significant meaning in isolation from the other."[11] Here, then, are two reasons why the voice matters tremendously. First, rightly or wrongly, people form distinct and emphatic impressions of a person's personality by the way he speaks. And, second, the way a person speaks is heard more constantly, and less critically, by himself than by anyone else—for which reason there is a tendency (not invariable, but persistent) for a person's personality to take on the attributes suggested by his voice, both for better and for worse.[12]

Rudolf Dreikurs, a psychiatric family counselor, provides a convincing illustration for his thesis that "communication takes place only to a small extent on the verbal level" but far more significantly through "intonation, inflection, volume, speed and other characteristics of the spoken word and sentence."[13] He cites the well-known instance of a mother calling for her child to come in from the playground for dinner, and having to call three or four times before the child actually does come in. However, says Dreikurs, this is neither an example of disobedience nor of failure of communication. Actually, he says, the mother does not mean it at first and would be as surprised as the child would be if he immediately came in. What she does mean is that dinner is about ready and pretty soon he must come home. Each call in succession is a warning that the time is drawing closer. Finally, when she really does want him to come, the quality of her voice changes distinctly and the child, recognizing that now she means it, instantly appears. In all manner of situations, participants realize when a speaker

[11] Wendell Johnson, "Speech and Personality," *ETC.*, 6 (1948), p. 84.

[12] Perhaps this is why Ben Jonson, the Elizabethan dramatist, made the oft-quoted statement: "Speak that I may know you, for speech most shows the man."

[13] Rudolf Dreikurs, "Communication within the Family," *Central States Speech Journal,* XI (Autumn, 1959), p. 13.

really means it; and it is often from his voice that they recognize what it is that he really means.

Adjusting Differences That Make a Difference

As has been indicated, every individual's voice is so different from others that friends have no difficulty in recognizing one another's voices even when there is considerable distortion from a cold, or external noises, or deliberate intent to disguise the voice. It has also been pointed out that different regions of the country have their own special dialects; and different social strata have their own identifying vocal attributes. In many ways vocal differences are natural and valuable. But there also are differences that interfere with communication (such as inadequate volume, or muffled articulation); and there are differences that lead to undesirable presumptions about the speaker's personality, or his ability. These differences should be dealt with in the following ways:

1. *Take care to have your voice accurately diagnosed.* To a degree this is done whenever friends or strangers respond to your speech, perhaps by indicating a failure to hear or to understand what is said, or perhaps with signs of displeasure with the quality of the voice. When it is feasible to have a recording made of your voice, you should study it as objectively as possible and with the aid of another person to identify the impressions which your voice creates. Your speech instructor or another expert in speech improvement may make a voice and articulation inventory for you and suggest factors in need of improvement.

2. *Learn to recognize significant voice and phonetic differences.* Improvement or correction does not follow from diagnosis alone. The way we speak is closely correlated with the way we hear. If you hear your own vocal pitch with satisfaction or even with acceptance, then it sounds like you, and you probably won't want to change it even though others may hear it as thin, high, and weak. Distorted articulation may be interpreted by the speaker's own ears as being marks of casual, natural, informal characteristics, which he associates with both his voice and his personality. However, if others interpret these same sound characteristics as indicating slovenliness, and if they result in misunderstanding of what is said, it is well for the speaker to learn to hear them as undesirable rather than as desirable attributes. Recording can help. So can a speech expert.

3. *Correct the problems that make a difference.* Some difficulties may be so deep-seated, either anatomically or psychologically, that

only an expert speech pathologist can help solve them. Others may be implanted firmly but less deeply through habituation. Still others may result from mere carelessness and inattentiveness. The careless errors may generally be eliminated simply by learning about them, by learning what is more acceptable, and by an act of will to replace the ineffective with the effective sounds. The habitual errors in voice production or in articulation will require considerable patient practice, based on sound exercises,[14] and supervised by a trained observer. Whether the problem is so deep-seated as to require clinical treatment, or may be dealt with by attentiveness or by exercises, a knowledge of the fundamentals of voice production will be helpful.

Voice

Physically, voice is produced by a column of air that is forced from the lungs and sets up a vibration of the vocal folds in the larynx as it passes between them. Thus, sound waves are produced, and as they pass up the throat, mostly into the mouth, some are screened by a number of vocal cavities responsible primarily for the ultimate quality of the voice. The result is that the human voice has the same characteristics as any sound—namely, pitch (frequency), rate (time), quality (wave composition), and loudness (intensity and energy).

Pitch

Audiences are sensitive to the pitch of a speaker's voice, for pitch not only is correlated with sex (lower for men than for women) and with age (lower for adults than for children) but is also an index of the confidence and poise of the speaker. You may well recall how, in times of emotional stress, your pitch tends to rise, making your voice sound strained or even shrill. A further point to keep in mind is that in normal conversational speech there are continuous pitch variations known as inflections. Mono-pitch, or the fixation of the voice on one pitch level, is wearing upon listeners and should be avoided. The best means of obtaining good pitch variation is to follow the advice given earlier—to be conversational and communicative.

[14] Many textbooks on voice problems have extensive exercise materials. One that is generally useful is Elise Hahn, Charles W. Lomas, Donald E. Hargis, and Daniel Vandragen, *Basic Voice Training for Speech,* New York: McGraw-Hill, Inc., 1957.

Loudness

The two principal faults of amplitude are speaking too loudly, thus blasting the ears of your listeners, and speaking too softly, thereby making it difficult for them to hear you. If you imagine you are talking to three or four individuals seated near the rear, and speak directly at (though, of course, not always to) them, you should achieve about the proper volume. Variations in loudness are of great value in achieving both over-all speech variety and emphasis. Remember that dropping the voice to a near whisper is often as effective for emphasis as raising it to a near shout, and in small groups may be far preferable. Some speakers tend not to vary the level of loudness, which prevents their using emphasis of this kind. And, like mono-pitch, the monotony of unvarying sound volume is wearing on listeners.

Rate

For most persons, normal speech tends to range from 125 to 160 words a minute; however, individuals vary considerably in this respect. There are two aspects of rate: the fundamental rate of speaking and the use of pauses between sentences and phrases to achieve good oral communication. Many individuals are warned by their families and friends that they talk too fast when their problem is more likely to be that they do not talk distinctly enough. Rate becomes a problem primarily when, because of nervousness, a speaker talks so rapidly that his words are jumbled together; or when he pours out his words at a uniform rate, without the natural pauses and variations that are required to lend their share of meaning to the ideas being communicated; or when interjections such as "uh" are interspersed through the speech; or when the sentences are broken up into relatively uniform breath-groups rather than into the naturally diversified groupings that relate to the meanings of the words.

Unduly slow speech drags, dissipating the listeners' interest. The rate should be energetic, varied, and suited to the needs of the occasion. When talking with a large group, or when speaking into a public address system, the rate normally should be somewhat slower than with a small group. Solemn or impressive subject matter also tends to require a slower pace. Scenes of excitement normally are described in rapid speech. As in other aspects of speaking, the standards of good conversation provide a generally safe guide.

Quality

The quality of a voice is one of its most individualized attributes. It is a leading cue to the personality of the speaker. When you recognize a voice over the telephone, it is probably the distinctive quality that provides the clue. This does not mean, however, that everyone should be satisfied with the quality of his voice simply because it is his. Speakers often develop a quality that is too thin. Another voice may be guttural or harsh or throaty. Confidence, friendliness, and a genuine interest in what you are saying and in your listeners have an immediate effect upon the quality of your voice, for it is peculiarly susceptible to psychological states and attitudes.

Articulation

After voice is produced by vibration of the air in the vocal folds of the larynx and resonated in the cavities of the throat and head, we still do not have articulate human speech. There remains the final process in which such organs as the teeth, tongue, lips, and hard and soft palates are instrumental in the actual making of the specific and particular audible sounds that are the speech symbols. This process is called articulation. In a broad sense, we may define articulation as meaning the distinctness with which speech sounds are formed.

No speaker can afford to be careless of articulation. He inevitably pays too great a price for such inaccuracies and faults. Although important in everyday conversation, it becomes more so in the public situation. For one thing, public speech must be instantly intelligible so that the audience will not be distracted from what is being said.

Although a speech is more important for its ideas than for the articulation and pronunciation used to communicate the ideas, faulty articulation and pronunciation may become grave barriers to effective presentation, as we have noted earlier. Since faults in articulation and pronunciation are widespread, it is important to analyze those most frequently encountered.

One meaning of articulation is *jointed.* The articulation of speech sounds, especially the consonants, is the function of the joint operation of two parts of the mechanism: tongue with hard palate, soft palate, or teeth; lip with teeth or the other lip; and, in the case of the sound [h], the vocal folds. This function is one of modifying the outgoing breath stream: squeezing it (as for [f] and [v]), and splitting it (as for [s] and [z]), stopping and exploding it (as for [p] and [b]). Another pair of articulators are the soft palate and back of the throat, which combine to keep the air stream from going through the nasal cavities. Among all English sounds, only those for the [n], [m], and the final sound in *ring* have this valve open to permit nasal resonance.

Errors of Articulation

There are many sources of error in articulation. The mechanism and the timing are so complex that it is truly amazing that we manage to stay within any norms at all. Physical and/or psychological effects in childhood, the emulation of an admired person, or even ordinary development of speech organs, can lead to articulation errors of distortion, substitution, or omission.

These and other characteristics of speech are not easily understood without the right kind of training. To the amateur ear, very often a slightly distorted sound, such as the [r] made through pursed lips, will seem to be a sound substitution, as, in this case, a [w]. Anyone can diagnose the voice quality that is heard when a person has a "code id his head" and the soft-palate-back-of-the-throat valve is closed, as "nasal," although the opposite is the case. What is being heard is *de*nasal quality, and the absence of normal nasal resonance.

As we have said, it is not important to learn all about voice and articulation, but it is important to know, as a listener, that voice and articulation errors may not indicate what they seem to about the speaker; and equally important for you to learn, as a speaker, is what faults, if any, you do have and how you can eliminate them.

Pronunciation

Correct pronunciation refers to the utterance of words within listener norms or expectancies for sounds and stress or accent. If you habitually make an articulation error, a particular sound is always distorted or omitted wherever it may occur. Thus, if you habitually say something like *dis* for *dish,* you are likely to say something like *sewer* for *sure*. On the other hand, you may not make this kind of substitution, generally, but may have learned to mispronounce *issue* as *iss-you*.

Pronunciation errors can be as damaging to the speaker's purpose as other speech deviations we have discussed. Listeners, usually without thinking, will respond to pronunciation errors as marks of ignorance,

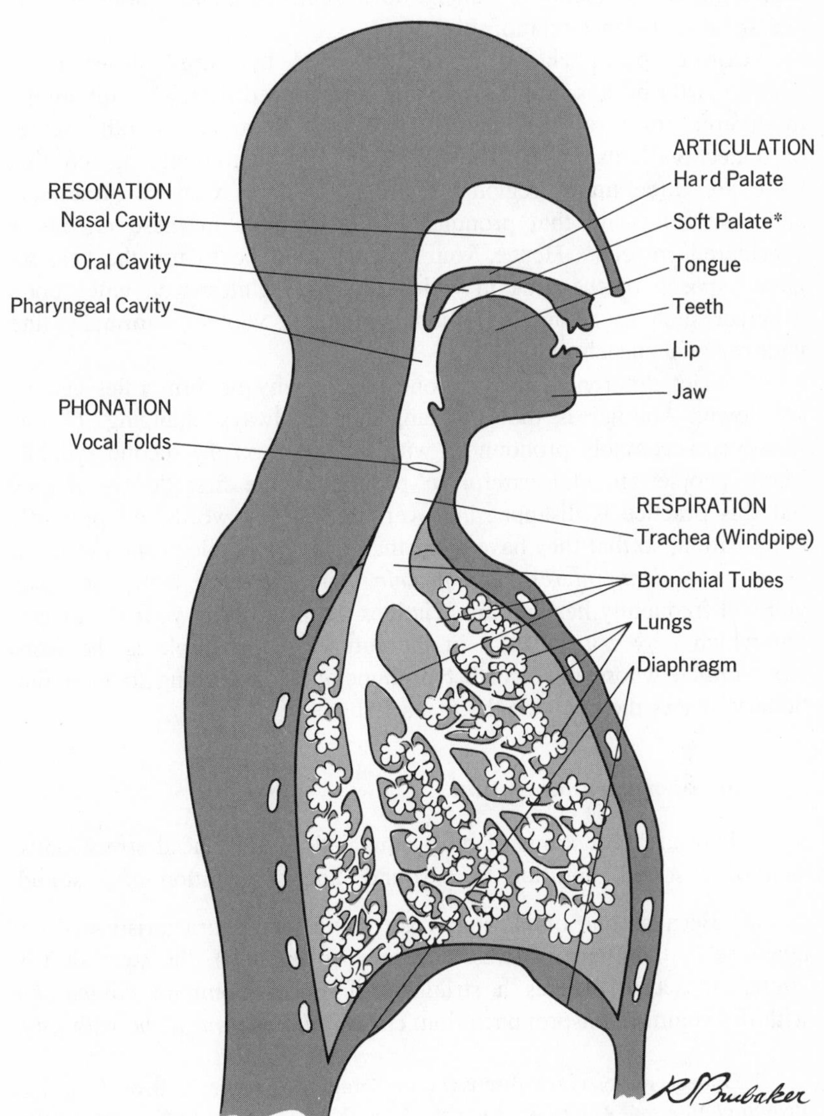

*For most speech sounds the soft palate is raised, separating the nasal cavity from the oral cavity. The soft palate is lowered when producing the nasals m, n and ng.

of lack of authority, of lack of common ground, and often very properly, as a sign of poor preparation. Just a small error in pronunciation can sometimes do irremediable damage to an initial communication in normal speaker–listener relationships.

Correct pronunciation is not governed by hard-and-fast rules. This is partly because some words are pronounced somewhat differently in different parts of the country. Although there are literally scores of dialect variants in the United States, it is commonly agreed that there are three major regional dialects—Eastern, General American, and Southern—and that pronunciation acceptable in these regions is considered correct.[15] Hence, your guide should be to use the best regional speech of the area in which you live. Unless you enter upon a career such as acting or radio announcing, you will normally find your regional speech satisfactory.

Dialect differences provide one reason why no firm rules can be set down. Another is that the language is always changing. *Canine* was once acceptably pronounced with the stress on the second syllable. Many people are still careful to pronounce the first "c" in *Arctic,* but this practice is disappearing over time. Many words are presently in transition, so that they have more than one acceptable pronounciation, as *advertisement, interest,* and *protein.* And there are words of which you will frequently hear pronounciations that are not in your dictionary, but which may appear in it in the future. An example is the word *comparable,* whose only correct pronunciation, according to your dictionary, places the stress on the *first* syllable.

Kinds of Mispronunciation

There are four kinds of mispronunciation: misplaced stress, omission of a sound, addition of a sound, and substitution of a sound.

1. Because one of the important identifying characteristics of our language is its pattern of stress (actually of *un*stress), the mere shift of stress, or accent, makes a striking difference. Compare *cómparable* with the common mispronunciation, *compárable,* or *mustáche* with *mús-*

[15] Dialect regions are discussed in detail in Arthur J. Bronstein, *The Pronunciation of American English,* New York: Appleton-Century-Crofts, 1960; and in Charles K. Thomas, *An Introduction to the Phonetics of American English,* 2nd ed., New York: The Ronald Press Company, 1958. Regional differences in pronunciation of specific words are recorded in John S. Kenyon and Thomas A. Knott, *A Pronouncing Dictionary of American English,* Springfield, Mass.: G. & C. Merrian Company, 1944.

tache. If your ear expects one pronunciation, it sometimes has difficulty in even identifying the word when stressed the other way. This is partly because, you will notice, you automatically change the vowel sounds.

2. Phoneticians identify many pronunciations marred by omission of a sound as typical of less-educated speech. Examples are: *guvment* for *government, ast* for *asked, blong* for *belong, recunize* for *recognize,* and *pitcher* for *picture.*

3. Similarly, certain pronunciations which have an extra sound added have been associated with less-educated speech. *Athelete* for *athlete, grievious* for *grievous, wunst* for *once,* and *filum* for *film,* are examples of such mispronunciations.

4. The fourth kind of mispronunciation is sound substitution: one sound made in place of another, as in the example of *issue* cited at the beginning of this section. Other examples include *git* for *get, imbred* for *inbred, emvelope* for *envelope,* and *expiriment* for *experiment.*

Sources of Mispronunciation

Sources of these errors are many. Sometimes the mispronunciations are simply easier, sometimes they are left-over childhood errors, or sometimes we just hear a word mispronounced and accept it and use it as correct.

Two related sources are important for every student of speech to understand and to guard against. One is the spelling mispronunciation and the other is the stock of words in your reading, but not in your speaking, vocabulary. The *ch* in *chasm* is correctly pronounced *k,* the *sch* in *schism* is correctly pronounced *s*, the *b* in *subtle* and the *l* in *calm* and *salmon* are properly omitted. Yet, sometimes you will hear words pronounced as they are spelled. Similarly, the speaker risks unnecessarily distracting his listeners by allowing himself to pronounce unfamiliar words as they are spelled without making sure of the pronunciation that his listeners expect. Or, if he has not practiced orally, a word with which he is perfectly familiar in his reading seems unpronounceable in the speaking situation; it is not yet in his speaking vocabulary.

The solution is simple. *Do* practice orally. And if in doubt about a pronunciation, find out what is correct.

Finding the Correct Pronunciation

You would expect that finding correct pronunciations is a simple matter. And in most instances, it is. A recent dictionary, recent because the language is changing and any dictionary is starting to become obsolete as it leaves the presses, will be dependable in most instances of doubt.

Often, however, the editors of dictionaries recognize more than one pronunciation for certain words. What then? You need to learn which is preferred, as well as which, among your listeners, is the pronunciation that they are least likely to notice. The pronunciation expected by your particular listeners will depend largely upon geographical location in some cases, upon specialized vocabularies in others, or on the influence of a teacher or even the President of the United States. President Kennedy in 1961 probably influenced the expected pronunciation of *Laos*. American politicians and newscasters have created doubt about their knowledge of Southeast Asia by differential use of the pronunciations, *Vietnahm* and *Vietnaem*.

In some cases it may be a toss-up between two pronunciations. In such an instance, play it safe with the preferred one in the dictionary.

To assure correct pronunciation of both the familiar and unfamiliar words that you may use, determine how they are expected to be heard simply because it is the way they are usually heard; and consult the dictionary freely when in doubt.

Conclusion

The auditory code has been discussed with particular concern for those acoustic aspects of speech delivery called voice, articulation, and pronunciation. Listeners associate certain faults in the use of these vocal processes with personality and communication traits that may or may not be appropriate to the speaker: ignorance, disinterest, lack of authority, incompetence. Further, any unusual characteristics of voice, articulation, and pronunciation are, at the least, distracting and, therefore, reduce the probability that a speaker will achieve his specific purposes. Before any improvement can be initiated, a speaker must learn to hear the differences that make a difference; it is not likely to help if he is merely told what is wrong. For voice and articulation faults, any improvement program is likely to require at least the guidance of a professional person in speech. The various kinds and sources of pronunciation errors are more easily identified and more easily remedied. In all cases, speakers need to bring or keep voice and diction within inconspicuous norms.

For both the visual and the auditory codes, the factor of chief significance is that the message a speaker conveys to his listeners is comprised of many cues in addition to the words that are spoken. Unless standards of acceptability are maintained for bodily and vocal delivery, the speaker may often arouse reactions which are far different from those he desires. By attaining communicative skill in the visual and auditory codes, one can add new dimensions of influence to his speaking.

Exercises

Questions for Discussion

1. What do we mean by *code?* Discuss the five functions of codes which we have identified. What, specifically, is meant by visual code and auditory code?
2. What unintended meanings may be conveyed when a code is misused? How are codes related to the principles of delivery?
3. Define empathy; illustrate your definition with examples. How may a speaker use empathy to help accomplish his aims? How may its effects counteract what he wishes to communicate?
4. How should the etiquette of speaking situations be adapted to your classroom? Have you noted instances on public occasions in which these rules of etiquette have been flouted? Were the results detrimental to effective communication?
5. What is meant by *gesture?* How many gestures have been identified? How many gestures do you use in your own speaking? How does your own use of gesture differ in varying circumstances?
6. To what extent and in what manner should gesturing be practiced? What dangers must be avoided in such practice? What is the fundamental source of effectiveness in use of gesture?
7. What is the importance of facial expressions in speaking? What is meant by the *poker face?* When is it helpful, and when detrimental?
8. Do you pronounce all of the words cited in the expected manner? If you found that you do have a pronunciation error, what would you say is its source?
9. Why do people hear themselves differently from the way others hear them? Is this a flaw in hearing? Is it learned?
10. What should you do if you find that some characteristic of your voice or articulation does not come within the inconspicuous norm?

• *Projects for Speaking and Listening*

1. The class may be divided into pairs and each student asked to give a brief speech analyzing the total delivery characteristics of his paired classmate. Each pair should talk over the project to ensure full understanding and to try to have each speech present suggestions and evaluations that will be truly helpful to the student whose delivery is being analyzed. The speeches should present constructive suggestions and avoid fault-finding. The purpose of this assignment is twofold: (1) to help you become a better critic of delivery, and (2) to give to each member of the class an objective and constructive analysis of his speaking manner by a classmate.

2. Select a well-known public speaker whom you have heard in person or on radio or television, and present to the class a brief speech in which you evaluate and characterize in some detail his qualities of delivery.

3. Analyze your own delivery in the speeches that you have thus far delivered, noting your elements of strength and the ways in which you need to improve. If a recording machine is available to you, record a two- or three-minute speech, and evaluate your own vocal qualities by means of a playback. Discuss your delivery in a conference with your instructor and determine to profit from the suggestions he makes to you.

4. Make recordings of each member of the class in which you each say exactly the same thing for the first four or five sentences. Play them back in a different order and see how easily each speaker will be identified by everyone but himself. Discuss with each other and your instructor the significance of this phenomenon.

5. During an evening of conversation, watch the other members of the group specifically to observe the way their meanings are conveyed through signs given off and by empathy. Be prepared to report to the class instances you observe in which visual, auditory, and linguistic codes used in the conversation either notably reinforce one another or notably contradict one another. Cite instances in which you believe one or more of the participants probably misinterpreted codes unintentionally used by others.

6. If facilities are available, have a brief talk recorded on video tape. Then view the tape and analyze your use of the visual and auditory codes.

Part Four

Communicative Functions and Forms

10 · *Sharing Understanding*

Our own generation, more than in any previous historic era, has been concerned with the acquiring, interpreting, and disseminating of information. So much that is new has been learned in both the physical and the social sciences that our age is characterized in part by what is called The Information Explosion. The demand for understanding has led to the very rapid spread of education, until college attendance today matches high school attendance of a generation ago, and graduate study has become as matter-of-fact as undergraduate study was in the 1940's. Yet there is nothing really new about the need to know. Over three thousand years ago the elderly author of the book of Proverbs was earnestly advising young men that, whatever else they might do to advance their well-being, "with all thy getting, get understanding. Exalt her, and she shall promote thee; she shall bring thee to honour, when thou dost embrace her."[1] The need to know is deep-seated and as old as the human race. But never before has there been so much that needed to be known. Never before has there been a society which absolutely demanded the widespread possession, understanding, and sharing of information.

[1] The Authorized, or King James, translation, Proverbs, 4:7–8.

The Need for Information

Francis Bacon, back in the Elizabethan Age, explained one reason for the acquisition of information when he wrote that "The human understanding is no dry light." It does not burn by itself. It requires fuel. The keenest of minds cannot operate effectively unless it is provided with the relevant facts. Cleverness, insight, imagination, ingenuity, originality, intuition are essential for genuine creativity, but they cannot operate in a vacuum. The judgment of one who knows is usually preferable to the hunch of one who merely thinks or feels he is right. A doctor, a physicist, a plumber, or a woman shopping in a supermarket are most likely to make wise decisions only on the basis of dependable knowledge properly interpreted.

The need for knowledge has become so urgent that a new occupation has been developed, known as "information retrieval." The research chemist working in the laboratories of a major industry not only works at problems of analysis and experimentation but also through library indexes, often programed on computer cards, to keep abreast of what others have discovered. In any kind of writing, or speaking, or thinking, a major problem is to locate the facts that are required for sound judgments. The problem is usually not that "so little is known" about a subject under examination but that "so much is known which I do not know." Some of these problems, as they confront speakers, have been discussed in Chapter 5. How to use reference materials has become an essential element in everyone's education. The sheer difficulty of sifting through the masses of available data has become one of the hardest challenges of our time.

The need for knowledge is always a need not for enough information but for the essential information. There is wisdom in an anonymous squib printed on the menu of a roadside diner: "Knowledge is power only if you know what facts to bother about." So important are the factors of selecting and evaluating pertinent elements of information that Chapter 7 has been devoted to this problem. As any almanac or encyclopedia attests, facts as such are available in confusing abundance. What is needed is accurate understanding in the selection, utilization, and adaptation to the occasion of the precise information that is required by the nature of the subject matter and the needs of the speakers and listeners who are participating in its consideration.

The need for information may be summarized in the statement: most problems can be solved only through the proper use of relevant data. This is true of all kinds of problems. We appreciate music, painting, or art photography when we know enough about them. Mathematics, physics, and chemistry may seem frighteningly complicated until one learns enough about them to be able to understand their principles. Problems of foreign policy may seem either too complicated or too simple before the facts involved are known. We may blame a friend for some conduct that seems strange until we learn why he behaved in that manner. A particular book may be too deep for understanding until more is known about its basic content. Even entertaining discourse depends more than we realize upon knowledge. For example, jokes about the Jewish religion or about humorous experiences in Istanbul make little or no sense except to those who know the meaning of the traditions and the terms being used. And for more serious problems, such as making up our minds what to think about race relations or economic policies, the first and overriding need is to get the facts.

Information as Shared Understandings

Facts may, of course, be known by individuals in isolation. Some kinds of facts are deliberately kept as secrets. But these are rarities. Most information is valuable precisely because it is shared. People's feelings toward one another depend to a large extent upon their having similar understandings. Their ability to work together depends upon their sharing of knowledge. Social and occupational groupings occur to a large degree on the basis of the amount and kind of education individuals have attained. So important is the sharing of what is known that sociologists have coined the term *the Sociology of Knowledge*[2] to indicate their view that people who share a particular body of knowledge form a distinct community. Thus, there is a fellow-feeling and unity of interests among philosophers, or linguists, or agricultural economists, or abstract painters, no matter what their nationality or where they live. The sharing of mutual information creates a universe of discourse; for the people who share understandings also share mutual interests and have both need for and pleasure in the exchange of ideas about the things they know in common. Such "knowledge-communities"

[2] The history of the work on this concept is traced by H. Otto Dahlke, "The Sociology of Knowledge," in H. E. Barnes, Howard and F. B. Becker, eds., *Contemporary Social Theory,* New York: Appleton-Century-Crofts, 1940, pp. 64–89.

not only knit together those who share information, but they also separate and divide members of one such community from all the others.

Moreover, all such communities become something of a threat to the stability of all the others who learn about it. As Merton phrases it: "Not only do there develop distinct universes of discourse, but the existence of any one universe challenges the validity and legitimacy of the others."[3] When the peoples of the Far East learned a hundred years or so ago about the science and technology of the West, their faith in their own humanistic civilization began to waver. And when the peoples of the West began to learn about the intuitive methods of Eastern thought, new approaches to Western logic began to multiply.

Effects of Shared Understandings

The facts that: (a) "information" differs from individual to individual and from group to group, and (b) these differences lead to competition, have a variety of consequences:

1. *Most problems can be solved only when the right information is viewed similarly by those who must jointly deal with them.* If a task is to be performed by a single individual acting alone, perhaps to solve problems in algebra, or to construct a birdhouse, all that is needed is for him to know what to do and how to do it. In every cooperative enterprise, however, what is essential is not only that the right facts be dealt with but that they be understood in the same way by all the participants. Mistakes occur when one or more of the group does not see the facts in the same light or with the same emphasis as do the others. So important is this commonality of understanding, in fact, that some political scientists insist that governing policies work effectively not when they are right but when they are widely supported by people who interpret them similarly. There is no right answer for a vast number of problems, such as how to eradicate slums; but social action becomes possible when, and only when, there is a general agreement about the whole panoply of facts, ideologies, ideals, ethical values, and political philosophies, which are involved in the problem. Similarity of understanding is what makes commonality of action a possibility. Problems that depend for their solution upon joint action inevitably

[3] Robert Merton, *Social Theory and Social Structure,* rev., New York: The Free Press, 1964, p. 457.

depend also upon the sharing of understanding. This is one reason why informative discourse is essential.

2. *Misunderstandings on matters of mutual concern lead to aggressive behavior.* It is not only true that a lack of shared understandings prevents constructive cooperation; it also breeds conflict. Individuals or groups become defensively hostile when they confront others whose knowledge is contrary to or even different from their own. This tendency is observable even on a college campus, where the students majoring in the sciences and in the humanities may tend to be defensively critical of one another. All religions are concerned with the same basic problems, but their differences of interpretation have historically had bloody consequences. When individuals are arguing (or nations are at war) and one of them exclaims, "I don't see it your way at all," the indication is that further argument is fruitless unless they are willing to proceed to the relatively calmer task of determining what understandings they have in common and why in other respects they interpret the essential information differently. This is another reason why there is an urgent social need for informative discourse.

3. *The sharing of understandings establishes and maintains social solidarity.* In the international realm it is notable that in recent years there have been wide splits between France and its normal allies, and also between Communist China and Russia, because of competing understandings concerning matters of vital importance. Alliances between nations or individuals depend upon mutual understanding. There is considerable substance in the proverb, "Birds of a feather flock together." Like attracts like. Those who speak the same language whether it be German, Japanese, or the language of literary criticism or of existentialism, feel a mutuality of relationship. The creation of social bonds is still another major function of informative discourse.

4. *The clarification of one's own ideas is aided by sharing understandings.* It is a commonplace that we know what we really understand about a subject more clearly when we explain it to another person. This is perhaps one of the most significant factors in the psychology of the audience. The presence of other minds to which one is revealing the content of his own constitutes a valuable challenge. Realizing that others may see the facts differently than we do, we tend to explore them more carefully and to analyze them more fully. For oneself it may be enough to feel the rightness of an explanation; but when presenting the explanation to others, it needs to be satisfactorily justified. This is a major reason why making speeches may seem to be difficult. You know what you understand or believe about a subject sufficiently

well to satisfy yourself; but when you must submit your understanding to the critical scrutiny of others, this means that you must also scrutinize it more carefully yourself. The challenge to convey information constitutes a prior challenge to validate it. And this, too, is a reason why informative discourse is important.

5. *The sharing of understandings heightens confidence in their correctness.* Social psychologists have established beyond reasonable question that individuals are unable, except in rare circumstances, to maintain their own understandings when these are manifestly contrary to those of the group.[4] An instance of this conformity trait is provided in an experimental situation where three lines are drawn upon the blackboard, one of which is slightly shorter than the other two. Then the professor and the class agree to call the short line the longest of the three, to test the effect of their combined testimony on the judgment of another student, who is not a party to their agreement. What happens is that the subject who is being tested will become disturbed and uncertain of his own judgment when he finds it is uniformly opposed by all the other supposedly unbiased observers. Aside from experimental situations, it is well known that individuals hold their opinions and have confidence in their presumed knowledge far more tenaciously when they know that their understandings are shared by others. A further legitimate function of informative discourse is to strengthen confidence in knowledge by making apparent its generalized acceptance.

The Nature of Information

Both the need for and the importance of informative discourse become more evident in consideration of the nature of information. A dictionary definition of *fact* is "that which has actual existence." For many purposes this definition suffices. One can say, "It is a fact that the population of the United States in 1967 reached two

[4] Many studies relevant to this conclusion are summarized in two chapters: Harold H. Kelley and John W. Thibaut, "Experimental Studies of Group Problem Solving and Process"; and Henry W. Riecken and George C. Homans, "Psychological Aspects of Social Structure," in Gardner Lindzey, ed., *Handbook of Social Psychology,* Reading, Mass.: Addison-Wesley Publishing Company, Inc., II Vols., 1954. See also, Theodore G. Grove, "Attitude Convergence in Small Groups," *Journal of Communication,* XV (December, 1965), pp. 226–38.

hundred million," and if challenged can cite the Census Bureau as the source. On closer examination, the nature of information becomes less clear and more complicated. If we are to become skilled in the transmission of information as speakers, and in receiving and interpreting it as listeners, it becomes important to understand some of the respects in which information itself is ambiguous.

"Anything which reduces uncertainty is information," Claude Shannon wrote in 1948 in his essay on "A Mathematical Theory of Communication." This became a basis for what is known as "information theory"—the reduction of information to measurable bits that can be indicated by mathematical digits and fed into a computer. The crucial consideration here is not what may be right or wrong, but what may be identified beyond reasonable doubt, so that different observers will perceive it as being the same. This approach is important not only to computer programers but also to speakers and listeners; for the emphasis is upon definiteness, clarity, and mutuality of understanding.

Another problem in relation to the nature of information was stated by a philosopher, Angus Sinclair, when he wrote: "Our knowledge of simple facts depends to some extent on the attitudes or views we hold about more general issues, in the sense that if these attitudes were different then the facts we know would be different also."[5] As he points out, the facts we notice are selected, out of the totality of the facts we might have noticed, by our interests and experience, and are interpreted in terms of our theories and abilities. What gets through this series of barriers is a tiny residue, or a small selection of a small selection of the universe of available facts. Yet for each individual, "It is the scraps and fragments of the independent reality that he knows directly."[6] Since each of us has his own interests and experiences, and each has his own theories and abilities, we share a commonality of knowledge only in a general way. Much that we know is part of the general social value system; some of it is our very own and is unlike what is known in this same intimate way by others. To this extent, the nature of information is also the nature of individuals in their own special social settings. There are as many different kinds of knowledge as there are kinds of people.

As we deal with one another, there is an urgent need for reliable knowledge, which will be true not only for one but for all, and also

[5] Angus Sinclair, *The Conditions of Knowing,* New York: Harcourt, Brace & World, Inc., 1951, p. 14.

[6] Angus Sinclair, p. 158.

true to the external and existent facts. Two highly regarded authorities who have specialized in the methodology of exact inquiry both testify to the difficulty of attaining a dependable certainty of understanding. "Civilized man," one writes, "has acquired a fear of not-being-thought-reasonable, and, in order to cope with it, has developed an astonishing repertory of rationalizations."[7] And the other adds: "The curious thing is that we have no clear knowledge of what our presuppositions are."[8] One problem, in short, in searching for objective information is that we really do not want it; we want a view of events and circumstances that accords with our own egoistic needs. Objectivity is a fine test to apply to others; as for ourselves, "We know what we know, and that's the end of it."

This, then, is the problem: information, or facts, is not so much what is true—for by what tests may truth be determined? Information is what the various people concerned agree to accept as being factual. But all such agreements are complicated because everyone has a marked tendency to see the world of events in his own individual manner: to notice what he notices, to ignore what he ignores, and to interpret as he interprets. When a speaker undertakes informative discourse with the single aim of explaining factually the nature of a value system or of a process or of a situation, he confronts the initial difficulty of attaining to a correct understanding in his own mind, and a second difficulty in presenting his explanation so that it will seem reasonable to his listeners.

Clarification as a Communicative Goal

As was seen in Chapter 4, there are many purposes involved in communication. It is never possible—nor would it be desirable—to separate them entirely. When the purpose of the speaker is to explain something—say, "The Nature of the Bolshevik Revolution of 1917"—he has the primary problem of searching through the historical record to determine for himself what were the crucial facts, and to understand them in their relationships to one another, with the proper interpretation and emphasis accorded to each. The fact that this is a selective process

[7] Harold A. Larrabee, *Reliable Knowledge,* Boston: Houghton Mifflin Company, 1945, p. 59.

[8] Michael Polanyi, *Personal Knowledge,* Chicago: University of Chicago Press, 1958, p. 59.

is indicated by the number of different explanations written by competent historians of the events. There is, then, an element of self-persuasion in the process of preparing one's own ideas as to what to say and how to say it.

In the next stage, while selecting out of what one has learned the items to be presented to listeners, and deciding how to arrange them, it is essential to consider the nature of the listeners in relation to this topic. What will they already know about it? What prejudices might they—or some of them—have which will present difficulties to the speaker in getting them to accept certain crucial facts? Again there must be a problem of selection and also of arrangement of the materials—this time not as determined either by the intrinsic nature of the subject matter or by the personal wishes of the speaker, but by the needs of the prospective listeners. In a sense this process also may be considered persuasive, even though the speaker's sole purpose is to help his audience attain a reliable understanding of the subject. The persuasion involves selecting, phrasing, and organizing the data in such a way that it will be accepted by the listeners in accordance with what the speaker believes to be a true interpretation.

A third consideration is that however important and compellingly interesting the subject may be to the speaker, there is always a chance that the listeners, or at least some of them, may be uninterested in it. After all, the speaker chose the subject in large part because of his interest in it. He may also have selected the subject in part for the very reason that he thinks his audience is unjustly prejudiced or ignorantly uninformed or even indifferent to what he knows to be a highly significant historic event. One of his problems, then, is to make sure that he does arouse interest in the topic—that he makes it appear vivid, compelling, and personally intriguing to his listeners. Thus, for even the most determinedly informative speech, when the speaker is trying very hard not to impose conclusions upon his listeners but simply and wholly to enlarge and clarify their understanding of the facts, the speaker will find it essential not *only* to inform and in part to persuade, but also to interest his listeners.

This is not at all to say there is no distinction of purposes in speaking. There are very important and obvious differences. On the subject of the Bolshevik Revolution, for example, one speaker might seek persuasively to win audience acceptance of the proposition that the blundering Kerensky was displaced by a brilliant Lenin who had a superior understanding of what was needed by the Russian people. Another speaker might seek to entertain his audience with an account of the dramatic intrigues and conflicts of the "ten days that shook the world," while Lenin was maneuvering to seize power from Kerensky. Still a third speaker might seek to enlighten his listeners so that they would understand the conflict of issues and personalities—to present the essential information in such a way that each of them could make up his own mind on the basis of far better information than he had previously possessed.

When informative discourse is presented, the test of its functioning properly is whether it does, in fact, enlighten the understanding of the listeners while leaving open to their individual determination a variety of optional conclusions concerning the merits of the matter being discussed. The discourse has been truly informative when the preponderant reaction of the listeners is, "Now I see what you mean; I understand the subject more clearly and fully than I did before."

In seeking to attain this clarification for his audience, the speaker will need to relate his informative purpose and materials to:

1. *Listener interest,* by motivating a desire to accept this information through appeal to listener wants and needs, in the introductory remarks and by continuous adaptation throughout the speech;

2. *Listener experiences,* by using examples and other supports that the speaker knows are drawn from or relevant to the experiences of his auditors;

3. *Listener language level,* by using a style of discourse that will seem appropriate to the listeners because of their own linguistic habits and because of its fitness to the occasion;

4. *Listener application,* by making clear, especially in the introduction and conclusion, but also throughout the speech, how the ideas and information presented are of interest, of use, and of importance to the listeners.

Objectivity: A Goal for Speakers and Listeners

Both speakers and listeners need to make very special efforts to be objective concerning whatever subject is being discussed, if their communication is to be effective. Subjectivity, as we have seen, is a characteristic of the human personality. Objectivity, therefore, requires special consideration and special conditions. The social psychologist Erving Goffman, who has adopted forms of the game-model for his studies of human behavior, concludes that whenever two or more people meet to discuss a subject of mutual interest, they enter into a special relationship that is governed by an unspoken but real agreement to work together to accomplish their common goal. This includes an agreement not to permit their thinking about the subject to be undermined by irrelevent considerations.[9] Goffman reinforces the point emphasized in this chapter, that both the development and the communication of clear understandings are difficult, but may be expedited by speaker–listener cooperation.

For the maintenance of an objective attitude toward the subject under consideration, both speaker and listeners should establish the following safeguards:

1. Inferences, opinions, and value judgments should be avoided or at least controlled. People are not informed by being told that "This engine is superior to most other six-cylinder engines," or "Of course, coeducational colleges are preferable to those limited to men or women." Such judgments as these call for proof and belong in the category of persuasive discourse.

2. An attitude of open-mindedness is desirable, even if it is no more than hypothetical. A speaker whose intention is to explain Buddhism by comparing and contrasting it with Christianity may not in actual fact be open-minded about the relative merits of the two religions. He should keep in mind, however, that he is not trying to persuade listeners that one is better than the other. He can in fact make his comparisons and contrasts more informative if he manifests no attitude of preference for either one. For the time being, and as a device to make his sharing of understanding more effective, he should concentrate wholly upon the single aim of showing how they resemble one another in some respects and differ in others, without affirmations of which one may be the better.

3. The emphasis upon portions of the explanation should be proportionate to their importance, rather than reflective of the speaker's feelings. In explaining the various ways of investing in the stock market, you might have a distinct personal preference for mutual stocks, or speculative issues, or blue chips, and if so it would not be amiss to mention this preference, with your reasons for it. But since all three types of investment are readily available, each having its own values and limitations, a balanced explanation requires avoidance of undue emphasis upon any one of them.

4. Consistent standards should be maintained when comparisons

[9] Erving Goffman, *Encounters,* Indianapolis: Bobbs-Merrill Company, Inc., 1961.

are being made. For example, a speaker comparing foreign cars with American built automobiles, might establish such categories as original cost, upkeep, repair costs and problems, operation costs, comfort, safety, and resale conditions. To select some of the categories for consideration when speaking of American cars and different categories when discussing foreign makes would result in a distorted comparison.

5. Concrete and specific information usually serves better than abstractions and generalities when the aim is the sharing of understanding. Generalized judgments are extremely useful, as in the comment that "Dance bands that have no distinctive style have little appeal." Yet such statements make only a vague contribution to the understanding of listeners except as they are supported by concrete and specific instances.

The Speech to Inform: Speaker–Listener Responsibilities

When a public speech is to be presented for the purpose of sharing understanding, or to inform listeners about some topic, there are responsibilities of a special kind, which devolve upon both speaker and listeners.

The responsibilities of the informative speaker include the following:

1. To attain for himself a clear understanding of what he will talk about.
2. To organize what he plans to say in a way that will be clear to listeners, remembering that his reason for speaking is that they are uninformed or misinformed on the subject he will discuss.
3. To commence with an introduction that places the subject in its essential context and that defines technical or complicated terms and concepts that must be used.
4. To arouse in the listeners a need and a desire for the information he will dispense, so that they will willingly make the intellectual effort to follow his explanation through its successive stages.
5. To provide perhaps an initial summary, and probably transitional summaries, as well as a concluding summary, to help the listeners see what to expect and to interpret the sequential relationships of what they hear.
6. To be alert throughout the speech to audience indications of puzzlement, if they do not understand, or of indifference, if they lose interest, so that the explanation may be adjusted accordingly.

7. To conclude with perhaps a summary, or an anecdote that contains the nub of the explanation, or with an indication of where further information may be obtained, or with a demonstration of how the information may be helpfully utilized by the listeners.

8. When practical it is helpful to follow the talk with an opportunity for the listeners to raise questions about aspects of the topic they may not have understood, and perhaps to comment on how the speaker could have aided their understanding by developing his materials differently. If this opportunity is unavailable, the speaker should undertake to query representative members of the audience in private conversation, to determine to what degree his exposition succeeded.

9. In everything the speaker does, during his preparation and during the presentation of his speech, he should be guided by considerations of what the listeners need to advance the breadth and the depth of their understanding of the subject. The purpose of the talk is served only in the effects it has upon the understanding of the listeners.

The responsibilities of the listeners to communicative discourse include the following:

1. To concentrate their attention upon attaining an understanding of the subject, rather than upon unspoken arguments with the speaker concerning its values or liabilities.

2. To bring to bear from their own knowledge and experience facts which will aid them to enhance their understanding of the subject.

3. To signal to the speaker unobtrusively but clearly, through facial expressions, bodily movements, and in other ways when they are confused, or when they have understood a point he is making.

4. To enhance their own interest in the subject by thinking of ways in which the information is particularly meaningful to themselves.

5. To identify points of vagueness or of complexity in the speech which they do not understand, and to try to formulate questions that might elicit the kind of explanation they require.

6. To note from their own reactions the needs they will experience when they become speakers, in terms of maintaining interest and applying the information to the past and future experiences of their auditors.

The Uses of Informative Speaking

The giving and receiving of information comprises a large proportion of all oral discourse. People ask for directions on how to get where they wish to go, or how to do what they must do. They inquire into the meaning of systems of philosophy and of political science, and the real nature of such social situations as criminology and the factor of race in unemployment. In business, according to a study made by Franklin H. Knower, "the ability to present clear explanations" was considered by businessmen to be the most valuable speech ability.[10] In our age of internationalism, it is important to note the judgment of one skilled diplomat that trying to explain problems of one culture to those who live in another poses a problem "akin to that of the public school teacher who heroically attempts to explain Einstein's quantum theory in simple terms that will be understandable to grade-school pupils."[11] Informative speaking is frequently used, often urgently needed, and sometimes badly presented or clumsily understood. What it requires above all is carefulness in both the speaking and the listening.

The emphasis in this chapter has been upon the sharing of understandings. Total meanings do not exist even in dictionaries. Meanings are discovered.[12] In a communicative situation, they are and must be shared. The question always is "What does this mean to you—and to me—to us jointly?" which is very different from, "What does it mean?" We speak informatively and we listen evaluatively in order to do our best to insure that speaker and listeners may together develop a set of meanings that will be identical, or at least closely similar, for both. The uses of such discourses are in part to give information, or to receive it, or to test the similarity of understanding of the various participants. As may be illustrated from many a conversation among students, through the exchange of views about a difficult reading assignment, they contribute insights to one another so that, eventually, all of them understand the meanings of the passage better than any one of them did before. Whether it be in public speaking, in conversation, or in formal group discussion, this is the basic use of informative discourse: to enhance and to clarify the understanding of the subject under discussion.

[10] Franklin H. Knower, in *Speech Education in Ohio,* Columbus: The Ohio State University, 1950.

[11] Ben C. Limb, "Speech: The Life of a Diplomat," *Quarterly Journal of Speech,* 43 (February, 1957), p. 60.

[12] Walter Coutu, "An Operational Definition of Meaning," *Quarterly Journal of Speech,* 48 (February, 1962), pp. 59–64.

Conclusion

The need for information is always urgent, for only with relevant facts can problems be solved. The mind, however brilliant, cannot operate in a vacuum. The sharing of understandings unites people in cooperative endeavors to solve problems, reduces aggressive competition, fosters social solidarity, and helps individuals by clarifying their ideas and by giving greater confidence in the soundness of their convictions. The reliability of knowledge is enhanced by subjecting it to the scrutiny of listeners, each of whom, like the speaker, will view it from a different perspective.

Informative discourse shares many characteristics with speech that aims to persuade or to entertain and interest; but it differs from these others in that its basic goal is the enhancement and clarification of understanding. Whereas, persuasion aims to win acceptance for a particular view of a subject, exposition aims to broaden understanding while keeping open for the listener the variety of conclusions which might be justified by the relevant information. Since informative discourse is a type of communication, it, like all other communicative types, must be closely adaptive to the needs, interests, and experience of its projected listeners. Both speaker and listeners have a primary problem in overcoming the binding effects of their own subjective interpretations of the subject matter. Five safeguards have been suggested as means by which objectivity may be enhanced. The responsibility for attaining a reliable mutual understanding of a subject rests upon both speaker and listener, though, as has been indicated, in differing ways. The ends toward which all informative discourse aim are threefold: to give information, to receive it, or to share it. For each of the aims, close cooperation is required between speaker and listeners.

Exercises

· *Questions for Discussion*

1. Review the discussion of purposes in Chapter 4. To what extent, by what means, and for what reason may the purpose to inform be distinguished from the purposes to persuade and to interest? Is it essential for effective communication that the speaker know what

purpose he is trying to achieve? Why? Is it essential that the listeners realize what the speaker's purpose is? At what point during the discourse should they be sure of his purpose? What difficulties might arise if the speaker's purpose is not evident to his listeners? Might the speaker himself encounter unexpected difficulties during his presentation if he becomes aware that his listeners have wrongly interpreted his purpose? What difficulties might exist if their interpretation is wrong but the speaker does not realize this fact? What kinds of assistance should the listeners extend to the speaker?

2. Using either the suggested topic, "The Bolshevik Revolution in Russia in 1917," or any other topic of your own choice, demonstrate the interrelationships among the various purposes of discourse. Show how the speaker's development of his topic will be governed by his own knowledge of what purpose he wishes to achieve. Show how listening is affected by the listener's decision as to what the speaker's purpose is.

3. Illustrate in class discussion by reference to talks presented in class some of the problems involved in sharing understanding. Cite means by which some speakers successfully solved some of these problems. Cite other illustrations that show how and why other speakers failed to solve some of these problems successfully. Offer suggestions for improvements in both the speaking and the listening.

4. Offer your definitions, with examples, of objectivity and subjectivity. To what extent do the discussions in your speech class indicate the value of an objective attitude, or show problems created by its lack? Are the speakers and listeners in your classroom exemplifying the recommended safeguards of objectivity? What improvements can you suggest to increase the objectivity of the discussions? In what sense and in what ways are subjectivity desirable in communication?

5. Compare yourself with a selected classmate in terms of how well each of you may be successful in bearing the recommended responsibilities for both speaking and listening. What suggestions occur to you for improving both yourself and your classmate in these respects?

· *Projects for Speaking and Listening*

1. The members of the class should select a problem area (such as American policy in Southeast Asia, or an ethical code for public officeholders, or any other of their choice) in which there is widespread interest and also a general lack of understanding of either the nature of the problem, or of desirable solutions to it, or of both problem

and solutions. In a preliminary discussion, the effort should be made to determine to what extent the lack of clear understanding results from lack of relevant information. After this has been determined, class members should undertake a search of library and other resources to find as well as they can the information that appears to be required. A subsequent discussion should be held in which new information should be presented and evaluated. A summary statement should be prepared indicating what shared understanding has emerged and what disagreements remain to be resolved or what areas of uncertainty still need to be clarified.

2. Each student should prepare a brief talk on a subject concerning which his understanding is superior to that of his classmates (perhaps because of specific preparatory reading, or because of his generalized background of experiences, or from a combination of these two). During the preparation, each speaker should concentrate his attention on what his listeners will need to be told in order to clarify or deepen their understanding of the subject. In the conclusion of each talk, the speaker should indicate through a summary what new level of understanding he thinks has been attained. The effectiveness of his analysis and of his presentation may be tested in a question–discussion period after his talk.

3. While listening to the speeches, each member of the class should make a careful evaluation of the objectivity of thinking being manifested during each talk, both by the successive speakers and by himself as a listener. These analyses may then be discussed by the class members after the round of speaking has been completed.

11 · Persuasion Processes

Freedom of speech is a heritage of vast portent in every facet of American living. Probably no other single factor has contributed so much to this country's continued stature and stability. Yet, for at least two reasons freedom of speech is widely misunderstood. One is that we take it for granted so much that we are not aware of its violation when it occurs. Secondly, it is thought of as speaker license, which it is not.

Freedom of speech was written into the first amendment of the United States Constitution to guarantee unlimited access of information to listeners and to readers—not to guarantee freedom of expression. No country can afford to protect and guarantee everyone's freedom of expression. Laws abound that necessarily place limitations on freedom of expression; for criminal acts are expressions, and the psychologically ill are confined both for what they do and what they threaten to do. The concept that in human affairs each kind of speaking and behaving has an appropriate time and place necessarily imposes restrictions on those expressions that threaten embarrassment or real harm to others. Thus, one may not and must not always practice freedom of expression.

On the other hand, Americans have a clear responsibility to practice freedom of speech: to determine what is right and what is to be done after consideration of all the available information, after exposure to all the available persuasion. George Orwell demonstrated clearly in his novel, *1984,* that the way to control a society is to carefully mold and limit information and persuasion. A society that controls itself is one which keeps open all of the channels of communication; it is a society whose members expose themselves to all available sources of information. Thus, in our society, we honor most highly a free competition of persuasion in order to guarantee decisions by an informed people, whether those be decisions to adopt new laws, to vote for a certain candidate, to buy a particular product, or to select a vocation or profession.

Practice of freedom of speech, then, involves all of the ways that people can find to make intelligent decisions—especially those decisions that affect the lives of others. One violates his heritage of freedom of speech no less by refusing to hear the opposition than by muzzling an opposition speaker. It is interesting to compare the relative sins of state legislatures or college administrations banning controversial speakers on the one hand and on the other hand those student activists who make it impossible for others to hear speakers of whom they disapprove by creating diversions or a din of their own.

In the American society of our time, freedom of speech is demanded and carefully protected in certain aspects of life and ignored or violated in others. In our courts of law, for instance, the competition of persuasion is structured so that contending parties each present the best possible case before judge or jury. In criminal cases, thanks in part to recent Supreme Court decisions, the accused is assured at least the machinery for providing that judge or jury will hear the most that can be said for him—whether he is innocent or guilty of the particular charge. Our freedom to choose on the basis of competing persuasion is no less protected in the field of advertising. Yet there are other areas in which we tend to be apathetic about demanding and protecting the benefits that accrue through a guarantee of freedom of speech. This is true in our political lives, especially in local politics, including student government in most places. Voting behaviors—including staying at home—based entirely on geographical or family traditions are violations of freedom of speech. This is not to say that one should vote contrary to these traditions but that, when he does, it should be because he has heard the opposition and found it wanting.

Persuasion is an essential field of study in order to assure freedom of speech and in order to both use and evaluate its processes effectively.

The Study of Persuasion

Persuasion processes are so important and so pervasive in American and western culture that it has become the focus of research and scholarship in many academic areas: philosophy, psychology, sociology, English, economics, education, history, business, journalism, political science, and religion, as well as in speech, and in newly developing programs and departments in communication arts and sciences.

An early landmark in the study of persuasion, it has been pointed out, is the work of Aristotle, in which he defined *rhetoric* as the study of "the available means of persuasion."[1] In modern study, however, persuasion means different things to scholars because various disciplines provide diverse perceptual frames through which to see the persuasion processes. Fotheringham notes four such frames of persuasion scholars:[2]

> Some stress the attempt to employ persuasive means [of influence], others the stimuli involved, others the ability to use those means, and some the effects of those means.

The speech student must be concerned with all these aspects, for they encompass the motivations and abilities of speakers, the messages they generate, and listener motivation and responses to both speaker and message. Yet there is more for the speech practitioner—and for any citizen—to consider; for what we have been saying in the introduction to this chapter is that persuasion is used not exclusively by speakers (or writers), but also by listeners (and readers) who must learn to make effective use of persuasion in a free society; that how listeners actively use persuasion affects the lives of us all.

Much of what follows in this chapter is based upon the research findings of scholars in the various fields noted above. But before turning to the processes of persuasion it will be helpful to consider the sometimes confusing relationships between persuasion and propaganda.

[1] See Lane Cooper, *The Rhetoric of Aristotle,* New York: Appleton-Century-Crofts, 1932 (paperback, 1960), p. 7.

[2] Wallace C. Fotheringham, *Perspectives on Persuasion,* Boston: Allyn and Bacon, Inc., 1966, p. 5.

Persuasion and Propaganda

Both persuasion and propaganda refer to efforts to influence or refer to messages that are the outcomes of such efforts. How should one discriminate between them? One way is to say that persuasion is good and propaganda is bad. Thus we can easily reject any persuasion which we do not like as blatant propaganda—whether it is valid or not—and turn off our listening. It is not a very dependable distinction. Another way to discriminate between persuasion and propaganda is to say that one is based on reason while the other is based on emotional appeals. As will be noted later in this chapter, very often when we think that an idea makes sense, we accept it, not because we have arrived at it through reasoning, but because it appeals to us. Thus, once again, it is natural for a listener simply to see what he likes as reasonable persuasion and what he dislikes as emotional propaganda. There is good evidence that listeners—even expert rhetorical critics—cannot consistently determine when a spoken appeal is to reason and when it is to emotions.[3] Further, as will be noted later, to reject as propaganda what is perceived as an emotional appeal is to deny an essential component of any effective persuasion—that while it should make sense it must also appeal and motivate.

A third basis for discriminating between persuasion and propaganda is that selected by the Institute for Propaganda Analysis during World War II. The Institute identified certain propaganda techniques[4] and suggested that the uses of these techniques or forms of messages could, in turn, serve to identify and distinguish propaganda from "honest persuasion." As Roger Brown points out:[5]

> Of course the devices are actually ubiquitous. They appear in the Bible, the Declaration of Independence, in philosophy, psychology, physics, and biology . . . .

Brown points out further that the effectiveness of the devices is contingent on many other factors and that often they are not effective at all. It can also be said that they are used, with variable effects,

[3] Randall C. Ruechelle, "An Experimental Study of Audience Recognition of Emotional and Intellectual Appeals in Persuasion," *Speech Monographs,* XXV (March, 1958), pp. 49–58.

[4] Name calling, glittering generality, transfer, testimonial, plain folks, card stacking, and bandwagon.

[5] *Words and Things,* New York: The Free Press, 1958, p. 301.

by able and good speakers in persuasion without violating any ethical or rhetorical code.

If the message does not directly reveal whether it is persuasion or propaganda, how then can one distinguish? Brown says:[6]

> Separating propaganda from good advice and useful information involves penetrating to the motives and knowledgeability of the person originating the message . . .

In other words, when we do not know the motive of the speaker we cannot say whether he is attempting persuasion or propaganda. When we know that he wishes to influence listeners to do or believe something that would benefit the speaker but not the listeners, he is, in this sense, a propagandist. And when we know that he desires a response that will benefit his listeners (and, perhaps, himself as a member of the group) he may be said to be engaged in persuasion.

The Uses of Persuasion

We use persuasion daily. While we are not called upon to make decisions of national importance, we do respond many times each day to the persuasive appeals of advertisers, teachers, relatives, and friends. The effective speaker or listener knows how to use this daily persuasion to advantage: both to his own advantage and to that of his society. He does so by making persuasion available to himself and to others, by intelligently evaluating the persuasion he hears, by developing his ability to persuade, and by responsibly applying that ability whenever the occasion demands.

Making persuasion available is often a simple matter of turning a television switch or turning one's attention to a speaker. At other times, making persuasion available requires extended effort, as when taking time out of a busy schedule to attend a local planning council meeting or insisting that a friend do so. Daily decisions are best confronted with maximum information. This does not mean that decisions are easier when all the pertinent persuasion becomes available. On the contrary, decision becomes more difficult. At the same time, validity of decision becomes more likely. Consider two professors we know who once served on a committee processing student requests for reinstatement, waiving of certain requirements, and the like. One faculty

[6] Roger Brown, p. 302.

member proposed that information from the personnel files of each petitioning student be made available. The other insisted, "Oh, no! If we know more about the student it will be harder to come to a decision."

Making persuasion available is both a necessity and a responsibility. At the same time, exposure to persuasion does not serve its purpose unless it is accompanied by intelligent evaluation.

Evaluation of persuasive efforts of others is not easy. Without an understanding of principles of persuasion, evaluation is apt to be made on inappropriate criteria. Persuasion can be accepted or rejected and a decision made on the basis of irrelevant factors as, for instance, when one allows a strange dialect to turn him against the speaker's proposal or when one buys a product only because he has heard about it most frequently.

By what criteria does the effective user of persuasion evaluate? The answer lies partly in the principles and factors discussed in detail in this chapter. But a few specific criteria may be useful at this point. These would be:

1. Is the speaker in a position to know?
2. Is the speaker led to his proposal partly out of concern for my welfare?
3. Does the proposal make sense?
   a. Would it solve the problem?
   b. Does it follow from what I know from other sources?
   c. If I agree, is it because I want to or because I am reluctantly compelled to by valid reasoning?
   d. If I disagree, is it because I want to or because the speaker calls for invalid reasoning?

These criteria are explained and supported in this chapter. But this chapter is also designed to help the reader learn to persuade others effectively: to help him invite others to the interaction that is necessary in influencing their attitudes, beliefs, or actions.

Developing the ability to persuade is, of course, essential to the effective use of persuasion. The principles are presented in this text, but the ability to use them comes with their application and practice both in class assignments and in daily living. The ability to persuade is basic to living successfully in any society, though the principles and related values are often quite different from culture to culture. Thus the principles detailed here are not universal but apply to our society and to our times.

In our society a person who has not developed an ability to persuade is handicapped or disadvantaged. He can know what he and others should do about a particular problem, but he may not be able to invite agreement to do it. Besides the ability to persuade, one more thing is required. That is a willingness and often an eagerness to apply the ability whenever the occasion demands.

Responsible application of the ability to persuade, then, is the ultimate aim of the speaker in persuasion. No ability is of use unless and until it is applied. For its very existence our way of life requires that members of society use their persuasive abilities; that they don't let George do it. The person who does not use his persuasive abilities when the occasion demands is not only handicapped, but he forces those who might otherwise make more valid decisions to be disadvantaged.

In the daily uses of persuasion each of us shares the responsibilities to make persuasion available to ourselves and to others, to evaluate it, to develop our own persuasive abilities, and to apply those abilities to the advantage of those with whom we live.

Contexts of Persuasion

A persuasive intent determines a speaker's behavior any time that he seeks to influence the attitudes, beliefs, or actions of listeners. Thus he may wish to share information, but at a given moment he may need to persuade his listener to want to learn; or he may, in a rambling conversation, pause to urge his listener to see a new film before passing on to other items of sociability. In other contexts entire speeches are designed to persuade, as in a final summation at court, or in debate on a proposal in a parliamentary group, or in a public speech on a controversial topic, or in numberless other circumstances, which call for speeches to persuade. Further, persuasive speaking takes place in contexts in which the particular speech is one of a series designed ultimately to achieve a persuasive purpose, though no single speech is expected to accomplish this purpose.

Thus, persuasive speech purposes may be momentary; they may be the point of focus for an entire speech; or they may be designed to help achieve long-range goals. The principles developed in this chapter apply in all of these contexts—not merely in classroom persuasive speech assignments. Further, persuasion has special relationships with the other purpose discussed in the previous chapter: sharing understanding.

Persuasion and sharing understanding have a relationship which causes students to be unsure or confused as to whether their purpose is one or the other. It should be noted that all speaking, regardless of how one may define the communicative purposes behind it, contains information. However, the essential question is: What communicative motivation led to the speaker's selection of the materials or ideas? Or, how does the speaker expect the listener to respond to the information? Thus, if a student would have his classmates understand the arguments against United States participation in the United Nations—whether he believes in such participation or not—he will automatically select and adapt one set of information. If, however, he wants his listeners to accept or believe the arguments, he will select and adapt different information and will talk differently.

Differentiating between persuasive and informative purposes is not so much a matter of what is said as of what moves one to say it; nor is it judged by a statement in a student outline, but by whether, fundamentally, the speaker wants his listener to respond with new attitudes or beliefs. There is a clear line to be drawn between the two purposes. Haziness comes only when the speaker himself does not fully understand his own purpose.

However, while the two general motivations for speaking can be clearly different, there are many important principles in common.

Persuasion leading to understanding takes place, for instance in the introduction of an effective talk whose purpose is to gain understanding. The persuasive purpose is to motivate the listener to want to understand and remember the central idea. Thus, the speaker attempts to strengthen or create the belief that what he is to talk about is worth knowing. If the speaker would have his listeners understand that the use of fluorescent paint is cutting down on mid-air collisions, he first makes it an attractive idea to learn by relating it to the fears of some listeners, to the curiosity of others, and to the concern of others for proper air safety.

Understanding that leads to persuasion becomes the goal of a speaker whose fundamental purpose is to persuade when he has determined that his listeners oppose an idea simply because they do not understand it. In such a case, the principles detailed in the last chapter apply. This goal has the added advantage that listeners are more receptive to persuasion that does not appear to be persuasion. "Let's look into this" opens channels of interaction, while "You have been wrong about this" invites listener defenses against learning, against adopting a new belief—even against listening further.

It must be kept in mind that for maximum speaker effectiveness principles of achieving clarity and understanding apply as much to persuasion as they do to sharing understanding.

Prerequisites for Persuasion

In our earlier discrimination between persuasion and propaganda we stated, in essence, a first prerequisite for persuasion: that the speaker propose something of value to the listeners. There are other prerequisites. These include apparent disagreement, the determination of a common premise, the assessment of feasibility of purpose, and a listening mode of creative problem solving. The latter serves also as a prerequisite for the listener who would make maximum use of persuasion.

Apparent disagreement refers to a situation in which a speaker perceives that his listeners are burdened with an attitude, belief, mood, determination, or commitment that is somehow handicapping to them. He may see that his listeners are led astray by their commitment to a political party or an old and no longer relevant tradition, or that they are unduly disturbed by misunderstanding of what the public schools are attempting, or that they are fearful of a developing situation only because they do not fully understand it. Examples of such daily disagreements are endless. In any of them, both speakers and listeners have responsibilities to use persuasion to determine what is the truth for them in given situations.

Arguments—often wasteful—take place in situations where this prerequisite is not met and where, after long harangues, it is discovered that there is essentially no disagreement. Often such debates end with a frustrated, "Then what are we arguing about?"

There is one purpose of speaking—often classified as persuasion—that does not involve disagreement. On the contrary, it requires full agreement between speaker and listener. This is the purpose of speaking that the ancients called *epideictic*. In modern parlance, this is speaking to stimulate or to strengthen present feelings and beliefs. This includes, for instance, the ceremonial speaking which takes place at certain celebrations and commemorations. Such speaking is discussed in the next chapter on enhancing sociability. However, it also has importance for the next prerequisite for persuasion: determining the common premise.

Determining the common premise is the discovery of what it is that both speaker and listener desire or value that can be achieved by agreement with the speaker's idea. Both the presence of a common premise and its discovery are prerequisite to the listeners' and the speaker's successful use of persuasion to arrive at decisions.

Some examples of common premises will serve to clarify this very important prerequisite:

—A speaker who would advocate abolition of capital punishment discovers that both he and his listeners put high priority on the deterrence of crime and would judge any policy on that criterion.

—A speaker who supports a policy of capital punishment may find that he and his listeners fear the return of murderers and kidnappers to society.

—A speaker in a civic organization opposes a campaign to "get out the vote." He knows that both he and his listeners value informed, thoughtful voting and plans to point out that such a campaign would succeed only in urging uninformed voters to the polls. A listener in the same situation may suggest a new proposal based on the same common premise: that the organization mount a campaign to urge voters to inform themselves.

—A student, urging a faculty committee to adopt a proposal for taking certain courses on a pass-fail basis finds that both he and they place a high value on students attempting difficult courses in fields outside (but possibly related to) their major interests.

—A fund-raiser for medical research finds that he and his listeners have a strong desire to do something that really makes a difference in the world.

It should be noted that this prerequisite is not just *any* area of agreement between speaker and listener but that special commitment which, if strengthened in the listener, is apt to move him to accept the speaker's proposal. This common premise becomes the essential starting point for persuasion; for the argument that must take place in the listener. It is to strengthen this commitment that the persuasive speaker can apply the process of speaking to stimulate or strengthen belief.

Where there is no common premise to be found, the speaker must reconsider his purpose, for his proposal apparently is of no value to his listeners. The speaker who perseveres in a proposal for which there is no common premise to be found is no longer a persuader but rather a propagandist.

The lack of a common premise may signal something about the third prerequisite for persuasion: assessing the feasibility of purpose.

Assessing feasibility of purpose is necessary in order to avoid attempts that not only fail but boomerang. A speaker who does not ask himself if it is realistic to expect his listener to reverse or modify a particular belief leaves communicative effectiveness to chance rather than to communicative ability.

There are two basic principles from current research which apply here. One is the theory of cognitive dissonance[7] and the other is the related principle of latitudes of acceptance, noncommitment and rejection.[8] Simply stated, the theory of cognitive dissonance holds that each of us, when confronted with inconsistent perceptions, tends to achieve balance by adjusting one or both of the perceptions. Thus, if we admire a man highly and someone reports that he takes candy away from children, we have a need to reconcile this inconsistency. We may do so by saying, "I was wrong about him," or (more likely) by rationalizing what we heard: we may say that the reporter is a liar, or we may say, "Of course, he wants to protect the children from tooth decay."

In persuasion, then, a speaker's proposal is at the outset dissonant with the listener's current attitudes and beliefs on the subject. Every listener will need to resolve that dissonance. One principle which applies is that—within limits discussed below—the greater the dissonance, the greater the likelihood that the listener will adjust his beliefs further in the direction the speaker proposes. For example, if listeners in an organization favor limiting a contribution to a particular charity to $1000, and the speaker would have them agree to giving $2000, he would be well advised, according to this principle, to propose a $4000 or $5000 contribution. Or, if listeners would like to contribute $1000 and the speaker feels that a $500 contribution would be more in keeping with the need and with the ability of the group to pay, he might propose that only $50 or $100 be contributed. Similarly, if listeners

[7] Leon Festinger, *A Theory of Cognitive Dissonance,* New York: Harper & Row, Publishers, Inc., 1957; J. W. Brehm and Arthur R. Cohen, *Explorations in Cognitive Dissonance,* New York: John Wiley & Sons, Inc., 1962; Shel Feldman, ed., *Cognitive Consistency,* New York: Academic Press, Inc., 1966.

[8] See Carolyn W. Sherif, Muzafer Sherif, Roger E. Nebergall, *Attitude and Attitude Change,* Philadelphia, Pa.: W. B. Saunders Company, 1965; also James O. Whittaker, "Resolution of the Communicative Discrepancy Issue in Attitude Change," in Muzafer and Carolyn W. Sherif, eds., *Attitude, Ego Involvement and Change,* New York: John Wiley & Sons, Inc., 1967.

are opposed to building a new school and a speaker would have them at least investigate the possibility, he would, under this principle not ask for the investigation (to which the dissonance-resolving response might be to agree to an investigation at a later date) but he would propose and support the idea of launching at once on the needed building program (to which the dissonance-resolving response might be to take the proposal seriously enough to set up the desired investigation of need).

Yet what if this principle of cognitive dissonance is carried to logical extremes? Should the speaker go all the way in order to assure the desired listener response? Should he propose a contribution obviously far beyond the ability of the group to handle? Or propose that there be *no* contribution? In the example of the school building, should he propose breaking ground tomorrow? Recent persuasion research suggests that the principle of cognitive dissonance applies only within specifiable limits; only within a range of proposals that fall within what has been called the listener's latitude of acceptance: those proposals along a continuum which the listener may not like as well as the one he is committed to but which he feels might be considered and that he might live with. However, should the speaker propose approval of an idea in the listener's latitude of rejection, the cognitive principle does not apply and the listener may respond by becoming more committed to his previous stand—or more extremely opposed to the speaker's proposal. Thus, two related prerequisites for persuasion may be seen from the examples above: feasibility of purpose and feasibility of apparent purpose.

The questions are: on the basis of analysis of the situation, can it be seen that the speaker's purpose is realistically achievable; and, on the basis of analysis of listener's willingness to consider various proposals, can it be seen that a more extensive proposal will, in the practical situation, serve the purpose?

Feasibility of purpose is related to one more principle from the same line of research: the concept of latitude of noncommitment. There are proposals which listeners would not necessarily reject but about which they couldn't care less: they have no feeling of involvement. Some people do not feel involved in local politics, for instance, and so may be easy prey to any persuasion which comes along. In speech classes, persuasive speakers may seem to be very successful when their listeners neither accept nor reject their proposals at the outset—proposals which fall in listeners' latitudes of noncommitment.

For feasibility of persuasive efforts, then, proposals must be selected that fall within listeners' latitudes of acceptance. This rules out at any given time propositions within listeners' latitudes of rejection (lest the response boomerang). It should be noted, however, that changes do take place and that persuasive speaking contributes to change; that conditions or speaking can induce changes in the latitudes and degrees of change in listener involvement, as when a speaker applies the factors of interest discussed in Chapter 8.

A listening mode of creative problem-solving refers to just one kind of listening out of the many in the repertoires of everyone. Every school child learns to pretend listening; every television viewer escapes to reverie; often our listening modes are signs of love or of hostility.[9] The creative problem-solving mode of listening, as a prerequisite to persuasion, is an active process of relating what one hears to one's own experiences and knowledge: actively engaging in the argument in order to discover the truth.

The listener with little or no involvement cannot offer this kind of listening. Yet it does not follow that if he is involved he will listen creatively, for he can be heavily involved and committed to hostile listening if he rejects the speaker's proposal.

Creative problem-solving listening is not only a prerequisite for persuasion to take place; it is also an essential for maximum use of persuasion by responsible listeners. Persuasion processes, then, from the points of view of both speakers and listeners, depend upon active listening, upon agreement to enter the argument. In turn, this pre-requires a difference of opinion between speaker and listener, a common premise which the speaker believes would be served by agreement with his proposal, and a situation and combination of circumstances that make the speaker's persuasive goal reasonably attainable.

Persuasive Processes

Persuasion takes place when, in a communicative interaction, the listener moves from one cognition to another—or from one attitude, belief, mood, determination, or commitment to another. The speaker invites change and the listener agrees to change.

In formal logic there is a similar movement from a premise (or

[9] See Paul D. Holtzman, "Modes of Listening," *The Psychology of Speakers' Audiences,* Chapter 2, Glenview, Ill.: Scott, Foresman and Company (in press).

set of premises) to a conclusion. Formal logic, itself, rarely if ever leads to changes in one's thinking, though it may be used to test the validity of a conclusion already arrived at. Aristotle, the inventer of the syllogism, pointed out that formal logic, dealing in certainty, has application only in scientific demonstration and in the game of dialectic.[10] However, the logical paradigm for hypothetical propositions of IF . . . THEN . . . , provides a useful model or analogy for understanding the persuasion processes. We refer to processes, in the plural, for it is a human characteristic to move from accepted premise to a probable conclusion through application of one or another of at least two thinking processes: the logical and the psychological, through reason and through emotions.

Logical Processes

One arrives at a reasoned conclusion reluctantly; it is not what he wants to conclude. For instance, a listener may accept the premise that there is easy access to firearms but he may not necessarily move to approve of strictly enforced restrictions on the sale of pistols and rifles. Further, if he should come to such a conclusion, one does not know whether he does so through logical or psychological processes, for the form is the same: for example, IF easy access leads to abuses, THEN restrictive laws would reduce the probability of such abuses. If the listener desires restrictive firearms legislation anyway, then he will not engage in reasoning but move easily from the premise to the desired conclusion. If the listener desires free and easy access to firearms but admits to himself that the irresponsibility of some people makes restrictive legislation necessary, then he is apt to move to the conclusion through the reasoning process.[11]

The logical (as well as the psychological) process begins with listener acceptance of the premise. No listening process in the desired

[10] For persuasion or rhetoric. Aristotle proposed the *enthymeme,* involving the various processes by which listeners move from accepted premises to probable conclusions. See Lane Cooper, xxv–xxix; also James H. McBurney, "The Place of the Enthymeme in Rhetorical Theory," *Speech Monographs,* III (1936), pp. 49–74.

[11] See Paul I. Rosenthal, "The Concept of Ethos and the Structure of Persuasion," *Speech Monographs,* XXXIII (June, 1966), pp. 114–26. Rosenthal proposes that the logical processes are predominantly a function of one part of the nervous system (central) and that the psychological processes are predominantly a function of another (autonomic).

direction can take place if the premises and the material, which are selected to validate them, are rejected by the listener.

To some listeners there may be a clear, logical step from the premise, "It is the lack of rigorous discipline in our schools which is leading to mounting juvenile crime," to belief in a program of rigid requirements for behavior and severe punishment for violators. But no reasonable, critical listener will take that step if he does not accept that premise. The probability that he would be willing to accept the premise and take the logical step is increased if he learns that the source is a well-known and respected psychologist who has recently completed a study of the problems of discipline in American schools. In short, the process of reasoning will proceed in the direction of the speaker's point only if the listener accepts the authority of the source and the idea.

It should be clear, then, that materials must be selected for their credibility, and they must be presented by whatever means will enhance that credibility. A statement of conditions in Red China presented on the authority of a student speaker or with a statement such as, "I read it in a magazine," impedes credibility; presentation on the authority of an Asian specialist or recently returned French or Canadian reporter enhances credibility.

We would not presume to provide in these few pages all that is needed in understanding the logical processes.[12] However, there are certain processes that should be noted. These include deduction, induction, causal inference, and analogy.

Deduction. IF any copper wire is a conductor of electricity, THEN a particular piece of copper wire will conduct electrical current. Similarly, IF it is accepted that all birds with a certain shape of beak are seed eaters, THEN it follows that a particular bird with a beak so shaped will welcome seed in the birdfeeder. Deduction is that logical process of reasoning which asserts that any member of a class will have the characteristics of that class; it is reasoning from accepted generalizations to specifics that must follow.

Speakers, before inviting deductive processes, and listeners, during

[12] For more detailed discussions of logical processes and their evaluation, see Douglas Ehninger and Wayne Brockriede, *Decision by Debate,* New York: Dodd, Mead & Company, Inc., 1963; Robert B. Huber, *Influencing Through Argument,* New York: David McKay Company, Inc., 1963; Elton Abernathy, *A Manual of Persuasion,* New York: David McKay, Company, Inc., 1964 (paperback).

persuasion, can test the dependability of conclusions with the following questions:

1. Is the generalization (premise) universally true?
2. Does the specific item really belong in the general class?
3. Or does the specific item represent an exception to the cited general class?
4. Is the conclusion confirmed through other logical processes?

Induction. More frequently, speakers call upon listeners to follow inductive processes from an accumulation of specifics to a general conclusion. IF in many cited, representative instances members of our community have become ill from fumes from our factories, THEN it is probable that we will have to go the expense of treating our manufacturing wastes. IF in many cited, representative instances graduates of large high schools tend to fare better than graduates of small ones, THEN it is probable that combining small school districts into larger ones will lead to increase in the quality of education.

Induction, then, is a means of predicting the probability that a conclusion is right. In essence, the preparing speaker engages in the induction process when he selects the specific information which he predicts will lead to acceptance of his idea by his listeners.

An effective critical listener demands many representative, specific instances before he will grant a general rule. If he hears of one person's experience with an advertised product, then he wants to know how others fared with its use. Statistical inference—an inductive process—is basic to all sciences, including the social sciences. The significance of any statistical conclusion is determined by the number and nature of instances tested. So it is with a listener who is asked to predict the probability that the speaker's conclusion is right. The appropriate advice, then, is that the speaker must provide an abundance of similar, representative, validating materials in ways that will make them acceptable to the listeners.

It should be noted that in the inductive process the direction of reasoning is not always clear-cut. Unless a speaker has examined for himself the possible logical conclusions that may be drawn, his efforts to gain this kind of response may backfire. IF in instance after instance students are finding it impossible to park their cars conveniently, THEN more parking facilities should be provided on campus. Or might it not follow: THEN more restrictions on student possession of automobiles are needed. For a given campus group both of these conclusions might follow, one logically and the other psychologically.

Tests for the dependability of conclusions derived inductively are:

1. Are the validating materials true?
2. Are enough cases cited?
3. Are instances representative of the whole being considered?
4. Are there exceptions which do not lead to the expected conclusion?
5. Are all instances drawn from comparable situations?
6. Is the conclusion confirmed through other logical processes?

Causal inference. The logical process of causal inference has importance to speakers and listeners in several respects. Listeners are often asked to reason from cause to effect: IF we approve of new student regulations, THEN these regulations will cause ill-will among students on the campus. Listeners are often asked to reason fallaciously from cause to effect: IF there is a high correlation between business success and breadth of vocabulary, THEN one should memorize long lists of esoteric words for success in business. In a parody of causal inference, historian Ari Hoogenboom cites as the cause of the American Civil War the aggressiveness caused, in turn, by the growing and wearing of beards.[13] More seriously, Marshall McLuhan cites media effects—independent of any messages—as causes of sweeping social changes.[14]

Both speakers and listeners need to be wary of two sources of invalid applications of this process. One is the neglect of plural causes; the other is a tendency to assume causes.

Human affairs are indescribably complex. It is seldom possible, through reasoning or any other processes, to determine the cause of an accident, a war, happiness, the winning of a game, or the failure of a course. This is usually because there is not a single cause; there are interacting causes. Thus, it is safest, most accurate and probably most effective for a speaker to acknowledge that a listener is asked to view armament races as one of the causes of wars, constant conflict in the home as one of the causes of juvenile crime, or the blocking ability of the all-American tackle as one of the causes of victory. The critical listener, too, must remind himself to look for other factors when he is asked to reason that a speaker's proposal would be the cause of the desired result.

The second caution in the application of this reasoning process

[13] "What Really Caused the Civil War," *Wisconsin Magazine of History,* XLIV (Autumn, 1960), pp. 3–5.

[14] *Understanding Media,* New York: Signet Books, 1966.

is against assuming cause from a sequence or coincidence of events. It is not considered logical to attribute an accident on the way home to a black cat crossing the road. But an ineffective listener may accept the fallacy when a speaker reports that the assassination of President John F. Kennedy caused the escalation of the Vietnamese war. Similarly, uncritical listeners may reason that the ignorance of a racial group is the cause for its poverty without recognizing that both facts have antecedent causes; that ignorance and poverty, though they may be coincident, do not necessarily have a direct causal relationship.

In the interest of persuasive effectiveness, speakers may call on listeners to reason either from cause to effect or from effect to cause, offering proof that a given policy will cause a future result or that a given condition was caused by specific events in the past.

Causal inference in preparation. Whether or not a speaker calls upon his listeners to engage in causal inference, in preparing to speak he is, himself, inevitably committed to causal inference in the processes of audience analysis and audience adaptation.

The crucial question in audience analysis is, "Why do the listeners believe as they do?" In other words, "What has caused them to hold their current beliefs?" Answers are apt to lead to discovery of the common premise discussed earlier. Thus, the preparing speaker engages in reasoning from effect to cause.

The application of audience analysis is audience adaptation. The basic question here is, "What will cause the listeners to believe as they should?" Again, the reasoning process is from effect to cause, for the preparing speaker must reason—given his particular audience—from the desired listener response to a probable cause of that response: from expected communication outcome to speaker and listener behaviors, which should cause that outcome.

Both speakers and listeners, then, must rely heavily on effectiveness in valid causal inference, often during speaking but especially in the preparation process. Tests for the dependability of causal inference are:

1. Is the cause really capable of producing the effect?
2. Was the cause really operating?
3. Are there possibly other interacting causes?
4. Is the conclusion (whether cause or effect) confirmed through other reasoning processes?

Analogy. As both a form and a method of proof, analogy is discussed in Chapter 7. Analogy is a basic process in all perception and learning, for we perceive and interpret new experiences and ideas by applying available perceptual categories. That is, we ask of a new idea, "What is it like (in my experience, knowledge, or beliefs)?" Further, when analogy is used as a logical process, we ask, "In what ways is it like and in what ways unlike what I have known before?" Such analysis of similarities and differences in the "internal argument" generally applies to literal analogies and seldom, if ever, to figurative analogies.

In persuasion, then, examination of comparable problems or solutions can lead listeners effectively to appropriate conclusions through reasoning. One may speak of needed improvement in his university by analogy with comparable institutions already benefiting from such improvements; or listeners may be asked to approve a program of state medicine by considering the results of such a program in a comparable nation.

The key to both effectiveness and to error lies in the term *comparable*. Two universities, for instance, are never identical in all respects. Still, a valid reasoning response can be expected to the extent that the two situations are nearly identical in the characteristics that are germane, whether they be size of student body, kind of support, public image, or amount of isolation from the community. It follows that if the two things or events or people are not comparable in the essential aspects, reasoning by analogy is not apt to be valid. The ineffective listener who accepts arguments based on invalid analogy is apt to be engaged not in logical but in psychological processes in arriving at his conclusion.

The model of ana*logic* is: IF two situations are identical in the essential relevant aspects, THEN what happens to one in given circumstances will happen in the other in the same circumstances. Tests for the dependability of conclusions drawn by analogy are:

1. Are the things compared related in essential details?
2. Does the comparison overlook fundamental differences?
3. Are the statements of similarity true?
4. Is the analogous situation representative?
5. Is the conclusion confirmed through other reasoning processes?

Deduction, induction, causal inference, and analogy are logical processes by which listeners may move intellectually to conclusions. Whether one moves through logical or psychological processes can usually be determined by whether he is drawn to a conclusion which he is reluctant or eager to reach. The unwary and uncritical listener can be drawn to a conclusion, however, not by valid reasoning but by fallacious reasoning. It is to help the listener avoid this possibility that questions have been presented for testing the validity of each process.[15]

Whether listeners move from premise to conclusion by logical processes or by the psychological processes discussed below, both are subject to the same tests, for whether one moves to a new conclusion reluctantly or because he wants to, it must make sense.[16]

Psychological Processes

The logical process has been discussed as one of the means by which listeners move from a premise (or fact or prior belief) to what is for them a new conclusion (or attitude or cognition). We pointed out earlier there are other processes. In spite of man's special ability to reason, his natural wants and needs are basic, and he lives by the dictates of what appeals to him, as surely as he does by reason. Of special importance is that "set" which might be called motivational or emotional. Motives are powerful driving forces in all human behavior and in all human decisions. The student of persuasion must recognize these psychological processes as both inevitable and essential in the effective use of persuasion: the speaker must involve the listener's motives. The listener should expect motivational appeals, and he should also carefully evaluate them in the internal argument. This is because motives may be ignoble or they may bring out the very best in man. They foster his ambitions, lead him to make choices, aid in cultivating his tastes and sentiments, and help to elevate him to the highest pinnacles of esthetic appreciation.

It is because of the fact that psychological processes are inevitable, essential, and effective in persuasion that an old idea must be rejected: that emotional appeals are somehow not worthy of the best kind of speaking. It is well known that we do not arrive at belief and action

[15] For examples of fallacies and further tests of the logical processes, see W. Ward Fearnside and William B. Holther, *Fallacy: The Counterfeit of Argument*, Englewood Cliffs, N.J.: Prentice-Hall, Inc., 1959 (paperback).

[16] For an alternate method of analyzing premise-to-conclusion reasoning, see the Toulmin "layout": data-warrant claim as applied to persuasion in Wayne Brockriede and Douglas Ehninger, *Decision by Debate,* New York: Dodd, Mead & Company, Inc., 1963; John F. Wilson and Carroll C. Arnold, *Public Speaking as a Liberal Art,* Boston: Allyn and Bacon, Inc., 1964; see also, James C. McCroskey, "Toulmin and the Basic Course," *Speech Teacher,* XIV (March, 1965), pp. 91–100.

through the logical processes alone. We must, in addition, be moved to such belief and action. Speakers should not hesitate, therefore, to discover and use materials and ideas that invite listeners to move from premise to conclusion through the psychological processes, and listeners should not reject motive appeals simply because they constitute appeals to the emotions. Of course, if the motive appeal does not stand up to critical analysis, then it should be rejected; not because it is an emotional appeal, but because it does not make sense.

It should be remembered that the logical pattern applies—by analogy—to the psychological processes. For example, IF it will save us some money, THEN let's build a student bookstore; or, IF we want an exciting new experience, THEN we would enjoy the Peace Corps.

Two sets of appeals or psychological processes are presented here for their applicability to the preparing speaker and to the critical listener: general appeals and special appeals.

General Appeals

People are generally moved to act, feel, or believe through what seems a vast variety of motives. One psychologist analyzed a wide range of persuasive messages for categories of values: the general desires of people.[17] He identified fifty "basic values and value symbols," including sets of goals (physiological, fearful, playful, social, egoistic, practical, cognitive) and sets of standards of judgment (moral, social, egoistic). The most common values reported were:

Goals	*Standards of Judgment*
safety	morality
independence	truthfulness
achievement	justice
recognition	obedience
dominance	religion
aggression	generosity
emotional security	tolerance
practicality	group unity
economic value	strength
work	determination
knowledge	carefulness
value-in-general	culture

These categories of values can be of practical help to the preparing

[17] Ralph K. White, *Value-analysis: The Nature and Use of the Method,* Society for the Psychological Study of Social Issues, 1951. See for examples of appeals based on each of these values found in persuasive messages.

speaker as he seeks means of inviting listeners to engage in the psychological process of moving from accepted premise to conclusion. Two things should be kept in mind: (1) values do not occur in isolation but in interaction with one another and in hierarchies of relative importance of values;[18] (2) hierarchies of values vary according to cultural constraints. This suggests that the preparing speaker may achieve his purposes if—in establishing the common premise—he successfully invites his listeners to rearrange their priorities of values. At the same time it should be noted that from time to time and from situation to situation, importance of values change in relation to each other. Nevertheless, application can be made with clarity and with good effect. For example, IF one values equally achievement and emotional security, and IF he becomes more committed to achieve, THEN he may risk emotional security in order to become a more effective person working hard on speech class assignments.

The reader may find advantages in a much simpler formulation of the wishes of man by William I. Thomas:[19] recognition, response, new experience, security.

Recognition. This set of values includes both the inner sense of achievement or accomplishment that one draws from his own knowledge of a job well done, and similar satisfactions from high regard by others. In other words, this is a psychological need for self-esteem. Listeners in our culture derive self-esteem, for instance, from the belief that they are being rational in an argument, from praise that is heaped upon them for their works, or from an internal sense that they are consistent—that their attitudes, beliefs, and actions are not dissonant.[20] Thus, a speaker may succeed with the general appeal: IF we wish to be consistent with our belief in helping the less fortunate, THEN we will approve of an expanded Head Start program.

Response. The human being wants the kind of love and interest that grows out of sensitivity to and understanding of feelings that one person may have for another. This is the appeal of a Martin Luther King: IF we meet physical force with "soul force," THEN all men can

[18] Ch. Perelman, *The Idea of Justice and the Problem of Argument,* trans. John Petrie, New York: The Humanities Press, 1963, p. 170.

[19] In *The Unadjusted Girl,* Boston: Little, Brown & Company, 1923, pp. 4 ff.

[20] For an interesting comparison of two psychological theories (dissonance and self-esteem) of the resolution of cognitive discrepancies, see William J. McGuire and Susan Millman, "Anticipatory Belief Lowering Following Forewarning of a Persuasive Attack," *Journal of Personality and Social Psychology* (1965), pp. 476–7.

become brothers. Or it is the appeal of a computer-based dating or matching service: IF you are matched with another on the basis of mutual interests, attitudes, and feelings, THEN you will find genuine understanding in the person selected.

New Experience. People are curious to explore. They want to see and understand new things, feel new sensations, hear a different kind of music or speech, experiment with tastes and smells, learn about far-off places and new ideas. In recent years the American people have become increasingly mobile. They have set new attendance records at world fairs, both at home and abroad. They have more leisure time to fill with interesting activities. They have been moved, in part, at least, by an adventurous spirit to join VISTA and the Peace Corps. New experience has probably risen in our hierarchy of cultural values over the past two decades. It is one of the appeals of the packager: IF we put our soap in a new, attractive, and interesting container, THEN more people are apt to select it instead of other, equally effective soap. It is one of the appeals of American college programs abroad: IF you want to experience living in new ways, making new friends, and seeing new places, THEN you will want to sign up for the junior year abroad program.

Security. This is not really an equivalent category with the others, for it is when the other values are satisfied that we experience security; when we know that continuously arising physical and psychic needs will be satisfied. Application of this process, then, is involved when listeners are offered an ability to cope with whatever problems they may meet in their lives. It is the appeal that was used to urge some readers to college: IF you want to be prepared to take advantage of the opportunities that life will offer, THEN you must continue your education at the college level. It is the appeal of many advertisers whose products offer the ability to cope with life's little and large emergencies: IF you have this, THEN you will be ready.

The reader is provided here with these two sets of general appeals (sometimes called vital appeals) that can be applied in inviting listeners to move from acceptable premises to the speaker's conclusion—the basic values and the wishes of man. For maximum effectiveness, however, the preparing speaker must learn as much as he can about the hierarchies of values and commitments that are special to his particular audience.

Special appeals. Listeners have special likes, hostilities, blind spots, ambitions, fears, attitudes, feelings, beliefs, and values. It is partly to learn about these and to understand why particular listeners have particular motives that the preparing speaker engages in audience analysis. In adapting to the particular audience, then, the speaker is able to offer special appeals. Examples: IF one is very fond of wild animals, THEN he will want to support a certain proposal for establishing a state park. On the other hand, IF one places high value on conservation, THEN he will want to support the same proposal for the state park. For still other listeners, IF one is hoping to find a place for a summer cabin, THEN he should support the proposal for a state park.

The application of special appeals calls for careful understanding of and respect for listeners' particular desires or values. This is important not only in identifying useful beginning points for the psychological processes but also in knowing what irrelevant fears and hostilities to avoid. A careless or unknowing remark, indicating lack of respect for members of a particular profession, though it have little relevance to the topic, may turn off listeners who hold such professionals in high regard. In such a case, the speaker may be establishing for himself an image. With this image of the speaker, listeners can easily move to the rejection of a proposal by anyone who would talk like that. This properly suggests an interaction between the logical and psychological processes and what we shall call speaker-image effects.

Speaker-Image Effects

Listeners necessarily respond on the basis of their own perceptions in any communication situation. They respond to their perceptions of the occasion, of the speaker's purpose, and of the premises that the speaker offers as beginning points for the logical and psychological processes discussed above. There is one inescapable beginning point in all speech-communication: that is the listener's perception of the source—what psychologists call *source credibility,* and what speech scholars refer to with the term *ethos.*[21] In the words of the late Carl I. Hovland, summarizing a number of experimental studies: "Who says something is usually as important as what is said in the determination of the impact of a communication."[22] Often cited, for example, is the study presenting a recorded speech on compulsory health insurance to groups of college students. Some heard the speaker introduced as

[21] See Kenneth Anderson and Theodore Clevenger, Jr., "A Summary of Experimental Research in Ethos," *Speech Monographs,* XXX (June, 1963), pp. 59–78.

[22] "Effects of the Mass Media of Communication," in Gardner Lindzey, ed., *Handbook of Social Psychology,* Vol. II, Reading, Mass.: Addison-Wesley Publishing Company, Inc., 1954, p. 1071.

the Surgeon-General of the United States; others heard the same speaker introduced as a communist. Listeners who heard Surgeon-General approved of the ideas in the speech and those who heard communist tended to reject the same ideas.[23]

The response processes in relation to the speaker-image also follow the logical model of IF . . . , THEN . . . : IF he says it, THEN it must be true (or false). The speaker, himself, becomes the premise from which the listener may move to a conclusion that may or may not be the one which the speaker proposes. Again, there are two sets of processes: the logical and the psychological.

Logical Responses to the Speaker-Image

"You may not like to hear me say this," a speaker might declare, "but I tell you from my own experience . . ." If the speaker-image is one of competence and trustworthiness, then the logical response is acceptance of his idea. When a listener moves reluctantly and consciously from speaker-image to a speaker's idea, he applies the logical process. More frequently listeners move easily and without awareness from speaker-image to either acceptance or rejection of the speakers' ideas: the application of psychological processes.

Psychological Responses to the Speaker-Image

Some analysts of the presidential campaigns of 1952 and 1956 attributed President Eisenhower's success to the image which the electorate had of his sincerity. Others said that his appeal was based on a father image. Both response patterns were probably operating. Yet many listeners attributed their favorable attitudes not to the effects of a speaker-image but to things that the presidential candidate had said: not to a reputation but to statements on the issues.

Speaker-image effects are potent, always present, and often underrated. This sometimes leads to errors of judgment regarding the consequences of what some may consider unethical behavior.

Speaker-Image Effects and Ethics

Quintilian insisted that an effective speaker is first of all "a good man" and secondly one who "speaks well." More—and often far more—than his validating materials, the speaker who is known as incor-

[23] Franklyn S. Haiman, "An Experimental Study of the Effects of Ethos in Public Speaking," *Speech Monographs,* XVI (1949), pp. 190–202.

ruptible has that image going for him. A speaker who risks passing along a little lie or an unconfirmed rumor in order to win an argument places much more in jeopardy than momentary regard or embarrassment. Ethical values in our culture are violated when we discover that someone has led us astray. One thinks immediately of the boy who amused himself by calling, "Wolf, wolf!" Right or wrong, we generalize that the speaker who would tell us something he is not sure about or quote out of context today is apt to be doing the same thing tomorrow. The potency of the speaker-image demands responsibility, then, on two grounds: the ethical and the pragmatic. A speaker is honest simply because he wants to be a responsible member of society or because he has learned that "honesty is the best policy." In the case of either motivation—though they are quite different—a speaker assures himself of future effectiveness at the same time that he attempts present persuasion.

The factors that contribute to speaker-image include some which have been identified in experimental research[24] and others which seem to be operating in actual speech-communication situations. The experimentally derived factors tend most often to be, on the one hand, perceived competence or authoritativeness in relation to the topic and, on the other hand, perceived personal trustworthiness or character. In addition to these, Aristotle identified a third factor—perceived good will: the extent to which listeners know that the speaker is motivated by good intentions; that he speaks without malice.

In addition to these factors of authority, trustworthiness, and friendship, other perceived aspects of a speaker attempting persuasion are apt to influence communication outcomes:

—Perceived common ground: the extent to which listeners see the speaker as being in the same boat with them.

—Motivational expectancies: how listeners see the purpose of the speaker. This is related to matters of latitudes of acceptance, rejection, and noncommitment.

—Ability expectancies: how listeners respond to the reputed speaking ability of the speaker. Listeners may admire fluency but be suspicious of glibness or disarmed by thoughtful hesitation.

—Language expectancies: how listeners respond to the appro-

[24] See, for instance, James C. McCroskey, "Scales for the Measurement of Ethos," *Speech Monographs,* XXXIII (March, 1966), pp. 65–72, in which independent factors of authoritativeness and character are reported. See, also, Andersen and Clevenger, cited above.

priateness of language used; whether it seems to suit the speaker-image, the occasion, the topic, and the listeners, themselves.

—Sponsorship of the speaker: in certain situations, how the listeners assess—consciously or unconsciously—the relationship between the speaker and the person or organization under whose aegis he is speaking.

In a given speech-communication situation, any or all of these factors can be operating to influence listeners to move—independently of what the speaker says—to conclusions in agreement with or in opposition to the speaker's idea. A speaker will often need to take them into account during his preparation and during his speaking.[25]

To summarize, the speaker-image is a most potent influence in determining persuasive effects. The student of speaking and listening must learn to assess speaker-image influence; to keep future effectiveness in mind, for what he says and does can change his own speaker-image; and to protect himself from irrelevant speaker-image influences.

The speaker-image is largely a matter of reputation, of prior perception. However, there is much that the effective speaker does—often automatically—that enhances his ethos or credibility:

1. He communicates his interest in his listeners.
2. He communicates his interest in his topic.
3. He communicates his interest in communicating.

Programing for Persuasion

What has been presented in Chapter 6 provides a general guide to organizing and outlining for persuasive speaking. However, there are some special principles that need to be taken into account here. These have to do with the order of presentation and with special methods of organizing.

Order of Presentation

Programing is, of course, a process of ordering information. While there has been a great deal of psychological research on the differential

[25] For a more detailed discussion of these speaker-image factors, see "What the Speaker Needs to Know about His Audience: General Listener Factors," in Paul D. Holtzman, *The Psychology of Speakers' Audiences,* Chapter 4, Glenview, Ill.: Scott, Foresman and Company (in press).

effects of ordering,[26] it is clear that there is no formula that applies in all situations. However, one principle is clear: for some listeners the common premise should be stated and supported first. Whether it be a common problem, a common need, or a common desire of both speaker and listeners, some listeners are not apt to associate the need with the proposal unless the former is presented first. For other listeners this ordering does not matter. They will seek, in their listening, to discover why the speaker is advocating what he is; to know what problem or need or desire would be taken care of by the proposal.[27] The safe bet, then, is from need-to-proposal; from common premise-to-speaker's conclusion.

A further implication for this ordering lies in the information on latitudes of noncommitment and rejection. If the speaker's proposal falls within his listeners' latitudes of noncommitment, listeners must be directed to focus on a common concern to which they are committed, so that they will then relate that commitment to the speaker's proposal when they learn what it is. If the speaker's proposal falls within his listeners' latitudes of rejection, only a careful programing from a series of premises can avoid a boomerang effect and the turning off of listeners.

In essence, then, a speaker is apt to be effective if he precedes any statement of his proposal with a clear statement of what is bothering both his listeners and himself. Thus, he may say—after a suitable introduction—"No matter how we may finally manage it, one thing is clear: we all want to avoid the human waste and suffering of futile, bloody riots." Gaining assent and building stronger commitment to such a premise, he is then ready to lead his listeners, step by step, to the point of accepting his plan.

Two warnings should be made here. One is that the speaker must

[26] See Carl I. Hovland, ed., *The Order of Presentation in Persuasion,* New Haven, Conn.: Yale University Press, 1957; note especially Chapter 6, "Need for Cognition and Order of Communication as Determinants of Opinion Change," by Arthur R. Cohen, pp. 79–97. For a recent review of pertinent research, see William J. McGuire, "Attitudes and Opinions," in Paul R. Farnsworth, Olga McNemar, and Quinn McNemar, eds., *Annual Review of Psychology,* Palo Alto, Calif.: Annual Reviews, 1966, section on "Order Effects in Persuasion," pp. 487–90.

[27] Cohen, in *Order of Presentation,* discovered that listeners with "high need for cognitive clarity" do not require the common premise-to-proposal ordering, while those with low need for cognitive clarity do. Both kinds of listeners are apt to be found in any given audience.

be sure that his proposal does follow from the common premise. Otherwise he may find himself in the position of a speaker in Cleveland who proposed a protest against the sale of a home to a Negro family. His common premise was a desire for maintaining dollar values of the homes in the neighborhood, and his proposed protest was the placing of For Sale signs in front of every home. An alert mayor then addressed the rally and pointed out, "If you do what is being proposed here your homes will nosedive in value. The way to hold up values is for every family to put out a sign which reads, 'This House is *Not* For Sale.' "

The second warning regarding programing for persuasion is the fact that often listeners know beforehand what the speaker will propose. In such a case, the speaker-image already contains the proposal before the speaker has a chance to say anything about the common premise. He must not adapt by pretending to be concerned with something else or by proposing something else. But he can draw attention to the fact that his listeners may not have thought of the connection between what concerns them mutually and the proposal which the listeners know is coming.

Whether or not the common premise is stated and supported before the proposal—and each instance must be determined on its own merits—the focus of the speaker's comments and of the listener's concern should be on that common premise. The methods detailed below are in all cases variations of the means of maintaining that focus.

Special Methods of Organizing

In discussing the order of presentation we have focused on one of the basic questions of organization: that of direct or indirect method of development. In the method of direct development the speaker deems it wise to state his idea first and then show how its acceptance would serve a common concern. In the indirect method of development the speaker begins with the common premise and leads his listeners, step by step, to discover that his proposal is the best way to deal with that need or value or problem. Of special interest and value is the problem-solving method, usually an indirect method.

Problem-solving method. In the problem-solving method of organizing persuasive speaking, listeners are provided with a sense of inquiry—with the speaker—into a problem of common concern. The basic organization, then, is that of the problem-solving discussion detailed in Chapter 13: analyzing the problem, its background history and causes, and examining the stakes of those involved; reviewing all possible solutions; establishing criteria for judging solutions; matching all solutions against those criteria; arriving at the solution which best meets all criteria. In the final step, then, the solution seemingly arrived at by listeners and speaker together becomes the speaker's proposal.

Although not applicable for greatest effectiveness in all cases, this method has many advantages that will enhance effectiveness whenever both speaker and listeners are deeply concerned about a problem to which there are solutions in addition to the one that may be commonly debated.

These advantages include:

1. The speaker who invites his listeners to confront the problem with him and cooperate in reaching the best possible decision creates an image of concern for the general welfare rather than that of a vested interest.

2. The speaker who has arrived at his solution to the problem through inquiry—a solution which he is now going to share with his listeners—is most likely to be convinced that he has found the best solution and to be confident that his listeners have much to gain. Further, the very experience of engaging in inquiry, as described in Chapter 13, prepares the speaker to talk with real understanding about the problem and its various solutions. Such a speaker stimulates an image of authority and involvement.

3. Since inquiry is apt to convince a speaker more forcefully than any other analysis of the problem or its solutions, it is also likely to provide the most effective method when recreating the experience with the listeners participating.

4. The problem-solving method of organization can be adapted to include the combined advantages of the other two special methods in persuasion: yes-response and this-or-nothing. The problem-solving method focuses the listener on the common premise; the this-or-nothing method helps the listener reject other proposals which do not effectively meet the criteria established to judge all solutions; the yes-response helps the listener compare the speaker's proposal with the criteria.

This-or-nothing method. The Citizens union of the City of New York is well known for its carefully considered recommendations in local elections. A candidate may be favored with the label, endorsed, or with lesser praise, preferred. It is for situations like the latter, in which no candidate (or solution to a problem) is totally satisfactory that the this-or-nothing method is particularly adapted. The speaker takes on an obligation to demonstrate that his proposition, above all those available, should be preferred. Alternative solutions to a problem are likely to have both advantages and disadvantages; to meet some criteria for evaluation and to violate others. The speaker is convinced, and seeks agreement from his listeners, that they may as well do nothing about the problem as accept other solutions which bring with them certain disadvantages and, therefore, new problems.

The procedure, then, is one of eliminating, one-by-one, all solutions—on the basis of their disadvantages—to arrive inevitably at the choice which the speaker is advocating.

Yes-response method. Yes-response is a method of avoiding conflict by gaining agreement in a series of favorable responses necessary before the speaker can gain assent for his proposal. It is, for example, the process of explaining to listeners what is to be gained before offering a proposal which may require money and sacrifice. If a speaker wants to increase the amount of money available for public education, he cannot abruptly tell overburdened taxpayers that they must dig deeper into their pockets to build additional schools and to raise the salaries of teachers. Still, he knows that parents want the best for their children (and for others') and he can count on their saying "yes" to his declaration that education is vital in our increasingly competitive society. He can also get them to agree that local schools must not be inferior to those in surrounding towns or neighborhoods, lest their children be thereby placed at a disadvantage. He can get them to accept the logic that, like it or not, an increasing school population naturally demands increasing school facilities. On these and similar grounds he may win a "yes" to his statement that present conditions must be remedied at once to meet the new demands.

Thus, step by step, the persuasive speaker strengthens not just one common premise but a chain of premises, leading logically and with some psychological appeal to a final "yes" in response to his main idea or proposal. This is the essence of programing: step by step progression through successive agreements to the ultimate agreement which the speaker seeks.

Programing for Action

A listener with new knowledge or understanding of a process is not necessarily able to engage in that process. Similarly, a listener with a new belief is not necessarily one who will act on that new belief. When listener action is the goal, the persuader must engage in special, specific preparation and programing in addition to that designed to invite new listener beliefs or attitudes. The action itself must be made clear, attractive, and perhaps easier. In addition, there is often a need to secure from the listener a commitment to action. Many have been the speeches on current controversies with a concluding plea to "write your congressman." Though the speaker succeeds in inviting a new belief on the subject, the action he calls for is another matter and almost always a forgotten matter.

How does the speaker elicit the needed action? In programing for persuasion he has asked, "How can I induce my listeners to believe what I think they should?" Now he must address a different question: "How can I induce my listeners with their new or strengthened belief to *do* something about it?" The speaker who would exert pressure on representatives in Washington in answer to this question might think of several programing possibilities:

—Support the idea of writing with information about effects of such pressure in some instances; with the idea that there is satisfaction in taking the trouble to do what needs to be done; with the prediction that listeners can expect a thoughtful reply from their representatives.

—Propose or distribute an outline as a guide for listeners to use in writing.

—Include in a distributed memo the request that you be given (or allowed to copy) all replies from the congressmen.

—Ask for carbon copies of the letters.

—Distribute postcards, already addressed, and ask for a commitment that the listener write and mail the card that same day (or, if there is time, ask that the cards be written and left with the speaker at the end of the class meeting).

—Ask for a commitment to write; announce that you must know, when the class meets again, how many letters were sent.

—Offer to stamp and mail the letters.

The imaginative, concerned speaker will think of ways—appropriate to each desired action—to effectively elicit needed action or commitment to action, but only if he remembers that action does not automatically follow belief or attitude and if he remembers to program specifically for listener-action.

Conclusion

Persuasion is an essential part of daily, democratic living. We will make freedom of speech work for us only if we are willing to listen to persuasion and to learn as much as we can about persuasion processes. As listeners we must seek the common premise, if any, from which to consider the speaker's proposal. As speakers, we must seek the common premise, if any, upon which to base our speaking—or risk the image of self-serving propagandist.

The formal logic model, "IF . . . , THEN . . .", is applied, by analogy, to the processes—both logical and psychological—through which listeners may be expected to move from the speaker's information to his idea and from the speaker-image to acceptance of his idea.

Programing for persuasive effects requires careful adaptation of available methods to particular circumstances. Whatever the method, one central requirement stands out: that the sequence of materials, ideas, and their development focuses listeners on the common premise and on how that premise would be served by adherence to the speaker's proposal.

Exercises

· *Questions for Discussion*

1. What are your attitudes toward persuasion? Toward controversy? Do you have one standard for political speakers and another for advertisers?
2. How many times have you been involved in persuasion as speaker or listener in the past twenty-four hours?
3. How do you distinguish between persuasion and propaganda? How is this different from the distinction made by Roger Brown?
4. What can be gained from listening to the other side? Even if your mind is made up?
5. Is it right for people to try to influence the attitudes, feelings, or beliefs of others?
6. Why is it necessary to plan specifically to induce action? Shouldn't strengthened feeling or new belief be enough to spark action?
7. How can you tell the difference between persuasive and infor-

mative speaking by your classmates? Does the speaker always know his purpose?

8. Do you think that psychological appeals by speakers are fair? Or do you consider them unethical?

9. Why is the study of inquiry so important to persuasion?

10. Why can't induction deal with certainties instead of probabilities? Do any of the logical processes mentioned deal with certainties? Why?

11. Why is it a mistake to assume that when one event follows another there is causality involved?

12. Do you believe that you can develop an ability to use stimulating, vivid, colorful language in persuasion? Why?

13. How is the problem-solving method of organization related to the other methods?

14. When might you organize persuasive speaking by direct development?

15. Do you talk about ideas in the same order as they appear in your outline? Why would you not follow that order?

16 What is meant by the *common premise?*

· *Projects for Speaking and Listening*

1. Listen to a televised speech that is designed to persuade the American public or some segment of it. Determine the speaker's purpose, his method of persuasion, his common premise, the listener processes of reasoning and appeal that were planned for, the effect of the speech upon you, and the effect of the speech on its intended audience.

2. Plan a series of two classroom talks to persuade which would culminate in a new listener belief. The first is to be designed to strengthen the attitude, feeling, or belief, which becomes the common premise for the second.

3. For your next assignment, program your ideas and materials as it might be done according to at least three different methods and then select the one which you think will be most effective.

4. List ten topics suitable for persuasive speaking, and phrase a specific purpose and central idea for each. Indicate what might be the common premises with different audiences.

5. List five recent decisions you have made. Try to determine what processes of reasoning and what processes of appeal led to each decision.

6. Plan with another member of your speech class to talk on a controversial issue in such a way that you will be, sincerely, on different sides of the issue. Have listeners ballot on how they feel about the issue before and again after both of you speak. With the help of the listeners, try to analyze what made the difference, if there is a difference.

12 · *Enhancing Sociability*

Much social talk, ranging from casual conversation to formal public speaking, has an aim other than to convey information or to achieve agreement on disputed issues. Individuals talk and listen to one another in part simply to enhance sociability—to increase their enjoyment in being together. Sometimes this is called speech to entertain, but this traditional label never has been very satisfactory. Social talk serves a more important function than merely to pass time enjoyably.

A great deal of the talking and the listening that occurs under casual circumstances may seem to be aimless, in the sense that the discourse is relaxed, relatively formless, and expressive of strong and intimate feelings. Nevertheless, such speaking and listening are highly valued. Normal individuals dread being deprived of companionship. If required to be alone for a time, they may turn on the radio or television, not to learn something, and not even to be entertained, but to feel the sociability of hearing human speech. The real purpose of much speech (including most conversation and many public speeches) is to knit together more closely and more pleasantly the ties of sociability.

Functions of Sociable Speech

The functions of speech designed to enhance sociability may be either highly personal or broadly social. It may serve special and personal needs of an individual, or it may contribute to the attainment of generalized social goals. These functions are: (1) to strengthen social solidarity; (2) to renew loyalty to common goals; (3) to accomplish the ceremonial needs of society; (4) to maintain courage under discouraging or threatening circumstances; (5) to stimulate individual and group endeavor; (6) to create and share pleasure; and (7) to nurture humanistic qualities, both individually and in the group.

To Strengthen Social Solidarity

Individuals value their separate identity, their differences, their special, or peculiar, or unique characteristics. They also value association and fellowship with their comrades. Everyone feels "an abiding sense of incompleteness . . . a social hunger . . . a craving for companionship."[1] A basic attribute which man shares with other species is that he is gregarious. Another basic attribute is the determination to be true to oneself, whatever the cost. The normal person insists stubbornly that he is a unique being, with a personality that is entirely his own, and equally stubbornly strives to be liked, accepted, and respected as a member of his group. Because of these two contrary tendencies, man's social behavior assumes a bewildering variety of forms, such as: "A man denounces his neighbor, a worker praises his foreman, a diplomat writes a negative evaluation of his assigned country, a husband and wife call each other vile names, union and management leaders excoriate the negotiator, a boy and girl declare their mutual love, and an angry crowd threatens an integration leader."[2] One set of feelings draws people together in friendly cooperation, while another set impels them to hostility and conflict. As the anthropologist Bronislaw Malinowski observes: "Each verbal statement by a human being has the aim and function of expressing some thought or feeling . . . in order either to serve purposes of common action, or to establish ties

[1] Paul Halmos, *Solitude and Privacy: A Study of Social Isolation,* New York: Philosophical Library, Inc., 1953, p. 4.

[2] Albert Pepitone, *Attraction and Hostility,* New York: Atherton Press, 1964, p. 3.

of purely social communion, or else to deliver the speaker of violent feelings or passions."[3]

Despite the homogeneous nature of man, harmony, comradeship, and cooperation are not to be taken for granted. There always are contrary factors inducing conflict, hostility, and competitive struggle. Much talk, therefore, is needed to reassure people of their friendly regard for one another, to heighten their sense of community relationship, to remind themselves of their need, respect, and liking for each other. This is clearly the motivation underlying much social conversation. It is a sufficient justification for time and effort devoted to conferences and discussions—in addition to their other fruitful results. It is the principal result of many talks given at businessmen's luncheon clubs and women's organizations. Whenever there seems to be a need for pep rallies, or for group meetings to hear talks on patriotism, or school spirit, or to boost employee morale, the aim to be served is the strengthening of the group's social solidarity.

To Renew Loyalty to Common Goals

The Fourth of July oration, which for over a century was an unbroken tradition in every American community, had as its purpose the renewal of patriotism. A professor of speech who read over 800 of the 2,500 such orations that he found had been published, reported: "The orator assumed it his obligation to remind his hearers of their unique identity as citizens of the United States, to restate national ideals, and to instruct all in the ways these ideals might be preserved."[4] The speaker did not decide for himself what to say; this was largely predetermined by the occasion and the customs concerning it. The same principle applies in much of the speaking done on the anniversary of famous events. Again, the aim of the speaker is to utter the sentiments of all: to restate and thereby to cement their common loyalities. "For so, if we learn aright the lesson of the hour," as President Chester A. Arthur said at the one hundredth anniversary of the battle of Yorktown,

[3] Bronislaw Malinowski, "The Problem of Meaning in Primitive Langauges," Supplement I of C. K. Ogden and I. A. Richards, *The Meaning of Meaning,* New York: Harcourt, Brace & World, Inc., 1923, p. 307.

[4] Howard H. Martin, "The Fourth of July Oration," *Quarterly Journal of Speech,* 44 (December, 1957), p. 394. See also Cedric Larson, "Patriotism in Carmine: 162 Years of July 4th Oratory," in *Quarterly Journal of Speech,* 26 (February, 1940), pp. 12–25.

"shall we be incited to transmit to the generation which shall follow the precious legacy which our fathers left to us—the love of liberty, protected by law."[5]

To Accomplish the Ceremonial Needs of Society

A great deal of private and public speaking aims to fulfill what Thomas Jefferson described in the Declaration of Independence as "a decent regard for the opinions of mankind." When a friend's daughter marries, or his wife is ill, or he has received a promotion, or is given an award to mark twenty-five years of service, or has been honored as an outstanding citizen, or his house burns down, or his father dies—on all these and on a great number of other occasions—it is important to say proper things in proper ways. On occasions marked by either sadness or gladness, there are ritualistic or ceremonial comments or speeches required by good taste and etiquette. When a person dies, his burial must be accompanied by suitable words spoken in a funeral address and in commitment at the cemetery. When a person is honored, the principal aspect of the honoring is the presentation of appropriate remarks to the appropriate listeners. On such occasions speakers strive for originality, not of sentiments but of ways of dramatizing them. What is desired is that the ceremonial requirements rather carefully established by social custom shall be gracefully met.

To Maintain Courage under Discouraging Circumstances

A famous example of a speech to incite courage is the remark alleged to have been said by a Marine sergeant in the Battle of Belleau Woods in World War I as he led his squad out of the trenches in an attack through heavy German machine-gun fire, "Come on, you SOB's, do you want to live forever?" Captains of athletic teams are usually selected because of their ability to inspire their teammates to special endeavor. In time of war, patriotic addresses are given frequently to maintain courage and zeal.[6] People who are ill, or communities enduring a depression or suffering from a disaster (such as a flood or a tornado) need to be cheered up with appropriate remarks. Perhaps Winston Churchill's greatest contribution as Prime Minister of Great

[5] Frederick Saunders, ed., *Centenary Orations . . . from Bunker Hill to Yorktown,* New York: E. B. Treat, 1882, p. 880.

[6] Cedric Larson and James R. Mock, "The Four Minute Men," *Quarterly Journal of Speech,* 25 (February, 1939), pp. 97–112.

Britain during World War II was his inspirational speaking, such as that he did on June 4, 1940, after the British army had been defeated at Dunkirk:

> "We shall go on to the end, we shall fight in France, we shall fight on the seas and oceans, we shall fight with growing confidence and growing strength in the air, we shall defend our Island, whatever the cost may be, we shall fight on the beaches, we shall fight on the landing grounds, we shall fight in the fields and in the streets, we shall fight in the hills; we shall never surrender. . . ."[7]

Words of comfort and inspiration are often needed; and those who can phrase and present them effectively perform a valuable function of leadership.

To Stimulate Individual and Group Effort

Apathy and indifference are as damaging to achievement as are fear and discouragement. Leo Tolstoy, the great Russian writer, in his short story, "God Sees the Truth but Waits," tried to dramatize the point of view that it is necessary not only to understand a problem but to feel also a sense of personal involvement to do something constructive about it. Teen-agers who derided the Vietnam War by carrying signs reading, "God Isn't Dead—He Just Doesn't Want to Get Involved," were making the same point. Many times people "who don't want to get involved" need to be stirred to active participation. Knowing what is right and wrong and thinking correct thoughts about it may characterize good people who stop short without committing themselves to action. As the English orator Edmund Burke said during the French Revolution, "All that is necessary for evil to triumph in the world is for enough good people to do nothing about it." One of the valuable functions of speech is to arouse feelings sufficiently so that people who know what ought to be done will feel that they ought to do it. William James, the philosopher and psychologist, wrote that people may be divided into two groups: those who say, "Someone ought to do it, but why should I" and those who say, "Someone ought to do it; and why not I?" Much of the speaking on such issues as civil rights, air pollution, and crime prevention is aimed precisely at the goal of stimulating individual and group effort. What should be done may be understood and agreed upon. The action stage of getting it done, however,

[7] Winston S. Churchill, *Blood, Sweat, and Tears,* New York: G. P. Putnam's Sons, 1941, p. 297.

requires speech that both arouses feelings of involvement and indicates actions to be taken.

To Create and Share Pleasure

Telling jokes, recounting amusing experiences, and relating dramatic or exciting or anticlimactic stories of human interest, of travel or of adventure constitute a large portion of social conversation and also may form the principal substance of speeches given on occasions where the primary aim is entertainment. The annual "Ladies Night" at Rotary and other luncheon clubs, or the spring banquet held by social fraternities, or the awards presentation dinner for bowling clubs or similar organizations are but a few of the many examples of community gatherings in which speakers are invited primarily with the hope that they will be entertaining. And, of course, even the most serious talk is enlivened and, therefore, holds attention better if it has entertaining qualities.

To Nurture Humanistic Qualities

An essential characteristic of human beings is the capacity to talk. We talk, among other reasons, simply to develop our humanity. A linguist calls man "the languagized mammal."[8] A philosopher attests that: "Man's conquest of the world undoubtedly rests on the supreme development of his brain, which allows him to synthesize, delay, and modify his reactions by the interpolation of symbols in the gaps and confusions of direct experience, and by means of 'verbal signs' to add the experiences of other people to his own."[9] A sociologist claims that "Man as a social being exists in and through communication; communication is as basic to man's nature as food and sex."[10] We talk because talking is a behavior characteristic of our nature; we talk together because our kind of society (distinguished by free cooperation—as contrasted with the instinctual automatism of an ant hill or a bee hive) depends upon the interactions of speaking and listening. And we talk also for the sheer exuberant pleasure of stating, and exploring, and

[8] Charlton Laird, *The Miracle of Language,* Greenwich, Conn.: Fawcett Publications, Inc., 1957, p. 16.

[9] Susanne Langer, *Philosophy in a New Key,* Baltimore, Md.: Penguin Books, Inc. 1948, p. 22.

[10] Hugh Dalziel Duncan, *Communication and Social Order,* New York: Bedminster Press, 1962, p. xxvii.

debating ideas and feelings. The inability to express oneself is rightly felt as a limitation upon one's independent identity. It is resented when such limitations are imposed by outside authority; and it is deeply regretted when such inability derives from one's own verbal incapacity. Human beings value the right to speak and the ability to speak well because in this they are most truly human. Good conversation is the mark of a cultivated society, and discriminative talking and listening are marks of discerning and intelligent minds.

These seven functions of speech, which have been described, are evident to some extent in all discourse, including that which aims primarily to inform or to persuade. They are, however, valuable simply and precisely as means for the enhancement of sociability. Taken together, they are means of preserving contact. When any one or several of these functions are being accomplished, the discourse serves to strengthen the ties by which speakers and listeners are bound together for their mutual satisfaction.

Types of Speech to Enhance Sociability

The kinds of speaking, which aim toward accomplishment of the seven functions described in the preceding sections, may be classified as echoic, ritualistic, inspirational, and entertaining.

The echoic speeches are those in which the speaker does not aim to be original or individualistic in his comments but has the primary function of representing what the group wants to have said in the manner in which custom decrees. Speaking that aims to strengthen group solidarity and to renew loyalties is basically of this type. The eighteenth century English poet, Alexander Pope, described this kind of discourse as consisting of: "What oft was said but ne'er so well described." The speaker excels by the sureness of his insight in saying just the right things in the right ways. Many commencement speeches and many sermons (though by no means all of either type) are largely echoic. Echoic speaking is appropriate on all occasions when the group desires a spokesman who will render its own sentiments suitably. Speeches of presentation, of acceptance of an award, of farewell, and of commendation are of this type.

Speeches that echo the sentiments of the group often have in addition to this function the characteristics of ritual. The sorrow of death must be ameliorated by the dignity and the traditionalism of a ritualistic ceremony, including an address that follows an expected form. Speeches of nomination to high office normally have a ritualistic quality. This is even truer of the customary speeches on significant anniversaries, such as Veterans Day. Ritualistic speeches are called for whenever the occasion is clearly ceremonial.

Inspirational speeches may aim to maintain courage or faith or to stimulate high endeavor. The inspirational speaker echoes the sentiments of his listeners in the sense that they agree fully with what he says; but he needs to accentuate or heighten their feelings, or to refine or clarify their beliefs. A preacher is being inspirational when he induces parishioners to live more fully in accordance with their religious beliefs. A football coach may give an inspirational talk to his team at halftime in a game to induce them to play with more intensity. A sales manager may hearten his sales force with an inspirational talk concerning the probabilities of their success. A teacher may inspire a class to see greater value or more interest in the subject matter being studied.

Among all the forms of talk that aim to enhance sociability, the most widely used and in this sense the most typical is the speech to entertain. For this reason it is discussed in greater detail.

To Entertain

Entertaining speech frequently is humorous, but not always. Humor is indeed its major wellspring. When a person who is known to be a good storyteller gets a sparkle in his eyes and a crinkle of humor around his lips as he fills a pause in the conversation with, "Did you hear the one about . . . ," his listeners lean forward with eager anticipation. Laughter draws people together and safeguards individuals from frustrated unhappiness. When it is announced that an entertaining speaker is scheduled, the audience gathers with the glad expectation of enjoying some hearty laughs. Nevertheless, despite the importance of humor, experience reminds us that not all entertainment is humorous.

Escapism. An individual who goes to a lecture on explorations in the Antarctic does not expect to laugh but does expect to be entertained. What is sought is relaxation through avoidance of the humdrum or demanding realities of everyday life. The principal function of such discourse is to help individuals to escape from problems. Talk of this kind may be melodramatic. It may be serious in its depiction of dangers and the toil of penetration into the icebound continent. But it also is marked by a high degree of unfamiliarity and of remoteness from the listeners' immediate concerns. This, more truly than humor, is the hallmark of speech that aims to entertain.

Good humor. Whether humorous or not, entertaining speech is marked by geniality and good humor. The tension of conflict and personalized competition is strained out. Good fellowship and the enjoyment of other people's company are emphasized, rather than the struggle to succeed or to excel. If this seems not to be the case in recitals of crime, often marked by extreme brutality (which comprise a large proportion of television entertainment), the fact is that such narratives are remote and unreal. They happen, but not to people such as the family viewers. When the point is made that such crimes are real and a real problem to be dealt with, the depictions cease to be entertainment and become exercises in persuasion. When violence is described in entertaining speeches, it usually is with a touch of ridicule, or exaggeration, or fantasy, giving the listeners to understand that the struggle is not to be taken seriously. In all speaking that is intended to entertain it must be clearly evident that "nobody is mad at anybody"; good humor is the first rule.

Unreality and exaggeration. The quality of unreality also stands among the basic characteristics of entertaining speech. A ludicrously exaggerated discussion of how to park your car in the busy downtown business district might be entertaining; its tone would be vastly different from a serious discussion of traffic problems. This element in entertainment is illustrated in the motion picture (now on the Late Late Shows), *Along Came Jones,* in which Gary Cooper, as a gangling, ineffective cowboy, is given the kindly advice: "Shoot 'em in the right eye first. It spoils their aim."

The unusual. The description of unknown facts or narrative of unusual experiences may be rendered with zest and with emphasis upon their strangeness, rather than upon any usefulness they may have, with the aim to entertain. More important in the result is the tone and spirit of the presentation than the nature of the facts discussed. A speaker discussing bees might give a great deal of information about how they live. If his purpose is to entertain, he will present the information with heightened drama and in a spirit of playful good humor. He will emphasize the most interesting aspects, not necessarily the most significant. The conclusion toward which he progresses may be fanciful, such as: "Thus, as we see, bees are much like people, only less quarrelsome"; or "The hive is like a home, with one mother, no father, some lazy brothers, and a lot of hard-working sisters." The accent is upon the unusual for its own sake, not for what it might teach.

Comedy. What has been said about entertainment not being confined to humor does not derogate from the fact that humor or other aspects of the comic do indeed constitute its principal form. Under many circumstances, to be entertaining is considered synonymous with being funny. The range is wide, from slapstick actions and crude jokes to refined wit and witticisms. True humor, it has often been said, cannot be well translated from one language to another. More than this, it cannot readily even be quoted in its own language. The best of humor consists not of gag-lines or of jokes but of situations that are gradually unfolded. Mark Twain's "The Invalid's Story," and Charles Dickens' "The Pickwick Club" can scarcely be related except in the words, and at the leisurely pace, of their authors. Genuine humor consists of the way in which people and events are viewed: with affection but with a keen awareness of their ludicrous incapacities; and also of how they are described: with a mixture of exaggeration and understatement, in which dire calamities turn out to be only minor inconveniences—as in the story of Pat, who stepped into an elevator shaft, fell ten stories, then can back up to warn Mike, "Watch out for that first step. It's a long one!"—or in which purely imaginary events have widespread effects—as in Thurber's story, "The Day the Dam Burst."

Sympathy. The characters in an entertaining speech may endure all manner of strange mishaps, but they don't get hurt. The cartoon comedies familiar in motion picture theatres show their characters subjected to incredible disasters, from which they emerge enraged or frustrated or surprised, but unscathed. The thin line separating humor from pathos lies precisely at this point. In pathetic stories the hero suffers pain; in humorous stories he suffers no more than a momentary loss of dignity. Such a master entertainer as Charlie Chaplin has been much admired for his ability to shift back and forth between tears and laughter. Humor, like pathos, depends upon sympathetic identification with the characters. In humor, there is a sudden awareness of the incongruity of a situation, accompanied by the certainty that no harm has been done. There is pathos in the public defeat of an admirable man; but when Adlai Stevenson, after losing the 1960 Presidential nomination to John F. Kennedy, wryly told his supporters, "A funny thing happened to me on the way to the election," they burst into appreciative laughter relieved and pleased by the assurance his quip gave them that he had emerged from the experience with his spirits unscathed. The humor depends upon the hearers' sympathetic involvement; they must care whether the character in the narrative is hurt in order to feel a burst of genuine relief when they learn he is not. As Max Eastman says in what is perhaps the best book on the nature of humor: "Like all of our emotional life, humor is deeply, and is indeed primarily, social. It flourishes best among the genially gregarious. . . . We find things funnier when we are in company than when alone."[11] Humor not only knits social bonds more closely but it also profits from the web of sympathy binding people together.

Wit. Irony, whimsy, paradox, puns, burlesque, and all forms of verbal play (even including baby talk and mimicry of drunken speech or of foreign dialects) comprise forms of wit, which have always been part of the stock in trade of skilled humorists. Oscar Wilde's distortion of familiar ideas, to display the modicum of truth in their opposites, is a familiar example—for instance: "When the gods wish to punish us they answer our prayers," from *An Ideal Husband;* or "In this world there are only two tragedies. One is not getting what one wants, and the other is getting it," from *Lady Windermere's Fan.* While most people may complain (or boast) about their operations, a man of wit curtains the pathos behind a thin veil of whimsy: "One of the advantages of surgery, to a man at loose ends in Boston, is that it entitles him to a night at a hospital in advance of the operation. In short, it gets him in off the streets."[12] Wit is one of the highest forms of humor, for it demands intelligence enough (in both speaker and listener) so that truths uttered obliquely may make more sense than if they were presented flatly and directly.

Irrelevance. Incongruity, or the pretense of finding logical relationships where obviously none exist, is another characteristic of entertaining speech. This quality was utilized by the speaker who said: "My reason for going to college is that I'm overweight, my father has crossed eyes, and my mother won't let us buy a blue automobile. These reasons may not seem convincing to you, but they're better than my roommate's claim that he came because he'd rather listen to lectures by professors than nagging by the girl next door. Now stay with me, and I'll try to make it clear why my reasons for being here are better than those of half the students on campus. In the first place, being overweight and dumb gets you nothing except to be the laughingstock of your home town. But when you get a college education you can begin to throw your weight around. . . ." Thus the speech proceeds, not quite making sense, though including tantalizing suggestions that it may, perhaps, deviate into logic, perhaps in the next sentence. Meanwhile, as

[11] Max Eastman, *The Enjoyment of Laughter,* Garden City, N.Y.: Halcyon House Publications, 1936, p. 68.

[12] E. B. White, *The Second Tree from the Corner,* New York: Harper & Row, Publishers, n. d. (1955), p. 3.

in other forms of humor, the speaker should manage somehow to help his listeners attain flashes of insight amidst the flow of good-humored nonsense.

Irreverence. Another major type of humor is that which aids "man's normal rebellion against restraint."[13] Serious sacrilege or selfish evasion of authority may be frowned upon and punished with disapproval or discipline. Because of such restraints, individuals feel so penned in by social conventions, regulations, and laws that permissible flouting of authority or of established codes is a frequent source of entertainment. This is why off-color stories and jokes about the minister or the absent-minded professor are funny. Mother-in-law jokes arise from this same enjoyment of the acceptably irreverent. Privates in the army like to jest about the alleged awkwardness or dumbness of sergeants. Pomposity is always a subject for wit. When irreverence breaks out of the bounds of the permissible, however, listeners wince at the speaker's bad taste. The aim in irreverent humor should be to release tensions, not to create them or to intensify them. The result sought is laughter, not embarrassment. So long as basic respect for law, morals, and authority is not affronted, jests at their expense are generally appreciated.

Delivery of Speech to Enhance Sociability

When the chief aim of discourse is to enhance sociability, whether it is echoic, ritualistic, inspirational, or entertaining, and whichever of the seven social functions it may seek to accomplish, the delivery should make apparent the speaker's poise, confidence, and full mastery of the situation. Speakers should also manifest an unmistakable aura of good will concerning their subject matter and for their listeners. Tension, uncertainty, and lack of command are always handicaps in speaking, but they are especially detrimental to the establishment of closer social bonds. The speaker should not have to struggle for thoughts or words. Listeners should not reveal distaste for the situation or boredom. If the auditors feel that the speaker is struggling to remember what he will say next, that he is unsure of his ability to command their interest, or that he is worried about his own lack of communicative skills, they will suffer with him and be less affected by the thoughts

[13] Albert Rapp, *The Origins of Wit and Humor,* New York: E. P. Dutton & Co., 1951, p. 110.

and feelings he is trying to convey. Similarly, in no other type of oral discourse is it so important that the audience show clearly the depth of their own sympathetic involvement in the situation. The enhancement of sociability is an exercise in mutuality and reciprocity. It succeeds only when there is a unity of intention, a commonality of purpose. Unless these factors are not only present but clearly recognized, the speaker cannot be the spokesman for the group.

A concurrent requirement is that the speaker make it plain that he realizes and accepts the nature of his responsibility. His purpose is not to inform those who do not understand nor to persuade those who may be opposed to his ideas. His purpose is solely and completely to enrich, enliven, or animate sentiments that are already widely held and accepted. He is not striving to wrestle with the judgment of his listeners, nor to inform their intellects, nor to change their attitudes. His purpose is to help them to be what they wish to become.

Adaptation to and rapport with the listeners are absolute necessities. The speaker must leave no doubt that his subject and his method of handling it are suited to the occasion. His speech should reflect the situation, the mood of his audience, and the mutuality of their concern with the subject.[14] A similar responsibility rests also upon the listeners. Discourse aimed to enhance sociability is necessarily a team enterprise. The speaker is not trying to sell; the listeners need not resist. The one is serving as the agent or the instrument for the many. Unless all are working toward the same end, the goal is not social enhancement but something else. The church service, the commencement exercise, the anniversary celebration, the award presentation, the after-dinner program, and all such community ceremonies are occasions designed primarily to enhance the sociability, the unity, the accord, of those who attend. Accomplishment of this aim is the responsibility which the speakers and the listeners jointly undertake.

[14] Bronislaw Malinowski, pointing out that words are not enough to stimulate and maintain social interaction, insists that communication designed to enhance sociability must be (as he terms it) *phatic*. His meaning is that people communicate their basic feelings to one another through a totality of nonsymbolic sounds and bodily tensions—none of which has definable meaning in itself, but which, cumulatively, make clear the attitudes and feelings that underlie the communication. See Harry Weinberg, *Levels of Knowing and Existence,* New York: Harper & Row, Publishers, Inc., 1959, pp. 40–2; and S. I. Hayakawa, "The Language of Social Cohesion," *Language in Thought and Action,* New York: Harcourt, Brace & World, Inc., 1941, pp. 69–81.

Conclusion

A great deal of oral discourse is not aimed to impose upon listeners the understanding or the conviction of the speaker; it is designed instead to enable the group to celebrate the fact of their cordial sociability, or to deepen and clarify their common goals and feelings. The speaker and the listener under these circumstances are very definitely on the same team, working together to accomplish the same general end. The speaker's endeavor is not to devise means of mastering his audience but of serving its needs. The listeners are neither seeking new knowledge nor resisting an effort to change their beliefs; they are uniting with the speaker to intensify shared feelings. These are the characteristics unifying the seven functions and the four types of speech that enhance sociability; and they are illuminated in the widely popular and frequently used speech to entertain. The study of this kind of speaking is valuable for its own sake and also because all discourse—including that which seeks to inform or to persuade—succeeds only when there is underlying it and finally evident the cardinal fact that speaker and listeners share common purposes and seek similar ends.

Exercises

· *Questions for Discussion*

1. How do the functions of the speech for sociability fit in the discussion of purposes in Chapter 4? In what other ways could you designate or describe the purpose to enhance sociability?

2. How does the speaker–listener relationship in this kind of discourse differ from that in the other purposes of oral communication? Is the difference largely a matter of degree? Is it a significant difference in the sense that it changes the communicative behavior of speaker and listeners?

3. How does the conflict between the sense of individuality and the sentiments of homogeneity affect the problems of oral communication?

4. If a speaker is saying what everybody already knows, is this necessarily a fault? What must he do to render it a virtue?

5. What is meant by *involvement?* What may speakers—and lis-

teners—do to intensify group and individual effort in matters of mutual concern?

6. Illustrate each of the seven functions of social speech from examples found on your campus or in your own community. Are some of them more useful or more desirable than others? Should any of these functions be discontinued or their pursuit discouraged?

7. Consider each of the nine characteristics of speech to entertain. Which ones do you find most often utilized by professional entertainers on television? Which ones are the most useful in conversation? Which may best be employed for entertaining speeches?

8. How does the responsibility of listeners to the discourse aimed to enhance sociability differ from that in regard to other kinds of speaking? How does this purpose affect the responsibility of the speaker?

9. To what extent and in what ways should speech to entertain be used in the more serious speeches to inform or to persuade?

· *Projects for Speaking and Listening*

1. Members of the class may suggest subjects for discussion on which they feel there is considerable unanimity of agreement but with variations of concern or involvement. For example, all might agree that there is general responsibility to aid the impoverished and otherwise disadvantaged; but there might be considerable differences of feeling as to the extent to which individuals should try to do something constructive about the problems. Or the class might find itself in agreement that the United States is unfortunate in its entanglements in Southeast Asia, but might disagree concerning many aspects of the problem and concerning what individuals may or should do about it. As the subjects are suggested, class members should discuss them sufficiently to enable them finally to select one that has considerable complexity yet concerning which there is agreement on the basic attitude toward it. Examples might include: the brotherhood of all mankind, affection and respect for parents, loyalty and liking for one's school, the responsibilities of good citizenship, the values of intellectual freedom.

2. Each student should prepare a brief speech on an aspect of the general subject which represents what he would most like to say and which he feels either does or should represent also a basic conviction of his classmates. In his presentation of the speech he should try to make it very evident that he is representing the feelings and beliefs of the entire group, while also seeking to clarify and intensify their reactions.

3. Alternatively, each member of the class may present a brief speech intended to entertain, either humorous or escapist, as he may prefer.

4. At the conclusion of the speeches, discussion should clarify the ways in which both speakers and listeners met (or partially failed to meet) their special responsibilities in this discourse aimed to enhance sociability.

13 · Group Processes

Today's communicator finds himself participating in a wide variety of discussion situations and forms, ranging from informal family gabfests at breakfast to staff conferences at work, or to club meetings in the evening. There is no question that man's maximum application of his communicative abilities is in talking things over as a participant in groups that might be as small as two or three persons and up to a size of ten, or a hundred, or even more. In these situations, he makes frequent use of his abilities as both speaker and listener, bringing to bear all the principles, methods, and techniques of the human communication process. Discussion, then, affords the greatest opportunities for adaptation, flexibility, and resourcefulness in relation to different people, subjects, and settings.

There often is neither need nor opportunity for formal preparation. Yet one tries always to call upon his knowledge of principles of good speaking and listening, almost without giving conscious attention to them. The larger the storehouse of these, and the better he has developed his ability to use them, the better discussant he will be. But there are many discussion situations of a more formal nature for which he may need to prepare more carefully. One of these may be in an approaching meeting where a certain subject is to be discussed and there is much controversy over it. He should read up on the subject so that he can supply facts and information, or shape his thinking in relation to arguments pro and con. Or, if a more formal situation lies ahead, such as a panel in front of an audience, he prepares in other ways.

This chapter is concerned with the principles and techniques for planning, participating in, and leading discussions. Many of these are adaptations of speech principles which we have already discussed; others are special principles peculiar to the discussion process. But we have frequently pointed out that we do not have new and separate communication principles and methods for every situation; we learn to adapt and to apply.

Thus our first principle of discussion is to suggest that all of the basics of good speech communication be reviewed, with consideration given to their use in preparing for discussions within the speech course and in the countless situations in daily living.

The Nature of Discussion

There are many ways to define discussion. Ours is a simple one: it is the communicative interaction and exchange of messages among two or more persons in a cooperative effort to accomplish a group objective.[1] Except for some social conversation where we have no particular goal except that of having a cordial and pleasant time, meaningful discussion is goal-centered. In a business conference or at the meeting of a club, the goal may be to arrive at a specific decision or to impart or develop information. In a public panel, the goal may be to solve a problem but not necessarily to reach a specific decision. The purposes of discussion, then, may be to solve a problem, to gather information, to learn, to make a decision, or simply to enjoy each other's remarks and company.

We are presently concerned chiefly with problem-solving discussion, as this is probably man's most frequent use of the discussion

[1] For fuller treatment of the nature of discussion, its uses and purposes, and the problem-solving method, see such books as H. E. Gulley, *Discussion, Conference, and Group Process,* New York: Holt, Rinehart and Winston, Inc., 1960; and R. H. Wagner and Carroll C. Arnold, *Handbook of Group Discussion,* Boston: Houghton Mifflin Company, 1965.

process.[2] This in essence is the application of scientific method or inquiry to the group solution of human problems. A scientist confronted with a problem, such as finding an appropriate metal for acid-carrying pipes or arriving at a hypothesis of a quantum theory, does not jump to the first solution that comes to mind. Yet, in areas of human affairs, we are all prone to do this. Mention the problem of parking or college grading and a solution immediately comes to mind.

When we limit ourselves to the acceptance or rejection of one solution, we curtail our ability to solve problems, for we give ourselves only two courses—to accept or reject it. When, on the other hand, we ask, "What is the best way to solve this problem?" we are in a position to consider all possible solutions and, like the scientist, to establish standards by which to evaluate each of them in arriving at what is truly the best one for achieving our objectives.

Group discussion for problem-solving requires, then, an attitude of inquiry, a willingness to investigate and to learn even at the expense of exploding a pet theory. It also requires that all the participants try to use the guiding principles of discussion. This means a mutual desire to explore and analyze the problem and to have opinions that are flexible and based on honest, open-minded, scientific inquiry. Further, the participants realize that their own individual preparation, their own investigation and study of the problem, is essential to assure maximum information on which to base decisions.

The Pattern of Discussion

The pattern of problem-solving discussion is the same as for all systematic and scientific inquiry, for which we are all indebted to John Dewey for first writing about and suggesting such a system:[3]

1. Determine the nature and importance of the problem, gathering necessary facts and information.

[2] The use of the discussion process in learning is considered in books on training, adult education, management development, and other sources, e.g., R. O. Beckman, *How to Train Supervisors,* New York: Harper & Row, Publishers, Inc., 1954; and Harold P. Zelko, *How to Get More Out of Training Conferences,* Santa Monica, Calif.: Assignments in Management, 1965.

[3] John Dewey, *How We Think,* Boston: D. C. Heath and Company, 1910.

2. Analyze the history, background, and causes of the problem.
3. Determine who is involved and their vital interests in the problem and its solution.
4. Offer all possible solutions.
5. Establish criteria for evaluating solutions.
6. Evaluate solutions.
7. Arrive at best available solution or combination of solutions (decision).

At the outset, when the problem or question is put before the group, it is important that the participants understand and agree on what, specifically, is really the nature and extent of the problem. Too often, both individuals and groups jump too hastily toward solutions with only a hazy understanding of what the problem is. The possibility is also sometimes overlooked that there may not be a real problem at all, or that it is not as important as it was first felt to be. If a group, while discussing a problem, finds that there is no serious difficulty, in spite of the strong beliefs that had prevailed that one or another possible solution should be applied, then the group has probably had a successful discussion and need search no further for a solution.

In the next step, many discussions encounter difficulty, the tendency being to give superficial attention to the analysis of the history, background, and causes of the problem. This may lead to serious consideration, later on, of a solution that has been tried and failed. Most persons in a discussion are too eager to offer solutions before the problem is thoroughly analyzed. The analysis should include answers to questions such as: What was the origin of this situation or problem? Who was responsible? When did it start? How did it start? What current data and facts are available as to its extent and whom it affects? What has been done about it to date?

No solutions should be introduced during this phase of the discussion. Both leader and participant have an obligation to be sure that the problem is first fully explored. In discussing a question like: What can be done to improve the parking situation in this community (or on this campus)? many in the group should have suggestions to make. But they first need to know certain facts, such as: the present available facilities, the number of cars to be served, the peak hours of need, the present regulations and fees, the growth-rate contributing to the problem, the apparent inadequacies and inequities, and other possible causes and contributing factors. Leaders also make the mistake of giving a brief summary of a problem and then asking, "What do you think should be done about it?" Obviously, this is a solution-centered question, which should not be raised until the group has contributed its knowledge and information, focusing on problem analysis. This analysis should lead to and include a determination of the persons, groups, and vital interests involved in the problem and of the extent to which the solution will affect them.

The offering of possible solutions should be started with a clear understanding that here, too, contributions by members are to be clearly understood first, and not debated until later. A major fault in this step is to start evaluating the suggestions too soon. As a speaker–discussant at this point, the goal is to explain and inform what the proposed solution is and how it will work. As a listener–discussant, the communication goal is to understand how the solution will work. Neither, at this point, should be evaluative.

If a group goes too directly into evaluation while solutions are being offered, this will tend to restrict the free offering of solutions. It is here that brainstorming is sometimes appropriate for finding the maximum number of solutions without fear of criticism or evaluation.[4] When brainstorming is practiced in the fullest sense, all members strive to be as creative as possible, with all critical comment and evaluation ruled out. The accumulated list of suggestions is then evaluated, usually by another committee or group. While of limited value in most practical discussions, the spirit of this method is helpful in many situations where it is wise to search for creative solutions while postponing critical evaluation as much as possible.

Criteria or standards for evaluating solutions should now be considered.[5] Specific attention of the group may be directed toward these, or they may emerge during the evaluation process of finding the best solution. If the standards are clearly understood, the group can more carefully evaluate by matching proposed solutions with them. The way the possible solutions will affect those involved with the problem should be a major factor in establishing criteria. Even though the final best solution may not meet all the criteria, it is important to list them as fully as possible, and to be inclusive of all individuals or groups in-

[4] Brainstorming was first proposed by Alex Osborne and developed in his *Applied Imagination,* New York: Charles Scribner's Sons, 1957.

[5] The value of postponing criteria establishment until after all solutions are obtained is shown in John K. Brilhart, "An Experimental Comparison of Three Techniques for Communicating a Problem-Solving Pattern to Members of a Discussion Group," *Speech Monographs,* 33 (June, 1966), pp. 168–77.

volved. The ideal goal would be to come as close to meeting these as the group can in working toward a decision.

During the evaluation of possible solutions, there will be argument and opinion, yet all should try to keep an open mind and a willingness to listen to the thinking of others. Listening should be especially alert and sensitive. This is the essence of good discussion, remembering that it is basically deliberative thinking and scientific inquiry which must include the thoughts and opinions of others.

The final step in the discussion pattern is to try to arrive at the best solution in the form of a decision or course of action, usually by concensus, in which members come to feel that they are in substantial agreement.[6] Votes are usually not taken in panels, forums, and business conferences, and parliamentary procedure is not employed. Consensus, then, is an attempt to reach a group decision without vote, but it does not imply unanimous agreement.

The Forms of Discussion

The form of discussion, and the setting, may determine to what extent the complete pattern described above will be followed, and particularly whether the group will actually complete the decision-making step. Unless there is a specific responsibility to do this, as in the parliamentary meeting or business conference, a decision may not be made on the best solution or course of action.

One way to classify the forms of discussion is as public and private. Public discussion is any group discussion open to a wider group in attendance, frequently as an audience to the chief part of the discussion. The major forms are the panel, symposium, and debate.[7] Each of these is usually followed by a forum of audience participation, thus constituting a panel-forum or debate-forum, all of which may be called group discussion. Private discussion includes those group situations which are completely self-contained and without a larger audience. The major forms of these are the conference, committee, and a variety of two-person situations, such as the interview or private conversation.

[6] Consensus and other factors of leader-group relations in conferences are discussed in Harold P. Zelko, *Successful Conference and Discussion Techniques,* New York: McGraw-Hill, Inc., 1957.

[7] For fuller explanation, see Joseph F. O'Brien, "A Definition and Classification of the Forms of Discussion," *Quarterly Journal of Speech,* 25 (April, 1939), pp. 236–43.

—The panel is one of the most common forms of public discussion, in which three to five persons sit in front of a larger audience and usually engage in problem-solving discussion with a leader as guide. Sometimes the panel is used for learning and instruction.

—The symposium similarly involves several persons seated in front of the larger audience to discuss a subject in a prearranged order, with each person making a speech presentation on some phase of the broad question or problem-solution sequence usually standing and facing the larger group.

—The debate is more formal than the panel or symposium and normally comprises a total of four speakers, two on each side of a clearly defined proposition or issue. Since the debate speaker is primarily an advocate and considers the pros and cons of only one solution without yielding to the views of his opponent, the debate is not typical discussion.

In any public debate, then, whether in courts of law or in a campus forum on academic freedom, speakers are not addressing each other. They speak in response to each other but to gain a particular response from the audience. The debaters, after all, are committed. Their role is to provide the strongest case for their position. They may not persuade each other, but they do try to persuade the other listeners or jury.

The Discussion Topic

In any of the above public discussion forms, the leader and the group have a responsibility to select and word the topic or problem. Sometimes the reason for the meeting itself provides the topic. In the average small staff or business conference, the topics or problems grow out of the work situation. But in planning a symposium, panel, or other form of public discussion, thought should be given to selection and refinement of subjects for discussion, with these suggestions in mind:

1. Select a subject of timeliness and direct interest to the persons who will participate as well as to the larger audience.
2. State the topic in question form.
3. Keep the question narrow enough so that it can be handled in the time available and by the particular participants.
4. Phrase the question clearly.
5. Avoid either-or questions, unless a debate is planned.

6. Phrase the question to include the problem and allow for maximum latitude in solving it.

In phrasing a good discussion question for the topic of student drinking, a wording such as, "What is the best solution to the problem of student drinking?" or "What should be done about student drinking?" is better than "Should student drinking be forbidden?" For the topic of the draft, the wording, "What should be the policy for providing men for the armed forces?" is better than "Should we stop drafting college students?" In addition to leaving the question open for a consideration of many solutions, the time factor should be considered in relation to the breadth of the question.

The chief difference in wording a question as a discussion topic or as a debate topic is that the latter poses a specific plan or solution (frequently as a resolution), on which either one side or the other may be taken. For the general subject of foreign trade, the difference might be like this:

DISCUSSION QUESTION: "How can we best develop our foreign trade?" This could be narrowed, such as "How can we develop trade with Latin America?"

DEBATE RESOLUTION: "Resolved, that we should follow a policy of free trade in Latin America," or "Should we raise our protective tariffs with Latin American countries?"

Outlining for Discussion

Most discussions follow the pattern of organization similar to the problem-solving sequence described earlier. The leader bears the primary responsibility for keeping the discussion organized, but each member should also make an analysis of the topic and determine what should be said in each phase of the discussion. The outline is a guide for keeping the discussion coherent and organized, yet this should be flexible and the leader should be ready to modify it as the discussion progresses.

Questions are usually used as the main and subpoints, instead of direct statements as in a speech outline. The subquestions should be shown as divisions of the main question, to make the meaning more clear and precise. The leader should direct his question either to seek information and facts or opinion and attitudes. Sometimes factual material supplying answers to questions is shown in tabular form in the outline to insure that this information will be brought out during the discussion.[8]

FORM FOR DISCUSSION OUTLINE

Topic or Question: What is the best solution to the student parking problem at this university?

Introduction

I. How can attention best be directed to the problem?
   A. What is the immediate relationship to the group?
   B. How can the participants best be introduced?

Problem Analysis

I. What is the nature of the problem of student parking here?
   A. Can it be defined?
   B. What is its scope?
   C. Whom does it affect?
      1. What students? How many?
      2. How many cars are involved?
   D. When did the problem start to become serious?
   E. What has been tried in the past? With what success?
II. What are the causes of the situation we have today?
   A. Insufficient parking lots?
   B. Poor access to lots?
   C. Too many cars owned by students?
   D. Other causes? University regulations as causes?

Possible Solutions

I. What are the various solutions to this problem?
   A. Can we relate solutions to some of the causes?
   B. Can we make a list of possible solutions?
II. Do these solutions represent all our suggestions at this time?

Evaluate and Choose Best Solution

I. What do we want the ideal solution to accomplish?
   A. Eliminate causes of the problem?
   B. Take care of all phases of the problem?
   C. Be more than a temporary expedient?
   D. Can it be accomplished in a reasonable time?

[8] A fuller treatment of the discussion outline is found in James H. McBurney and Kenneth G. Hance, *Discussion in Human Affairs,* New York: Harper & Row, Publishers, Inc., 1950, pp. 170–85.

E. How much will it cost?
F. Will it satisfy the interests of all people involved in the problem?

II. Are we sure this is the best solution?
A. What advantages does it have over other solutions? What criteria does it meet?
B. Will it bring new disadvantages? What criteria does it violate?
C. Is it the most practical?
D. Does it (or could it) gain the support of the various interests, such as university administrators, faculty, and students?

Decision and Proposed Action

I. Can we make arrangements for putting this plan into action?

II. To whom should we communicate our proposals?
A. In what form?
B. When?

III. What further steps should we take?

Leadership

The role of the leader in discussion involves a great deal more than merely sitting at the head of the table and having the participants speak. If the topic is interesting and stimulating, if the sequence is well organized, if questions are clear and thought-provoking, if the members offer meaningful contributions, the leader should probably receive more credit than he often does. Good discussion is rarely accidental. Although each participant has many responsibilities, the leader usually has more to do than anyone else. These major responsibilities may be considered under the headings of planning and preparation and leadership responsibilities and methods.

The factors to be considered in the function of leadership are numerous and complex. They include personal characteristics and qualities, attitude, relation of leader to group in terms of permissiveness or control, and more specific methods and techniques to be used.[9]

[9] The subject of leadership has been studied in many ways, from the traits and characters of a leader in society in general, the ways leaders develop, leadership in relation to organizations, to the specific methods of the leader in group discussion objectives. Some references of value include Kurt Lewin, "The Consequences of an Authoritarian and Democratic Leadership," Alvin W. Gouldner, ed., *Studies in Leadership,* New York: Harper & Row, Publishers, Inc., 1950; Robert Tannenbaum, Irving R. Weschler, and Fred Massarik, *Leadership and Organization: A Behavioral*

While the role of leader is somewhat the same in all forms of discussion, the way one discharges it may be quite different for a panel, a symposium, a staff conference, or a large parliamentary meeting.

It is not possible here to consider all the factors and problems of leading a discussion as they may emerge in the many different types of meetings and group objectives. The committee chairman may be a very informal leader; the staff conference leader may sit back and let the members around the table do most of the talking very informally, or he may have to exercise considerable control; the public forum leader may be somewhat formal in introducing members of the panel or symposium and very alert in guiding discussion; the leader of a business meeting using parliamentary law has to be concerned with correct procedure in addition to all the other principles of discussion. But fundamentally every good leader assumes the following responsibilities while carrying out his major functions to stimulate, guide, and control or focus discussion.

1. Establish a pleasant working relationship between himself and the group, and maintain the same among the members.
2. Introduce the subject, topic, problem, or agenda.
3. Introduce members or participants.
4. Start and stimulate discussion.
5. Guide the discussion.
6. Encourage all to participate.
7. Control or focus the discussion.
8. Conciliate and resolve tension.
9. Use the blackboard, charts, or other visual aids when appropriate.
10. Make transitions and summaries throughout the discussion and at the end.

The leader should give careful thought to his opening remarks in any group meeting, for they set the tone for the entire session. They should be brief, appropriate, and thought-provoking. They might include the timeliness, importance, and purpose of the meeting and

---

Science Approach, New York: McGraw-Hill, Inc., 1960; Franklyn S. Haiman, *Group Leadership and Democratic Action,* Boston: Houghton Mifflin Company, 1951, and "Concepts of Leadership," *Quarterly Journal of Speech,* 39 (October, 1953), pp. 317–32; and R. Victor Harnack and Thorrel B. Fest, *Group Discussion: Theory and Technique,* New York: Appleton-Century-Crofts, 1964, especially Chapter 12.

the subjects to be covered, while trying to motivate and develop interest in the listeners and to establish a cooperative mood. In a public discussion, members of the panel should be introduced to the larger group, and in a conference to each other. Sometimes this is best done by each member introducing himself. The discussion should be started by posing a question to the group as a whole so as to get a spontaneous response, or to an individual, or by introducing the first speaker, as would be done in the symposium.

Questions are the chief tool of the leader, along with internal transition and summaries.[10] All questions should be purposeful, toward developing subject-matter content and working toward group goals. Questions that are vague, abstract, or too general lead to a lack of response. Broad or general questions should be avoided, or they should be followed by more precise ones that break down the general to the narrower or more specific. If this is done, members will usually respond more spontaneously, which is generally better than a response obtained by a direct question to a specific person. The direct question is valuable when the member seems eager to respond or has knowledge which the group should have at the time. Or if a member has been silent for some time, the leader should direct a question to him if it appears quite certain that he would not otherwise respond. Questions raised by group members toward the leader should preferably be thrown back to the group to answer. Although the leader may occasionally answer a question, he should not do this continuously.

Stimulating, guiding, and *controlling* discussion are the chief responsibilities of the discussion leader. He stimulates interaction by his own manner and enthusiasm, and by his use of questions, examples, and other devices. He encourages all to participate. He limits the few who want to speak too much by adroit use of humor, summaries, and transition remarks. He carefully guides the trend of the discussion through an appropriate logical sequence. He does not allow too much time to be spent on any one phase of the subject at the expense of other phases. He keeps the group informed and focused on a clear understanding of broad goals and goals of each point at a time. He intercedes when an argument between two members becomes tense, and he tries to resolve this by according them both some credit, by tactfully turning to another member, or to another phase of the subject. He summarizes frequently, and particularly in making the transition

[10] One of the older books discusses the use and types of questions in great detail: E. S. Hannaford, *Conference Leadership in Business and Industry,* New York: McGraw-Hill, Inc., 1945.

to the forum period of participation by the larger audience. He then encourages clear brief questions and answers, and he tries to spread the participation to as many in the audience as possible, and among the panel members.

The size of the discussion group itself and then of the larger audience will affect both the leader's methods and the interaction within the group. It is obvious that there will be more and livelier interaction when the group is small. And in regard to the forum period, when the total audience group is also small, the leader will tend to be informal and let panel members themselves receive questions from the audience and respond to them. But if this is done, the leader should be alert to guide or control the situation when necessary. In a large audience forum he would stay in control and himself accept the questions and turn them over to the panel for reply, usually restating the question clearly so that all in the audience can hear it.

Planning is an essential responsibility of leadership. Good discussions don't just happen; they are usually the result of careful planning. This includes attention to the program itself, the agenda of a conference, the topics and how they are stated, the members of the panel or group, the facilities and physical arrangements, and the outline of the discussion.

The leader should plan in accordance with the type of meeting and program. When the choice of topic or agenda is also the leader's, he needs to consider whether to do this himself or meet with a committee of the members to help select and phrase the subject for discussion. If he is also responsible for the make-up of the panel, he should try to invite people who are informed and whose points of view on the subject or problem will differ. In planning for a symposium, he should meet with the members and determine how the subject should be divided and who will represent each part. In a problem-solving symposium, the sequence of speaking will be something like this: speaker 1 introduces the background and present state of the problem; speaker 2 might continue to develop the analysis and scope of the problem and its causes, and he might propose a solution; speaker 3 proposes a solution and develops it; and speaker 4 presents another solution and develops it, along with a summary, depending on whether the chairman will himself make a summary statement. Other aspects of planning with the members of the panel include an understanding of the length of the discussion by the panel before starting the forum period, and the length of the symposium speaker's individual remarks.

Arranging the meeting or conference facilities is a major aspect of good planning. This may appear simple, but a chairman who has not planned properly may find himself at the last minute frantically trying to locate chairs, fix lights, arrange for blackboard or chart easel, look for a pointer or extension cord, and many other details too often taken for granted. The room should be neatly arranged, with the best possible visibility for the entire group in relation to the panel, good hearing range, and good lighting. Name cards for each panel member, in clear view of the audience, will add to the nicety of the total facilities. These are also desirable in a conference where the members all sit face to face but do not know each other.

In a public discussion, such as the panel or symposium, all participants should be in view of the larger audience, preferably on a raised platform if the room is large, and seated in a semicircle with the leader in the center or at one end.

The leader's outline is an important part of planning. He should include in it the names of all the panel members and pertinent information about them, which may be useful. Sometimes it is helpful to give each member a brief version of the outline to have before him, taking care that this should not appear to the audience to represent too many notes. In some instances, the leader may want to go over the outline with the panel members in advance of the discussion.

Participation in Discussion

All the principles of good speaking and listening apply to discussion and conference. There must be careful analysis of the occasion and group, study and research of the subject, determination of purpose, coherent organization of ideas and subpoints and questions, logical and interesting support and evidence, and effective communicative manner. Many additional factors bearing on effectiveness in discussion deal chiefly with the interacting relationships that develop among members of a small group. Recent research on small group process and phenomena shows that factors such as role, self, and emotional involvement (with subject and other people) tend to influence a member's behavior and contributions more than do logical factors of thought process.[11]

[11] Much attention has been given to small group process in research and writing. See, for example: A. Paul Hare, *Handbook of Small Group Research,* New York: The Free Press, 1962; Gerald M. Phillips, *Communication and the Small Group,* New York: Bobbs Merrill, 1966; and T. M. Newcomb, R. H. Turner, and P. E. Converse, *Social Psychology,* Chapters 10 to 15, New York: Holt, Rinehart & Winston, Inc., 1965.

Some of the specific factors are attitude, adaptation and conciliation, orderliness, brevity, directness, and listening.

Attitude. Any group communication situation requires an attitude of respect for the information, opinions, and feelings of others. Open-mindedness and a sense of humor help maintain this attitude. One should not be too dogmatic in stating and advocating his position, which might be in direct opposition to that of another member. And if new information is presented showing his original position to be wrong, he should be ready to change it. If he continues to believe it, however, he should do all he can to defend and advance his position. The effective member of a discussion group maintains a happy balance of open-mindedness, patience, tolerance, and respect for others while striving to reach group goals. And these must be put ahead of personal goals.

Adaptation and conciliation. Most contributions in a small group are made in relation to something said by another member. There must be a constant striving to adapt and to integrate one's own thoughts and opinions to those of others. The principle of common ground should get much attention—the attempt to arrive at common thinking, common feeling, and common agreement. Here are some specific suggestions in replying to a point with which you may not fully agree:

1. *Start your response with an attitude of conciliation.* Try to give some credit for the point, find some area of agreement. Avoid such statements as "I disagree completely," "I don't agree with a thing you say," or "You are entirely wrong."

2. *Take issue with the point, not the person.* Such statements as "You show utter ignorance of the subject," or "If you'd only read the newspaper . . ." do nothing but attack the person of the speaker. Both he and the rest of the group will be offended and antagonized.

3. *Restate the other person's point clearly and accurately.* Do not be vague and abstract regarding what you are refuting. Do not overstate or exaggerate what has been said. Do not put words in your opponent's mouth. (And do not call him or think of him as opponent.)

4. *State your own position in relation to his clearly.* First give whatever credit you can to his position and refer to areas of agreement. Then state your position in a strong and positive manner. You have a right and a responsibility to be persuasive at this point.

5. *Support and prove your position.* You should make use of the principles of validation, proof, and support.

6. *Do not extend your discussion once your point is made.* Con-

clude your remarks by clearly restating your position and summarizing what has been said, avoiding the tendency to go on to another point.

7. *Be tactful.* Tact involves sensing the mood and atmosphere of the group, being pleasant in manner, using judgment in the frequency and length of one's remarks, maintaining an air of modesty rather than boastfulness, and practicing the virtues of refinement and culture.

Orderliness. This is the quality of thinking clearly and systematically, of trying to contribute to the chairman's efforts to keep the discussion in a logical sequence, and of paying close attention to the goal of the group.

Brevity. Each individual contribution in any group situation, including conversation, should be brief and to the point. Normally, only one point at a time should be made. It is better to make repeated short remarks than one long-winded speech in group discussion, and the tendency to develop a chain of different points, going on from one to another, should be avoided.

Directness. Good speech communication in the group requires speaking with a degree of projection and enthusiasm so that it can be easily heard and understood by all present. The tendency to let the voice drop to a normal low conversational level should be avoided. Be alert to responses and look at different people on the panel from time to time, and occasionally at members of the larger audience. The ceiling or floor gazer gets little respect or notice from others. And do not make the mistake of speaking only to the chairman or to your immediate neighbor.

Timing. Contributing early in the discussion will help toward getting recognition from others in the group and toward feeling more involved for better interest and involvement throughout the rest of the meeting.

Listening. More time is spent in listening than in any other activity in group discussion. Listening well has at least two major values: it conveys to the speaker your own interest in what he has to say; and it affords you the opportunity to analyze the views of others as you develop your own thoughts toward further speaking. In a remarkable display of listening in the U.S. Senate in the debate on the extension of lend-lease in World War II, Senator Robert Taft permitted the interruption of his remarks by six other senators, each of whom made a point of refutation at some length. He listened intently to each one, then resumed the floor and wove into his further remarks his own adaptation and refutation of the point each had made, with remarkable clarity. He had taken no notes, but he had trained his mind to do this. Good listeners are very much needed in discussion. It is unfortunate that so many discussants just sit and stare aimlessly outward or at the floor or ceiling, in apparent boredom while others are talking, giving the impression that the only reason they are there is to make an occasional comment.

The Conference

Group process takes its most consistently used form in the staff or business conference in the work setting. Whether one is a teacher, lawyer, manager, or worker, he will spend a considerable amount of time in conference. Large corporations and small businesses are using the conference regularly to accomplish the greatest number of communication objectives possible in the effort to improve organizational communication.[12] Within the average conference, matters can be explained, company policies can be clarified, problems can be solved, and decisions can be made, all while affording an opportunity for participation and recognition of members and to contribute toward upward communication. The increased emphasis on the consultative aspect of modern management has made the conference an even more important tool of modern business and professional organizations.

Conferences differ from public discussion in several significant ways. *First,* they are private, not intended to influence a larger audience. *Second,* they are frequently concerned with more than one subject or problem. *Third,* there will be more variation in the use of the typical discussion process and in leadership methods. A manager may wish only to consult and seek the counsel of his staff. He may ask them to help determine the cause of some problem, such as a slowdown in production, or poor morale, or slackening consumer demand for a product. He may need to explain a new company policy and work out methods for its implementation. *Fourth,* the practical considerations

[12] The many recent books on management and communication all emphasize the use of the conference for these objectives. See, for example, Lee O. Thayer, *Administrative Communication,* Homewood, Ill.: Richard D. Irwin, Inc., 1961; Willard V. Merrihue, *Managing by Communication,* New York: McGraw-Hill, Inc., 1960; and Fred H. Blum, *Toward a Democratic Work Process,* New York: Harper & Row, Publisher Inc., 1953. The latter writer stresses the use of committees and informal group process in modern management's efforts to maintain a more participative social climate.

of time and relations within the organization (and others) frequently result in more leader control than in public discussion groups.[13] Since the leader is usually in a position of authority and is responsible for decisions, he may have to exert more influence in reaching them, or he may use the conference chiefly to ask advice and to consult, then later make the decision himself.

Most committees are run very much like a conference, in that they are private and without a larger audience, are usually quite small in membership, and have specific goals to achieve. Although these are chiefly problem-solving and aim for a decision as the recommendation of the committee, they may be fact-finding and information-seeking. The committee chairman is normally impartial and exercises little control over the decisions reached by the members. Although he is ideally democratic, he may have to use considerable influence to help the group move in the direction of proper goals and particularly in discharging his task functions of keeping the discussion orderly, on the track, and functional. He is usually responsible for drawing up and submitting a report to the larger group, thus again providing opportunities for influence.

Participation in conference requires preparation both of attitude and of subject matter, as in all other discussion situations. Sometimes the position one holds in the organization or professional setting makes his involvement in the subject and the outcome of much more direct importance than in a public discussion. It is necessary to exercise special care and effort toward understanding the feelings and frame of reference of others who might be at parallel work tasks and in competitive relationships. Interpersonal conflicts should be avoided, although persuasion and exchange of opinions are vital. Conciliation assumes even more importance than in public discussion, for in the conference it is quite likely that there will be continuing and permanent relationships among the members, and any deep frictions developed within the group could carry into the work scene and be extremely difficult. A conference is no place in which to suggest by word or manner a criticism of the competency or motives of others. What is needed is teamwork and cooperation, working not only for the conference goals but for the larger goals of the department or organization.

[13] Robert S. Tannenbaum and W. H. Schmidt, "How to Choose a Leadership Pattern," *Harvard Business Review,* 36 (March–April, 1958), pp. 95–101, presents a good analysis and explanation of various leadership styles and behavior in relation to group goals and leader control.

Parliamentary Law

Parliamentary law (or procedure) is a system of principles and rules for making decisions in groups. It is used in most business meetings of clubs and organizations to facilitate the decision-making process by supplying a consistent, orderly and fair way of taking up subjects and moving toward a democratic discussion of them and to a final decision. Whereas, in public discussion, as described above, most groups do not need to come to a decision, and in the private business or staff conference the group is small and can reach a decision by consensus, the parliamentary group is usually larger and must follow a procedure that can be uniformly understood and applied. In our form of democracy, our legislative bodies are the prime users of such procedure, which we carry over into a variety of settings.

A Senate committee engages in inquiry into problems like foreign aid, law enforcement, or education needs, and then proposes legislation appropriate to those problems. A labor union committee inquires into the need for educating its members on grievance procedures and proposes a program. A committee of your student government tackles the problem of housing and reports its proposal. A fraternity group considers what to do about study hours. The members, convinced through their experiences in inquiry, now become advocates for a proposed solution; they are ready to debate, in a parliamentary situation, for or against a proposal or solution. Frequently, they may try to recreate that experience in the minds of their listeners and will be applying the problem-solving method of development in persuasion.

This relationship of discussion and parliamentary debate is the core of democratic procedures as we know and live them. Inquiry followed by discussion or debate are the fundamental tools with which people direct their own affairs.

The Purpose of Parliamentary Law

It is therefore important to understand something about parliamentary procedures and, most of all, to understand the philosophy of parliamentary law. That philosophy may be stated thus: It is not the rules which are important, but the process of finding, quickly and fairly, the intent of the group. A working knowledge of the rules will help each member cooperate with others to achieve group intent.

In the first place, parliamentary procedure provides a regular and fixed order for taking up the business of a meeting. It next provides rules which help the group to make decisions with regard to any item of business which comes before it. The purpose of parliamentary procedure, then, may be summarized as the provision of an orderly method for taking up business one subject at a time and in proper sequence, expediting the will of the majority, protecting the majority and the minority, and according equal rights to each member of the group.

The presiding officer of a business meeting is a combination of discussion leader, chairman of an assembly, and parliamentarian. He must be alert both to rules of procedure and to good discussion methods. A group, which has been informally discussing a problem and its solution, can crystallize its opinion and adopt a course of action by proposing the solution as a motion and taking action on it.

Forming a Permanent Organization

Most permanently organized groups conduct their meetings according to established parliamentary procedure. If a group of people decide to form a permanent organization, they should proceed in the following order:

1. Call a preliminary meeting of interested persons.
2. Ask one member to preside and call the meeting to order.
3. Elect a temporary chairman and a temporary secretary.
4. Appoint a committee to draw up a constitution.
5. Call a later meeting at which the constitution committee submits a proposed constitution.
6. Adopt the constitution by considering it paragraph by paragraph, amending and discussing each section and article, but not voting on the acceptance of the various parts until the whole document has been considered and amended.
7. Elect permanent officers and hold meetings as provided in the constitution.

Order of Business

The usual sequence for conducting the business of any meeting is as follows:

1. Calling the meeting to order.
2. Reading of the minutes.
3. Reports of officers and standing committees.
4. Reports of special committees.

5. Unfinished business.
6. New business.
7. Adjournment.

Some Common Terms

There are some widely used terms of parliamentary procedure which should be remembered.

MEETING: A meeting is one convening of the group.

SESSION: A session is a series of meetings.

VOTING: Voting involves the indication by members of a position for or against the matter on the floor. Voting is usually oral, or *viva voce*. If this method is impractical, votes may be cast by show of hands or by standing. If the group wishes, voting may be by written ballot.

DIVISION: The term division is used when a voice vote is not clear and a show of hands is taken. Any member of the assembly may call for a division.

MAJORITY AND PLURALITY: A majority is more than half of the votes cast; a plurality is a vote in excess of that for any other one candidate or issue but less than half of the total (occurring most frequently in elections of officers.) For example, in a body of 50 members, one candidate may receive 22 votes, the second 18, and the third 10—in which case there is no majority; another vote may then be taken on the two top candidates. Some motions require a two-thirds vote—that is, two-thirds of the members voting.

QUORUM: A quorum is the number of members necessary to transact business. This is usually determined by the constitution. If not specifically stated, a majority of the members constitutes a quorum.

GENERAL CONSENT: Many times the chairman will make a proposal, or a member will suggest a course of action, on which no vote is taken but the group's assent is assumed. The chair usually says, "If there is no objection . . . ," and in the absence of objection he assumes general consent of the group. This practice often facilitates business.

Motions

Parliamentary procedure is a system of motions. The main business is placed before the group by a main motion, and it is out of the discussion, amendment, adoption, rejection, or postponement of this motion that other motions grow. In addition to the main motion, the various kinds of motions are classified as *subsidiary, privileged, incidental,* and *renewal motions.*

It is well to remember that a knowledge of ways to use the various kinds of motions is often as vital to the members of the group as it is to the chairman. A common misconception about procedure is that the average member need not be concerned with it so long as the chairman knows what to do. But this is the very reason why many members of a group are not active participants but sit back wanting to contribute but not knowing just how. It is of course difficult to keep in one's head all the rules about motions, but everyone can remember the basic principles and then familiarize himself with a handbook on procedure in order to be able to consult it as a ready reference.[14] We cannot provide a complete discussion of all the motions here, but we shall look briefly at the various classifications of motions and then present a composite table.

It is well to be able to answer the following questions about each type of motion:

1. What it its purpose? What is the use of the motion? What will it accomplish? Most of the subsidiary and privileged motions affect the main motion by enhancing, retarding, or preventing its passage.

2. What is its precedence or rank? This has to do with the relation of the motion to other motions which may be on the floor or which may be made after it. Which motion has higher rank, or precedence? In the composite table, the motions are shown in order of rank, which means, for example, that the motion to refer to a committee would be acted upon before a motion to amend, even though the latter had been on the floor first.

3. Is a second required? Most motions require a second.

4. Is it debatable? In other words, can the motion be discussed, or must it be voted on as soon as proposed?

5. Is it amendable? May amendments be made to it, or must it be voted on in the form submitted?

[14] Among the many handbooks available, the following are recommended: Joseph F. O'Brien, *Parliamentary Law for the Layman,* New York: Harper & Row, Publishers, Inc., 1952, for an interesting, clear, and complete treatment; Henry M. Robert, *Rules of Order, Rev.,* Glenview, Ill.: Scott, Foresman, and Company, 1967, for a generally accepted authoritative treatment; and Alice Sturgis, *Standard Code of Parliamentary Procedure,* New York: McGraw-Hill, Inc., 1966.

6. What vote is required for passage? Does it require a majority or a two-thirds vote to be passed?

The *main motion* is the core around which most parliamentary procedure operates. It is made after a member has been recognized by the chair, when no prior business is on the floor. He may say, "Mr. Chairman, I move that we hold a dance." The wording should be clear and brief and should contain one central idea. Most of the business of a group centers around the discussion of main motions.

When parliamentary law is applied strictly, no discussion is permitted until after a main motion has been made and seconded, and then the discussion must deal directly with the motion before the group. However, this rule is often not observed, and members frequently find it advantageous to explain a situation or a point of view before making a motion setting forth some definite proposal. Even in formal groups, it is sometimes advisable to provide for a period of free discussion in which all conflicting points of view may be discussed and a general basis of agreement reached before any specific motion is presented. The proper procedure then is to move that the assembly resolve itself into a committee of the whole. This motion has to be seconded and may then be adopted by a majority vote. While the committee of the whole is convened, parliamentary rules are suspended and only main motions and amendments to them, appeals from the decision of the chair, parliamentary inquiries, and questions of personal privilege are in order.

Among the *subsidiary motions* are the two which, with the main motion, are the most important to understand, the *motion to amend* and the *motion to commit* (refer to a committee). Joseph F. O'Brien wrote, in *Parliamentary Law for the Layman,* that in groups "of fairly small size and closely knit memberships, the only motions wherein actual proficiency is imperative are the main motion, the motion to amend, and the motion to commit."

The *motion to amend* is the means whereby a main motion is perfected by the group before it comes to a vote. It requires a second and is discussed and voted upon before further consideration is given to the main motion. If the motion is "that our organization petition the University administration to establish a University bookstore," it may be amended by adding something or deleting something or striking out any of the words and substituting others in its place. For example, a member might address the chair and move to amend the motion by striking out "University administration" and substituting "Board of Trustees." After the motion to amend has been debated and voted upon, if it is passed, the amended motion is up for consideration; if it is rejected, the original motion is up for further consideration. A motion to amend may, in turn, be amended by the same process, but no more than one primary and one secondary (i.e., amendment to the primary) amendment may be pending at the same time.

The *motion to commit* could very well apply to the example of the university bookstore. A member may perceive that the problem is not clear or that there may be a better solution. He might address the chair and move that the motion be referred to a committee for investigation, study, and recommendations. It is wise to specify what committee, and, if it is to be a special committee, how many shall serve on it and how the members are to be selected. The motion to commit usually includes instruction on when the committee is to report. The form might be: "Mr. Chairman, I move that this motion be referred to a committee of three, appointed by the chair, with instructions to report at our next meeting."

Other subsidiary motions consist of actions that may be taken on the main motion other than a direct vote for its acceptance or rejection. In the table that follows they are listed as: to postpone indefinitely (which is an indirect way of defeating the main motion and sometimes may win the votes of some who would not vote against it directly); to amend (as previously discussed); to refer to committee (as previously discussed); to postpone to a specifically stated time (when it will come up again as a main item, taking precedence over other questions); to limit or extend the time allowed for debate; to proceed to a vote on the main question (for which purpose the procedure is to "move the previous question"); and to table the motion under consideration (which cannot then be taken up until another motion is made to take it from the table).

As the name implies, subsidiary motions are related to the main motion and therefore may be introduced while the main motion is under discussion. They take precedence over it and must be disposed of by a vote before any further discussion of the main motion is permitted. If a subsidiary motion is defeated, the main motion is again before the house; if a subsidiary motion is adopted, the main motion is handled in accordance with the intent of the subsidiary motion.

Privileged motions consist of all points by which the welfare of individuals or of the group is protected. For this reason, a member may secure the floor at any time by addressing the chair and asking

Chart of Parliamentary Motions

The motions are listed in order of rank or precedence, with the highest motion on the list having highest rank down to the main motion. Incidental motions have no order of precedence among themselves but are considered when made, with precedence over the motion they relate to.

Motion	Debatable?	Amendable?	Vote required?	Second required?	Interrupt speaker?
PRIVILEGED					
Fix time to which to adjourn (when other business pending)	No	Yes	Majority	Yes	No
Adjourn (when unqualified and time for next meeting is set)	No	No	Majority	Yes	No
Take a recess (when other business is pending)	No	Yes	Majority	Yes	No
Raise question of privilege	No	No	Chair decides	No	Yes
Call for orders of the day	No	No	Chair decides	No	Yes
SUBSIDIARY					
Lay on the table	No	No	Majority	Yes	No
Previous question (end debate)	No	No	Two thirds	Yes	No
Limit or extend debate	No	Yes	Two thirds	Yes	No
Postpone to definite time	Yes	Yes	Majority	Yes	No
Commit or refer to committee	Yes	Yes	Majority	Yes	No
Amend	Yes	Yes	Majority	Yes	No
Postpone indefinitely	Yes	No	Majority	Yes	No
MAIN MOTION	Yes	Yes	Majority	Yes	No
INCIDENTAL					
Appeal	Yes	No	Majority	Yes	Yes
Division of assembly	No	No	Chair decides	No	Yes
Division of question	No	Yes	Majority	No	No
Withdraw a motion	No	No	Majority	No	No
Point of order	No	No	Chair decides	No	Yes
Suspend rules	No	No	Two thirds	Yes	No
Object to consideration	No	No	Two thirds	No	Yes
Parliamentary inquiry	No	No	Chair decides	No	Yes
RENEWAL					
Take from the table	No	No	Majority	Yes	No
Reconsider	Yes	No	Majority	Yes	Yes
Rescind, repeal	Yes	Yes	Two thirds	Yes	No

permission to "raise a question of privilege." If a member feels that the time has come for consideration of a motion that has been postponed to a definite time, he "calls for the orders of the day." The secretary then examines the record to see whether the time has come when a postponed question must be taken up.

Motions to take a recess or to adjourn are privileged motions and may be made whenever another member is not speaking. A question of personal privilege may be made at any time, even though a member interrupts a speaker to make it. Such a question would be raised if one member were insulted by a speaker, or if the public-address system failed to work so that the speaker could not be heard, or for any other similar reason requiring immediate decision.

Incidental motions cover a number of miscellaneous items concerning which the chairman may give a ruling or may call for a vote by the group. Included among them is a request for a secret ballot (instead of a vote by a show of hands); the division of a motion into two parts for separate voting on each; an appeal from a decision rendered by the chairman; objection to consideration of a question; an inquiry concerning parliamentary procedure; a request for further information on a matter being discussed, or a request for permission to withdraw or modify a motion which the speaker himself has submitted.

Renewal motions are those to reconsider a motion that has been acted upon or to rescind a motion that has been adopted, or to take from the table a motion that has been tabled.

Conclusion

This chapter has pointed out the close relation between discussion principles and the general principles of effective speech. Although all principles of good speaking apply with certain adaptations to discussion, there are some, such as proper attitude, conciliation, brevity, directness, and listening which should be especially developed for discussion purposes. We have emphasized the application of all these principles to problem-solving in a cooperative group effort. The need for an attitude of inquiry and open-mindedness is essential.

When you serve as discussion chairman, you will be concerned with proper selection and wording of the topic as a question, and the planning and development of the discussion outline as a guide for leading the group, and your leadership responsibilities include those of stimulating, spreading, and guiding the participation of the group members. As a participant, your responsibility is to help the leader accomplish these objectives and be a cooperative and enthusiastic member.

When business is conducted and decisions are reached under the rules of parliamentary procedure, the members as well as the person in the chair need to be familiar with the basic rules and the philosophy behind them.

Exercises

Questions for Discussion

1. In what ways are the general principles of effective speech communication applicable to discussion?

2. Do you think that the classification of discussion as public and private is a logical one? What are the bases of this classification and the distinguishing characteristics of each form?

3. What are the forms of public discussion? Distinguish among them. In which one would it be easiest for you to participate? Why?

4. In selecting a discussion topic, what principles are applicable that are different from those applicable to selecting a topic for a speech? How should the discussion topic be worded?

5. Do you think that leadership or participation is the more important for you to learn? Consider this from the standpoint of your abilities and your future use of the discussion process.

6. What are the basic requirements of problem-solving discussion?

Projects for Speaking and Listening

1. Bring to class prepared statements of five discussion topics which you think would be appropriate for class discussion projects.

2. Prepare a discussion outline for one discussion topic showing the sequence to be followed and key questions you might use as a leader. Plan to make a two-minute introductory statement that would be appropriate in starting the discussion of the topic.

3. With the instructor's aid, select a topic and choose four members of the class to participate in a panel discussion of which you will be the chairman. Meet with the group, and determine which panel members will respond to certain questions and discuss major areas of the subject. Be prepared to lead the discussion for about twenty

minutes, then open the topic to the entire class for a forum and group-discussion period.

4. Plan a program similar to that described in the preceding project, but as a symposium in which each participant will make a four-minute talk on some phase of the topic. Make a discussion outline, then meet with the members of your group and decide the sequence of speaking, who will handle each phase of the subject, and how the speeches will fit together into an over-all discussion of the entire subject. Each speaker will prepare an outline of his own talk, showing as his specific purpose the point of view he will maintain and also showing how he plans to adapt to preceding speakers in his introduction as well as throughout his talk.

5. Make an analysis of the ways in which a discussion leader handled a program which you attended, showing his assets and weaknesses.

6. Analyze a discussion program you have heard, either personally or on radio or television, covering its organization, topic, speaker participation and adaptation, and leadership.

7. Organize the class into a business meeting run under rules of parliamentary procedure. Bring to class several ideas which you will present as main motions. Practice addressing the chair and making main motions. Let the chairman practice proper restatement of the motion to the group.

8. Hold a practice session in which members of the group offer various kinds of amendments to main motions. Keep the discussion of the amendments to a minimum so that the greater part of the practice can be on the proper phrasing of and action on amendments.

9. Plan a session of the class in which a controversial subject is up for discussion and opposite points of view are expressed. In answering a point of another speaker with whom you disagree, practice the principles of conciliation as discussed in this chapter. A formal debate, with two persons upholding each side of the proposition, might be the basis for this practice session.

10. Assume a business or organizational setting and plan a staff conference of about eight to ten members with an agenda of one subject to be developed as information and explanation and another as problem-solving.

14 · *Special Applications*

In the total effort toward being an effective communicator, one is always making special applications of the principles of speaking and listening we have discussed throughout this book. Every communicative act requires the judgment and flexibility of application needed to accomplish the purpose of the immediate situation. There are few principles that may not be universally applied with wise adaptation to particular circumstances. This chapter singles out several important speech communication settings or problems which deserve special consideration in making the kinds of adaptations needed to accomplish their goals effectively. These are the chairmanship function, informal conversations, interviews, and the use of the manuscript.

The Presiding Officer or Chairman

In the preceding chapter, we discussed the duties and functions of the discussion leader in relation to group process, chiefly from the standpoint of how he plans for, guides, stimulates, and affects the general conduct of the group interaction and the achievement of group goals.

Our concern here is more generally with the many responsibilities which a presiding officer or chairman of a meeting has to assume and some suggestions for discharging these duties.[1] They include planning, presiding, and introducing speakers. The president of any organization, such as a fraternity, PTA, or Kiwanis Club, may have such responsibilities. So does the master of ceremonies at a dinner, or anyone who is asked to preside at meetings of public groups for particular purposes, such as a group of parents to discuss scouting, or little league baseball, or plans for a community project. Whether or not a meeting of this kind is productive depends in large measure on the chairman's initial attention to his basic responsibilities and then his skill in presiding, introducing speakers, and handling group activities.

Planning

Preliminary arrangements for most meetings need not be elaborate; but if they are neglected confusion results and both the neglect and the confusion are depressing to speakers and discouraging to listeners. The chairman should manifest an air of calm assurance—and he can do this only if he actually is efficient in having the necessary details properly arranged.

The meeting place. Ideally, it should be just large enough—neither too large nor too small—for the size of the group. A bit of crowding is preferable to many empty seats. If twenty people are seated in a room that just holds twenty, there is a general feeling that the meeting is well attended; but if those same twenty people are scattered in an auditorium that seats 150, the atmosphere suggests lack of interest. Besides, it is far easier for a speaker to talk with his audience when it is seated close together and close to him. Unless cleanliness, orderliness, and proper heating, lighting, and ventilation may be taken for granted, the chairman should insure them by preliminary arrangements. A disordered, dark, and stuffy (or cold) meeting place gets any gathering off to a very bad start.

Facilities. If a speaker's rostrum, or blackboard, or easel chart, or slide projector is needed, the chairman should make sure it is on hand. If there are to be several speakers for a large gathering, the

[1] Fuller treatment of the duties of the presiding officer is found in Frank Snell, *How to Hold a Better Meeting,* New York: Harper & Row, Publishers, Inc., 1958; and Bert and Frances Strauss, *New Ways to Better Meetings,* New York: The Viking Press, 1951.

chairs should be arranged on the stage, where a pitcher of water and glasses alongside the lectern will often be welcome.

Public address system. If the audience numbers more than 200, a public address system may be required. Since loudspeakers and microphones need to be in perfect adjustment, they should be checked in advance of the meeting. If the speech is to be recorded, the recorder should be in place, perhaps on a table in front of the stage, and with an experienced operator in charge. The microphone should be multidirectional and sufficiently sensitive so the speaker will not need to handcuff himself to it. If a lapel microphone is available, this will give the speaker maximum freedom of movement. If the speaker is unfamiliar with microphones, the chairman should reassure him that he may speak normally, perhaps with some special care to articulate carefully.

Placement of speakers. If there are several speakers, for a large meeting, the chairman should seat himself in the middle, but leave available to them the space behind the rostrum. Order of speaking may depend on the topics of the speakers; but the most important speaker is always the last on the program.

Preliminary arrangements with speakers. When speakers are invited, they should be told the nature of the audience and of the occasion, the expected size of the audience, the purpose the talk is to serve, and how long it should be. If there are to be several brief talks, to be followed by a longer one, the preliminary speakers should be informed politely but firmly how much time each is to have, and requested to conform strictly to the time limit. Speakers should be met by the chairman at the door as they arrive and treated with the courteous attention appropriate to honored guests.

Presiding

Whether the meeting is large or small, formal or informal, much of its success depends upon how well the chairman presides. The job is not too difficult, but it needs to be done with firm assurance and efficiency. Many meetings fail because of the bumbling inefficiency and self-consciousness of unskilled presiding officers. The sequence of duties is as follows:

1. *Start the meeting on time*—either precisely at the time announced, or within five or ten minutes. If there is need for a delay, an explanation should be made to the audience. If an adjournment time has been announced, try to adjourn the meeting on time.

2. *Establish an appropriate atmosphere in the opening remarks.* Once again, a calm assurance—a signal to the audience that the situation is being well handled by a chairman who knows his job—is the basic requirement. The audience should be greeted with warm friendliness. Reference to the reason for the meeting may be appropriate. The chairman is expected to establish the tone for the meeting, whether it is to be one of deep seriousness, of informal good fellowship, or of gay and relaxed enjoyment.

3. *Serve the essential needs of both speakers and listeners.* The speakers may appreciate a prearranged system of signaling to them when their allotted time is about to expire. The audience is entitled to protection from speakers who blatantly ignore time limitations. Sometimes the chairman is obliged to interrupt a speaker to tell him pleasantly but firmly that his time is up. This may be embarrassing, but need not be if prior to the meeting the chairman has warned the speakers that each will be held strictly to the agreed-upon time limitations.

4. *Plan appropriate remarks between speeches.* These should normally take the form of a complimentary remark on the speech just ended, with a transitional sentence introducing the next speaker. At a banquet, when the chairman is serving as toastmaster, brief humorous stories often make appropriate interludes, provided they fit the occasion, relate to the speeches, and are well told.

Introducing Speakers

Speeches of introduction are often so ludicrously ineffective that experienced public speakers (and audiences) will be deeply grateful for simple efficiency in this role. Actually, the mistakes that are commonly made ought to be easily avoided. What needs to be done is as follows:

1. *Remember that the speech belongs to the speaker, not to the chairman.* The introduction should be brief (seldom more than two minutes) and should *not* summarize the chairman's views on the topic the speaker is to discuss. His job is to present the speaker to his audience, briefly, directly, and with a respectful cordiality that will help make them eager to hear him and his message.

2. *Be prepared to say what needs to be said.* It is disconcerting to a speaker to be asked, a few moments before his speech, "What do you want me to say about you?" The chairman should take care

to have well in advance, from the speaker, from his associates, or perhaps from his secretary, the kind of information establishing the speaker's authority to speak on the subject. This may include his education, travel, and experience with the problem to be discussed. If he has written a number of books, it is appropriate to refer to him as a distinguished author, and to cite the titles of such of his books as are appropriate to the subject. The timeliness and importance of the topic may be mentioned—but, again, carefully avoiding expression of opinion on the subject, for this is the job of the speaker, not of the chairman.

3. *Avoid saying what ought not to be said.* The chief thing to avoid is describing the speaker as a good speaker, or declaring that he is entertaining, or a master of platform arts. If he speaks well, the audience will soon discover the fact. To announce in advance that he is a skilled performer centers attention on his performance and interferes with his communication of ideas. Neither should the introduction outline the points he will make—nor be an admonitory lecture on what he ought to say. There should never be an apology for the smallness of the audience; however, if circumstances such as a blizzard have reduced the number well below expectations, it might be appropriate to explain that many wished to hear the speaker, but have been prevented from coming.

4. *Close the meeting appropriately after handling the forum-question period.* What is often most appropriate is a brief but sincere statement of appreciation. If the speaker has presented one side of a controversial issue, it might be appropriate to thank him for expressing his views and to announce that in a subsequent meeting the other side of the question will be discussed. If a question-forum period is to follow the talk, the chairman's duty is to insure that a first question is secured quickly and readily. If no one immediately rises with a question, the chairman should turn to the speaker and ask a question himself. If the gathering is small, the chairman then retires to his seat and the speaker receives and deals with subsequent questions directly. If the audience is large, it is more courteous for the chairman to receive the questions as they are offered, to restate them clearly enough so everyone will hear, then turn the question over to the speaker.

As will readily be seen from the foregoing pages, the varied responsibilities of a chairman are in reality simple and natural. There would seem to be no need to review them—except that everyday observation demonstrates how badly the job of presiding and introducing speakers is often bungled. Anyone with reasonable poise and clear-mindedness should be able to preside over meetings with unobtrusive effectiveness.

Conversation

All the principles of good speech apply with proper adaptation to social conversation. Conversation is so varied that it is difficult to lay down any set prescriptions for it. It may consist of two friends chatting briefly on a street or bus, or of a dozen people gathered in relative formality to talk seriously about a new book or a current political campaign. It could be between two lovers exchanging ideas on plans for their future life together, or two businessmen arguing a matter of business ethics. It could be in the form of "kicking ideas around" or of analytical or persuasive discussion of them. In other words, the situations, the purposes, and the content of conversations vary widely. But there is almost as wide a variation in public speaking—which may range from a score of alumni hearing a humorous recital of their collegiate escapades at a reunion dinner, to an hour-long lecture to 5,000 people on conditions in Soviet Russia or a nationwide televised debate between rival candidates for the presidency.

What we have been concerned with in this book is to help you to attain skill in analyzing what you plan to talk about, to determine what is true about it and what your convictions concerning it may be; in analyzing the occasion and the listeners who will hear your talk, so that you may properly develop the means of making your ideas effective; and of organizing, illustrating, and supporting what you have to say so that it will be clearly understood, interesting, and attractive or appealing to those whom you seek to influence. All these skills are essential not only in public speaking and in formalized group discussions but also in social conversation.[2]

As a brief guide, we suggest the following cautions:

1. *A good conversationalist pays careful attention to all his listeners.* He tries to observe their reactions to what he is saying. If he meets strong opposition, he tries quickly to analyze the reasons, which quite probably relate less to what he says than to his manner of saying it. He should be quick to modify his manner and to approach topics

[2] For a detailed study of conversation see *Conversation: The Development and Expression of Personality,* by Robert T. Oliver. Springfield, Ill.: Charles C Thomas, 1961. Also of interest is a Student Affairs Research poll taken at The Pennsylvania State University, in which social conversations, daily social contacts, and personal contact with instructors were ranked at the top level of importance, as reported in *The Daily Collegian,* June 1, 1967, University Park.

with respectful consideration for the sincerity of the views of others who are present.

2. *A good conversationalist is sensitive to the desires of the group.* It may be that the topic he introduces is obviously of no interest to the others. In this case, he will either drop it, and find what the group does wish to talk about; or, if the topic is one he feels ought to be discussed, he will try to make it interesting by linking it to subjects in which they do feel a present interest. Similarly, if the others are in a mood for frivolity, he will not introduce a serious or argumentative note—at least not without successfully maneuvering a transition of mood to the one his topic calls for.

3. *A good conversationalist listens and yields the floor readily to others.* There is always a danger that exuberance of mood or determined intensity of feeling about a topic may lead one conversationalist to seize the floor and to pour forth what he has to say with little awareness that others present also wish to express themselves. An extreme egotist is seldom a good conversationalist. He may be a good entertainer at such times as he can dominate a group, but this kind of entertainment is not true conversation—which always requires give and take and the exchange of ideas. Sensitivity to the feelings of others is essential.

4. *A good conversationalist will try to abide by the principle that the purpose of conversation is to engage the full participation of all present.* On occasion, even lengthy monologues are appropriate, as when someone has had a genuinely interesting experience the others are eager to hear about. But even in such instances, it is wise to be brief, and to suggest a ready willingness to cut off your remarks quickly. If the others really do want you to keep on talking, they will see that you do by asking questions. The chances are very great that your best course of action is to lead as quickly as you can from your experience to that of others. For example, if you are telling about an evening you had in a Paris nightclub, try to get to the point quickly, then add that this reminds you of the local night spot, thus inviting others to relate some of their own homebound experiences. If they are eager to know more of Paris, they will ask you; there is no need for you to force the issue.

Conversation is talk, and talk has been the subject of this entire book. There is no principle of communicative speech that does not apply when you gather for social chit-chat. The relaxed and informal character of conversation encourages you to speak freely and without tension; but it also permits you to engage in many violations of clarity and even of simple good taste. A good conversationalist is always so highly regarded that it is worth a great deal of concentrated attention to try to master the art. And it is well to remember that the foundation of success in it is to be deeply and broadly interested in other people, not immersed in your own feelings and ideas. As we have said in other connections, the chief general requirements are self-respect and respect for others. Out of this combination, healthful social relations are built.

Interviews

The interview is more formal, purposive, and sometimes more structured than social conversation. Skill in interviewing is becoming more and more essential in all walks of business and professional life. Examples are interviews between lawyer and client, doctor and patient, and manager and worker (or superior).[3] For the college student, interviews with a professor or administrative officer may assume great importance in seeking information, seeking advice and counsel, or discussing his academic record. One of his most significant interviews, usually during the spring term of his senior year, is with a prospective employer. Typically, he will probably have several such job-seeking interviews, in which he may be evaluated more for his conduct and manner than on any other aspect of his record.[4]

The employment, or job-seeking, interview requires careful preparation by both persons. The employer's representative studies the record of the applicant fully, and the applicant prepares with a number of considerations in mind. He should have his exact purpose clearly established: Does he really want this job? On what basis? What information does he want to obtain? What points about himself does he want to make? Careful analysis of the company and its representative should be made in advance as much as possible. And the main ideas to be brought out should be determined.

[3] See such books as R. L. Kahn and C. F. Cannell, *The Dynamics of Interviewing,* New York: John Wiley & Sons, Inc., 1960; and W. V. Bingham and B. V. Moore, *How to Interview,* New York: Harper & Row, Publishers, Inc., 1959.

[4] This conclusion and many valuable principles in this kind of interviewing are found in Milton M. Mandell, *Employment Interviewing,* Washington: U.S. Civil Service Commission, 1956.

The *personal manner* should start with punctuality, for coming to an interview late will set one back considerably even before starting. One's poise, ease, tact, confidence, and respect for the other person will be carefully observed and count heavily.

The personnel interviewer for the company will probably take the lead in introducing topics for discussion, usually by raising questions. They should be answered directly and concisely. The interviewer's manner may indicate whether he wants fuller answers, or he may of course show this by further questions on the same point. He may want to determine how well the applicant thinks on his own, without guidance, and he may then ask extremely "open-ended" questions, such as, "What are you most interested in?" It is thus wise to have collected some ideas about life goals and what kinds of work will best achieve these goals and ambitions.

As a general rule, the applicant will not want to talk too much about his own record and qualifications, except when asked. The presumption is that the interviewer will already have a summary of his general training and will have procured statements of recommendation from teachers and others. What is most important is that the applicant demonstrate interest in the company the interviewer represents, indicating that he knows something about it and its products or services, and that he appreciates its possibilities, opportunities, and requirements. It is of course proper to ask questions that will both reveal this understanding and elicit particular information.

Do not go into an interview just to find out what will happen, in the variety of situations in which you are called upon to talk with someone in a relationship important to you. If you are summoned by the Dean to discuss your college record, you already know whether it is good or bad, and whether you are likely to be praised or reprimanded. If the latter, it is well to have in mind measures you might suggest in this kind of a counseling situation, in which both persons are trying to work toward a mutually helpful and satisfactory solution. If you are to interview your academic advisor about your course of study, you should identify in advance the problems that need to be solved and distinguish between the decisions you will have to make yourself and those in which you need his counsel. In the many counseling situations between manager and employee, both persons have to keep these or similar considerations in mind both before and during the progress of the interview.

The final consideration is the termination of the interview. Normally, this will be done on the initiative of the person by whom you are being interviewed. He will usually give a small but definite cue that he thinks the time has come for it to end. But it is well to watch for such a cue, as this can be an embarrassing point where he does not wish to say overtly that the interview is over. Such manners as shifting of posture, leaning slightly forward, or seeming to be about to rise may indicate a desire to close. While listening carefully, you may note that his words may hint that the purpose of the interview has been accomplished. Any of these cues should be heeded by rising or getting ready to do so. Sometimes the exact conclusions reached will be stated, but more frequently they will not be revealed during the close and will be communicated later. Thank the other person warmly, and leave.

The Manuscript Speech

The emphasis throughout this book has been upon extemporaneous speaking: that is, careful preparation of the ideas and their organization, using the language that reflects the immediacy of the speaking situation. This is the kind of speaking that is vastly to be preferred as a vehicle for learning the varied skills and insights needed in communicative speech. It is also the kind of speaking that is almost always done on the various community occasions when you may be asked to speak.

Nevertheless, in twentieth-century America the manuscript speech has an important place.[5] You may be asked to present a written report to your class or to your professional fraternity. If you are to give a talk over the radio, almost certainly you will write and then read it. On television, you may well be obliged to write out your talk, whether you then read it (perhaps from a teleprompter) or extemporize with the written text in mind as a guide. If you enter a profession or do research in a natural science, you may be invited to present a "paper" (actually a written speech) at a convention. On formal occasions of some types—typically in a eulogy at a memorial service, at a club meeting commemorating a deceased member, or even when awards are being presented—it is common for the talks to be written and read.

Many lawyers write out extensive briefs, in effect summarized

[5] See Harold P. Zelko and Frank E. X. Dance, "Speaking from Manuscript," *Business and Professional Speech Communication,* Chapter 9, New York: Holt, Rinehart and Winston, Inc., 1965, for a discussion of this emphasis in business and professional speaking, and for helpful suggestions.

speeches, which insure that the facts and the law are properly explored and interpreted, and in some courtroom speaking, especially before a judge, they may follow these briefs rather closely in their extemporaneous speaking. Many ministers write out their sermons, some to read them, some to extemporize from the written text before them. Executives in government and business often use written speech texts, partly to insure that they do not speak unwisely on crucial issues, partly to assist the press in quoting them accurately, and sometimes to have the complete text available for publication.

These are some of the reasons why skill in composing and reading of manuscript speeches is likely to be useful to many who expect to enter the professions or who may play increasingly important roles in corporate and community life. There is still another reason which applies to all of us. Extemporaneous speaking has above all the virtue of immediate adaptability to a live audience situation; its chief demerit is that it does not help greatly (and may actually hamper) the development of stylistic excellence. The development of compelling paragraphs, the skillful transition from one idea to another, the sweeping progression of an idea through successive stages to a culminating climax, and the choice of exactly the right words and phrases are all qualities of style that are best developed at the writing desk, where time is available for careful thinking and for second thoughts on better ways of phrasing.

Every writer has a full wastepaper basket, reflecting the number of times he has to rewrite in order to achieve a final composition that shows marks of naturalness and the inevitability of precisely the right words in the right order. Speakers seldom have this kind of opportunity—though nothing prevents them from parallel development as writers. But speaking itself, with all its extemporaneous liveliness and seeming spontaneity, can profit from experience in stating and restating ideas until they finally are cast into the most effective form.

Even speeches presented in a genuinely extemporaneous manner may, on occasion, properly be written out in advance. In this case, the writer of the speech develops with far greater care than he could by any other means precision of structure, a parallelism and vividness of imagery, and a cogency of concise statement. He has time to meditate upon turns of phrasing, upon metaphors and similes, upon witticisms and fresh ways of restating common ideas. When he then rises to deliver his talk, not by reading it, and not from memory, his mind is nonetheless prepared to utilize qualities of communicative speech which otherwise would be unattainable. Much of the objection to memorized speeches derives from the fact that they cannot possibly be immediately shaped to the atmosphere and events of the precise situation in which they are presented. Aside from this, many other objections arise from their being poorly written and poorly presented. If it is complained about a speech that it sounds "like an essay trying to stand on its hind legs," the complaint is not due alone to its having been written and memorized, but in part also to the fact that it was not written with the directness and spontaneous style of good talk. Once again, for students of speech, whose primary business is to acquire qualities of communicative speaking, our advice very strongly is to avoid written speeches and to follow strictly the extemporaneous methods of preparation that have been developed in the preceding chapters. Nevertheless, there are occasions when a speech should be written, and some occasions when it also should be read. To help you to prepare for such occasions, the following counsel is suggested.

Writing the Manuscript

The principles of good organization and the methods of achieving clarity, purposiveness, and interest that have been discussed in connection with extemporaneous speaking also apply directly to the writing of a manuscript speech. It is highly advisable to cultivate the ability to "talk your ideas" onto paper. Many people find their thinking processes inhibited when they sit at a typewriter or take up a pen. The important consideration is to know clearly what you want to communicate, then (with your knowledge, your purpose, and your expected readers in mind) say it. Theoretically, there is no reason why writing should be any harder than speaking. If it is more difficult, it is because when you put words on paper, they stare back at you; you can see what you have just said. If it is confused, or inexact, weak, or incomplete, falling far short of what you intended, these factors naturally concern you and may arouse a positive fear of putting down other words to follow them. The problem, however, is not that writing is difficult. The problem is that you have found yourself out. You know, now, that your ideas are not as clear, or precise, or well-founded as you had fondly thought them to be. If, on the other hand, the ideas you write down do make good sequential sense, the ability to look at them should be a positive help in moving forward with the further development of your thinking. Nothing and nobody can put ideas into your head except yourself—through your own reading, observing, listening, and thinking. But after you do have materials worthy of development, the following suggestions may help:

1. *Start with outlining.* Chapter 6 is just as pertinent a guide to writing a speech as to extemporaneous speaking. Ideas and materials should be organized in outline form before any writing is done, and the tendency to sit down and just start to write should be avoided. You have to know what you intend to do, and how you are to accomplish it, before you can do it. Without a plan you are as helpless as would be a ship's captain setting out to cross the ocean with neither a chart nor a compass.

2. *Develop your plan to accord with your purpose, your audience, and the length of the speech.* For a twenty-minute talk to be given to your local club on the occasion of your election to the presidency, you will have to consider carefully what must or should be included, and how much time (or space) can be allotted to each portion of it. Then you can block out your materials to serve as a guide in the writing.

3. *Try to write with an oral style.* This is difficult, for the tendency is to be more formal in writing than in speaking. It may help to imagine you are writing the speech as a letter to a close friend. It may help to think of yourself as conversing with a friend, and putting down on paper the words and phrases you would speak.

4. *Plan to rewrite your draft, perhaps several times.* The best of professional writers do a great deal of rewriting; it is highly presumptuous for an amateur to think he himself need not do so. President Franklin D. Roosevelt, who was famous for the warmly intimate and personal style of his "fireside chats," and who (despite his corps of speech-writers) did a great deal of work himself on the polishing of his speeches, often revised a particular speech six or eight times—always in the effort to make it sound more spontaneous and conversationally direct. It is helpful to read your speech manuscript aloud, trying to use the natural rhythms of spoken sentences; wherever it is difficult to do this, the passage should be revised.

Speaking from Manuscript

Reading a speech that you have written requires all the qualities of good extemporaneous speaking style, plus the ability to "pick up" from the page what is written there. The manuscript stands between you and the listeners and can be a substantial barrier to communication.

On the other hand, you will recall that in Chapter 1 we discussed various ways of converting barriers into bonds. The fact that you have gone to the trouble of writing out your speech is a guarantee to the audience that you have taken the speaking occasion seriously and that your intention is to give them your best. You should not permit the use of the manuscript further to suggest that, perhaps, you are afraid to trust yourself to speak extemporaneously. You will profit from the good effects and avoid the bad ones if you are so familiar with your manuscript that you can read from it with great ease and not remain bound to the text. Often it is wise to insert an extemporaneous addition from time to time, particularly as a method of bringing the present audience situation directly into your speech. The following specific suggestions may help you:

1. *Think of your written manuscript as a sequential development of ideas.* In other words, do not think of it as pages of words. Be idea-conscious, not word-conscious.

2. *Be thoroughly familiar with your manuscript.* Actual memorization of it may be impractical—and even if you do memorize it, you should still follow the mode of reading from it. It is not difficult, however, to become so closely familiar with the speech as written that you know where on a page a new idea begins, where transitions are located, where important points of emphasis appear. The speech should be typed up in such a manner that each new page starts with a new paragraph.

3. *Underlining or marginal marks may be used to help you note what you intend to emphasize.*

4. *Keep in mind that your function is to communicate.* Most faults in the presentation of manuscript speeches result from the style of reading them—as though the speaker were reading to himself. Your mind, and therefore your voice and manner, should propel your words out toward the audience, to reach them and bring them into the communicative process. Your voice and manner should reflect the urgency to communicate your ideas. What sometimes happens is that the desire to communicate your message has been substantially satisfied in the writing of it; then, when you come to read it, the communicative fire has burned out. As a matter of fact, whatever work you have done up to this point, nothing constructive happens to the audience except as it is carried to them by your presentation. If you stand with your eyes glued to the pages and your voice droning on in the monotone that signals you are talking to yourself not to them, your audience

will turn its attention elsewhere. You perhaps can recall occasions when you have drowsed through the dull reading of a lackluster speech. If you are lucky, you may also have heard some manuscript speeches presented with such lively communicativeness that you may never have realized they were not extemporaneous.

Conclusion

This chapter has attempted to show how the principles and methods of preparation, attitude, organization, development, and communicative presentation may be brought to bear in the special situations ranging from the informality of conversation to the formal manuscript speech. We have pointed out that each speaking and listening occasion is a special one, with each situation analyzed and treated with the greatest possible adaptation. Whenever the challenge to use oral communication to the fullest effectiveness presents itself, it should prove helpful to study all the factors involved and select those principles which best apply. Since human communication is such a complex process, and since so much importance is attached to it in striving toward life's goals, the need for constant review and study of the process and the methods for achieving results should be obvious.

For both speaker and listener, the responsibility is enormous, and the special situations are endless. Speaking and listening effectiveness carry with them a heavy social responsibility: to apply one's knowledge and ability for the benefit of others as well as for oneself; and to enter into every communicative transaction with insight into its nature, its probable or potential effects, and the means by which its proper ends may be accomplished.

Exercises

. *Questions for Discussion*

1. What are the duties of the chairman, and how should he perform them?
2. What would you identify as the particular characteristics of the speech of introduction?
3. What elements of good speaking should be manifest in conversation?
4. How may you plan for an interview? How should you comport yourself in an interview?

5. As chairman, what responsibilities may you expect to have in a conference? How should you fulfill them?

6. Discuss the similarities and differences between preparation and presentation of the manuscript speech and the extemporaneous speech. What are the advantages to be sought through practice in writing speeches?

· *Projects for Speaking and Listening*

1. Have half the class assume a role as speaker with a specific subject in mind and representing a specific well-known figure in public life. Have the other half of the class serve as chairman-introducers, each introducer in turn introducing one of the speakers.

2. Bring in the text of a speech from a recent newspaper and practice reading parts of it to the class.

3. For one of your extemporaneous speeches in class write out the development of one of the main points in full.

4. Analyze several conversational situations in which you participated on a given day, some with two, some with more than two participants. With regard to each, record the purpose of the conversation and the general subject or subjects. What part did you play in the conversation? How often did you speak? When did you supply information? When were you expressing opinion? Who was the most talkative in the group? The most argumentative.

5. Plan to hold a conversation with a friend in front of the class, as though you met casually on the street. Initiate the discussion as you would in such circumstances. Exchange ideas for several minutes, and then ask the class to analyze the manner and remarks of both you and your friend.

6. Prepare to participate in an interview in which you have a specific persuasive purpose to accomplish, such as selling something or getting the other person to agree to a plan or proposal. Make the following written preparation: a one-page analysis of the other person; an outline of the sequence of the interview in which you give the setting and the exact statement of purpose on the title page, followed by an analysis of what you will do in each of the steps. Your analysis should show the major points you intend to stress, the major objections you expect to be raised, and the supporting evidence you will use. The interview will be conducted before the class, but as though you did not have an audience. Both participants should talk as they would in an actual interview situation, the person being persuaded interrupting frequently with questions and objections.

Index

Index

Notes

Notes

Notes

Notes